The Heart of the World

The Heart of the World

Nik Cohn

ALFRED A. KNOPF NEW YORK 1992

Grateful acknowledgment is made to the following for permission to
reprint previously published material:
Donald Baechler/Ajax Press: Excerpt from pamphlet "Wasted Time
and Money" by Donald Baechler (Ajax Press, New York, 1989). Re-
printed by permission.
Def Jam Recordings: Excerpt from "Miuzi Weighs a Ton" by Carlton
Ridenhour and Hank Shocklee. Copyright © 1987 by Def American
Songs. Reprinted by permission.
New American Library: Excerpt from *The Fabulous Showman* by
Irving Wallace. Copyright © 1959 by Irving Wallace. Reprinted by
permission of New American Library, a division of Penguin Books
USA Inc.
Street News: Excerpt from "How to Make Pigeon Stew" by Cleve-
land Blakemore. Copyright © 1990 by Street News. Reprinted by
permission.

Library of Congress Cataloging-in-Publication Data
Cohn, Nik.
The heart of the world / by Nik Cohn.
p.   cm.
ISBN 0-394-56869-9
1. New York (N.Y.)   2. New York (N.Y.)—Social conditions.
I. Title.
F128.55.C64   1992
974.7'1—dc20   91-53128 CIP

Manufactured in the United States of America
First Edition

This book is the partial record of a walk I made up Broadway, starting at the Battery and aiming for the Bronx. Originally, I had planned a voyage round the world, but my friend Jon Bradshaw talked me out of it, turned my face to the Great White Way. "It is the world within itself," he said. So I started walking. Then Bradshaw died. But I kept on walking still, his spirit crouched on my shoulder.

One

of Broadway and Canal, a sheet of stray paper snagged my
trouser leg and would not let go. On it I read a life history,
neatly typed in single spacing: "Well this is the story of a young
girl by the name of Carmen Venus Colon, shes 8 years old, very
pretty living with her mother her name is Felicidad, brother his
name is Hector, and mother's boyfriend Charlie.

"This is the year of 1981, this young girl is very trouble. This
is a real life story, this is very emotional, this may have been
your own life story, but this is an ordeal for a young girl that
wants to be the best that she can be, but she had to go through
all the obsticles that got in her way.

"So please enjoy the book."

It was early January. The morning was bright but bitter cold,
far too cold to stand reading life stories on Broadway street
corners. So I tucked the page into my overcoat pocket, took
shelter inside the Plum Blossom, and called for duck soup.

While I waited, I locked myself in the bathroom and took
out Carmen's story, spread it flat across my knees. "This all
started in the Bronx, NY. Well I guess I use to be a good
student but after I was seperated from my big brother Hector
I was always in my own little world. Well I guess you can always
say every kid was in their own little world but I was different,

I was the real weird one. I loved my mother alot and also her boyfriend Charlie, the best friend and boyfriend in the world, but I was constantly beat on. I didn't know what I did wrong, it seemed to make no differents. Then by the age of 9 also I was sex molested by Charlie. This really had me in the dumps. But after awhile I got use to it. I mean love comes in all shapes and sizes, you just take it as it comes."

There the manuscript ended.

When I came out into the restaurant again, my soup was waiting on the table but some other man was drinking it, and this man was Sasha Zim.

Alexei Alexandrovich had sent him. If I meant to walk all the way up Broadway and live to tell the tale, he'd said, I would need a guide and minder, and Sasha Zim was the very man. He drove a Checker cab by day, played drums at night, and he was in love with streets, all streets, but Broadway above all streets. "So where do I find him?" I'd asked.

"In my bath. With his drums," said Alexei. "They've been sleeping there for weeks."

Neck-deep in my soup, he looked about twenty, a loose-limbed and gangling sort, big-boned and reddish blond, with a tangled mop of hair spilling out from under a cheese-cutter cap. "I am sorry abusing your duck but I am tired, very starving," he said. "In my taxi, crazyman goes crazy, declaims he is Trebitsch Lincoln, Abbot of Shanghai, master spy, second coming of John Baptist, and I have to take him to Turkish bath, steam away sins for all mankind. Oh, brudder. Turkish bath is closing during AIDS, so now I have to take him to bar, drink away sins for all mankind. Bar he is in Passaic, New Jersey." He wiped his lips; he shook himself. "So when do we Broadway?" he asked.

"Any time you're ready."

"Oh," said Sasha Zim, "how good is this duck soup."

High on his right cheekbone was a small strawberry birthmark shaped like a tattooed scimitar. In repose, it was so faint, it might have been just a bruise. But as the heat of the soup rolled through him and his blood rose, so did the mark. Now it glowed like a flaming brand: "*Broadway*," he intoned, reciting by rote, "*is mother of Broadways all over world, mother of lights of Piccadilly Circus and of Place Pigalle and Teatralny Plo-schtchad. Great White Way is greatest white way.*"

"Been here long?"

"Six years, ten months."

"And before that?"

"Moscow. Novokuznetskaya," Sasha said, as if that explained everything. "Till then I was seventeen, and now I have twenty-four."

I ordered duck soup of my own, and for some minutes the two of us wallowed in silence. Each bowl was half a basinful of fatted broth, piled high with bones and noodles, so that all day afterward a film of grease would coat our mouths like spikenard, a magical saline solution, strong to ward off evils. "So you're staying with Alexei Alexandrovich?" I mumbled.

"Is my drums," Sasha said. "Zim, he can be sleeping in taxi, in street, with woman, with woman in taxi, with woman in taxi in street, forgeddaboudit. But drums need get their rest."

God's Mutt, Alexei Alexandrovich had called him. In bomber jacket and Hawaiian shirt, jogging pants, lumberjack boots, a buffalo-head Western belt and a small silver crucifix, he was a walking flea market. Yet his face looked brand new, never used. "What it is," he explained. "I'm Soverican."

He had first learned English from daytime TV, *General Hospital* and *As the World Turns* and *The Young and the Restless, Hawaii 5–0* and *Fantasy Island*, washing-powder and paper-towel commercials, reruns of *I Love Lucy*. Now he worked days, but his education continued. "Am picking off street, like scavenger," he said. "In taxi is university of all mankinds, what you don't know won't hurt you, what you do is killing you dead."

The Plum Blossom was safe harbor. Once it had been Dave's Corner, famous for its egg creams. Then it was crammed with punks easing their cocaine nerves; now it catered to taxi drivers and juries, also a few Chinese. Ranks of Peking ducks, gleaming purple and umber, filled the plate-glass windows. Within was a room full of Formica tables, penned in by blank, mirrored walls, and the steam heat came up like a blanket, blotting out filth and rage, the frenzied hucksterings of Canal Street: "Whole world is going Helen Handbasket," Sasha said. "And Zim is drinking soup."

One oceanic bowl dispatched, he promptly ordered another. "Is like nymphomania of ducks, the more I'm full, the more I'm not," he said, beatific. "*One Life to Live.*"

Scrabbling in the depths of the bowl, he fished up an alien presence, some slimy something that might once have been an eraser head or a diseased Band-Aid. "What hell is this?" he muttered. But he looked delighted, slipped the relic into his shirt pocket, like a trophy. "My hobby," he explained. "I am collector of farces."

It was past ten; the Plum Blossom was almost deserted. Pleasantly drowsy, we nodded over our last bones and broth like unemployed sorcerers. "Broadway," I reminded him.

"Is going no place," Sasha Zim replied.

In out of the cold came an itinerant North African, a schlock peddler dressed in assorted rugs and bedding, a blue towel knotted loosely about his skull and a large tribal basket on his arm. Inside the basket was a wide range of trumpery—scarves, glass jewelry, batteries, joss sticks, Menudo buttons, Mets and Giants caps. But his staple was Darkie Toothpaste.

Darkie's trademark was a watermelon-grinning Sambo in a top hat and bow tie, his face full of glittering teeth. The African, who had no teeth of his own, was tall and immensely grave, his blue-black face ageless, his bandaged feet long and splayed like frogman's flippers, and he held up five tubes of Darkie in a fan. "What hellshit is this?" Sasha demanded, outraged.

"I am of Senegal," the African said. "I call Ousmane."

"Where d'you get it? *D'où vient le Darkie?*"

"My brother calls Ismaila. He steals by the Pearl River."

The Pearl River was a Chinese supermart, directly across Canal Street. I could see it from where I was sitting, a cinder-block barracks masquerading as a temple, festooned with streamers and dragon flags. "All. My brother steals all," said Ousmane. "My brother calls Ismaila, he steals the world away."

evening we drove round town in Sasha's cab, and after midnight
we drank. Right down at the foot of Broadway, in the back
streets behind Bowling Green, there was a Killarney Rose that
stayed open till four. It was a fine, clean place, and the bar itself
was prodigious. An old man sitting drunk at the dark end said
it was the longest bar in all Manhattan. The Irish Olympic
swimming team was trained in a pool the exact same length.

The drunk's name was Barney. He was a wizened old party,
a satchel of bones and parchment, and he had no teeth. At one
time, he claimed, he had been a top-rated messenger on Wall
Street. For forty years nobody was faster, no one more respected.
"My aim was true, all right," he said, "but I lost my teeth."

"Couldn't you have got dentures?"

"I could of. Course I could. I wouldn't sully my mouth, was
all."

In his fat days, he said, the Killarney Rose had been his
personal kingdom. He couldn't walk in without he was mobbed
by this man or that man; his money was no good here. "I was
the wicked messenger, all right. Wicked," he said. Then his
teeth went, and with them his friends. Overnight, it seemed,
the bar was full of strangers. "Summabishes. Scum. Low-life
summabish pantywaists," he called them. And these new bar-

tenders were no better. "Donkeys, friggin' Harps, straight off the friggin' boats." Now he had to buy his own drinks.

Come closing time, I followed Sasha Zim down to Battery Park. The night streets were hushed, our footfalls rang hollow, but a few strays were still about, sudden looming bodies.

This neighborhood had used to be a graveyard. After dark, it was said, you could empty a machine gun and you'd hit no man you hadn't aimed at. But that was before the Age of Realty. Now, luxury high rises blocked out the night skies, their lit windows making up new galaxies of their own. Even Lower Broadway tossed and turned.

"Aim was true," mumbled Barney, lurching along behind us. "Summabishes got my teeth." It was a raw night, the damp so clinging that it seemed to leech at my flesh and suck, a vampire kiss. But Sasha didn't feel it. Bundled safe inside a one-dollar flea-market greatcoat three sizes too big for him, he looked like the child warrior in the first scenes of Abel Gance's *Napoleon*, spoiling for a snowball fight.

At South Ferry, we ordered coffee and doughnuts from an Italian stall, where the counterman wore a chef's toque, shocking white in the blackness. He greeted Sasha Zim as a regular. So did the customers—ferrymen, garbage workers, assorted night crawlers. "Is everybody knows me, in New York, on Broadway, every place," Sasha said. "Of course, is not all their fault."

A large black man in a long leather coat and a Russian-style fur hat stood off to one side. He had a penitentiary face, set rigid as Mount Rushmore, and a cast in his right eye, the whole orb washed milky white. But Sasha waded straight in, slapped him five high and low. "Yo, Rickey O," he cried, "what it is!"

"The ship be sinkin'," Rickey O replied, impassive.

"Hellshit happens," said Sasha. "Is natural fact."

Rickey O seemed used to him; almost to take him for granted. As if signifying that Sovericans, talking jive and kicking butt, were his natural homeboys. "What's Russian for mo'fucker?" he demanded.

"*Yob tvoyu mat*, 'fuck your mother,' " Sasha told him. "In Soviet is friendly greeting, good way to saying 'hi,' like 'have nice day.' "

"Yo, Tofumeat."

"*Yob. Tvoyu. Mat.*"

Rickey O laughed out loud. Just for one moment, he let his sufferhead slide, and he unleashed a high-pitched squeal, almost a young girl's giggle. "*Yob tvoyu mat*," he pronounced, each syllable soft and clear.

"You're welcome," Sasha said.

We retreated into the park. All along the embankment, in the shelter of the harbor wall, derelicts slept on benches or were bedded down in cardboard boxes.

It was still drizzling, still rank. Far across the harbor, the floodlights trained on the Statue of Liberty made the faintest smothered glow.

The statue was one of Sasha's icons. In 1986, her centennial, he had worked this park on her behalf, vending burgers and Italian sausages, sweet or hot, under the slogan LET'S CELEBRATE MISS LIBERTY WITH MEAT-O-MAT BEEF PATTIES, and it was his insistence that we start our pilgrimage from her feet, so that we'd come to Broadway *tempest-tost*, the wretched refuse of alien shores.

The morning's first ferry left at nine. Most of the passengers were Japanese, with a smattering of Germans, Scandinavians, and Texans. But the star attraction was a group of schoolgirls from upstate New York, fifth graders decked out in full uniform—white socks and gray skirts, plum-colored blazers.

There was also Rickey O. We found him on the lower deck, lurking by the food counter. But when we approached, he stared straight through us, had never seen us in his life. "Working. Is not to disturb," Sasha explained.

"What work?"

"Is Liberty Booster."

He dragged me upstairs, out into the sun and freezing cold.

Slung from his shoulder was a satchel full of guidebooks, histories, and pamphlets, painstakingly marked for quotes. "Is like color commentation. Little touch of class," he explained.

The great harbor, which had once teemed with tugboats and tramp steamers, freighters, ocean liners, now lay almost deserted. Only a few oil barges remained and, on the horizon, a lone yacht, its white sail dazzling, bent almost parallel to the waters.

The whip of the wind sent me staggering, spun me clean around. But Sasha, snug in his greatcoat, would not let me go hide. Trapping me against the rail, he forced me to look up. And there she was, gigantic and sheer above us: *Liberty Enlightening the Nations*.

Up close, she looked more daunting than inspiring. "This substantial figure of lady," Sasha read out, snout buried in his gazetteer. "Nose is four and half feet long, fingernail is thirteen inches by ten, and waist is thirty-five foot, more length than football first down."

It was no use. Viewed from underneath, a hugely pregnant housewife in a nightgown and brandishing a candlestick, Liberty's expression was blank, her features vaguely sneering, with a sullen twist to her thick lips—a dead ringer for early Elvis.

Behind us, the deck was full of schoolgirls. Their teacher, snug inside an anorak, made them line up in rows, as if for a class photograph. Eyes front, they posed with straight backs and feet together, their knees raw-red and tears of cold streaming down their cheeks; and sang *America the Beautiful*, while the Japanese took pictures.

Halfway through there was a small disturbance. One of the Japanese, in search of a wider angle, edged back toward the companionway. Right in front of him stood a young man dressed in drabs, a racial hybrid who looked half asleep. As the Japanese brushed by him, the hybrid turned, their faces just inches apart. For a moment they seemed frozen, locked in each other's gaze. Then the Japanese appeared to stumble. Threshing for balance, he lurched, then bounced off like a pinball, caroming out of control. Luckily, Rickey O was there to catch him.

The boat had swung around, begun the journey back, and now we faced the Manhattan skyline. At first it looked no different from its movies. Then the stone wall began to separate, resolve itself into planes and curves and spirals, rank after rank rising up like a city of cards. Sunlight caught on glass and steel, squares melted into oblongs, bowbends into angles until, as we moved beneath it, the whole prodigious construct seemed to swell up and shatter, kaleidoscopic, into myriad shards and flints, refractions, highlights, voids. At its heart, a bottomless gorge appeared: "Broadway," Sasha mumbled. His birthmark flamed, bright crimson, and he crossed himself. "*Yob tvoyu mat*," he said.

So we came to the Great White Way.

Down below, there was no sign of Rickey O, but the hybrid was wolfing down a hot dog with mustard, sauerkraut, and double ketchup. He still looked half asleep.

When the ferry docked in Manhattan, we followed him, tracked him inland through Battery Park. He ambled idly, aimless, as if stoned, and when he reached the foot of Broadway, he didn't duck into Roy Rogers so much as he oozed, slipslid away.

A group of four awaited him—three Hispanics of varying shades and one light-skin black. Sasha Zim knew them all. "Refugio and Willie, Indio, Sinbad, and this here is Stoney, you saw him already on ferry," he reeled them off, then introduced me in turn. "Nikolai Normanovich, he comes with," he said.

"He cool?" Stoney asked.

"Is total dummy, believe me."

These were the Liberty Boosters. They met downtown on Broadway one morning weekly, either in Roy Rogers or some other fast-food joint, the more impersonal the better. Then two of them, picked from a hat, would go pick pockets on the ferry.

Technically, they were misnamed. Boosters were meant to

be shoplifters, not street-workers. But *Liberty Booster* was too fine a title to pass up: "It got that ring, that certain smile," Stoney said. "Make any man proud to partake."

The boosters came in two distinct styles. Indio and Sinbad wore hooded tracksuits, Nikes, and dead-eyed stares, the props of streetfighting men. But Stoney, Refugio, and Willie were decked out as civilians, in tans and drabs and beiges, outfits as neutral as Spam. The contrast made them look like opposing teams—Saints vs. Sinners—on some TV game show.

Stoney was their leader, their self-anointed spokesman. Physically, he was hard to define, could have been almost anything, a light-skin black or a dark-skin Mediterranean—a Syrian, say, or an island Greek. His features were bland, his expression blander. But when he got to talking, his authority was absolute.

Liberty boosting, he said, was not stealing, just carrying out the statue's own intent. "Listen up to the lyrics, the message be in the song," he said. "Liberty mean freedom, just like the man say. Give me Liberty or gimme Dead. So everybody be free. So every *thing* be free." He flipped his wrist, he smirked, like a conjurer calling forth rabbits. "Stand to reason," he said.

"Liberty, free for all," Willie said.

"Is Heartbeat of America," said Sasha Zim.

Stoney's father, the Reverend Abraham Lincoln Bisonette, had been a preacher near Rocky Mount, North Carolina, and Stoney was his true-born son. "The neighborhood where I was raised, we had a self-service market right down the boulevard, and every night when I was small I used to go by that store with my mamma, help buy the family's dinner," he said. "I was the youngest out of nine, two sisters and six brothers, three living, so I was kind of my mamma's pet, she liked to keep me safe by her. Anyways. At the market, right out front, they had a big painted sign, it was a picture of the three little pigs, and they was styling in front of this steaming bowl of swill, fixing to jump head in, and these three little pigs, they wearing these signifying, shit-eating grins, I mean we talking *raptured*, like they just died and went to heaven *first class*. And on that painted sign, the man with the plan, he wrote up just two words."

"What words?"

"HEP YO'SEF," Stoney said. "So I did. So I do."

The other Liberty Boosters had clearly heard the fable before, many times. While it was unfolding, they passed time by pulling faces and pouring salt into each other's sodas. "We just like a rock band, only we don't play no music," Stoney explained.

They'd been together for almost a year. Before the Liberty Boosters, they'd known each other in Spanish Harlem, had run the same streets together. They had belonged to the same gangs, graduated from the same holding pens. Above and beyond all that, they shared one problem—none of them were crackheads.

In their own place and time, it was a fatal lack. Within El Barrio, just the same as other ghettos, crack now ruled with such a tyrannical fist that any blood who opted out was ostracized as an alien, and aliens on these mean streets did not live to be old. Refugio's kid brother Ozzie had been shot dead outside a bodega over $3.50; one of Indio's cousins, Conchita Concepcion, had had acid thrown in her face. There were murders on every block, in every cup of news. So the boosters had moved out, come downtown to Loisaida, the Lower East Side, where failure to get hooked was only a misdemeanor, not yet a capital crime.

Their exact personnel and numbers varied, said Stoney, according to availability. "He mean who be in jail," Refugio supplied.

"Correctional facility," Stoney said sternly, making it sound a privilege. But facility or jailhouse, getting locked up was no big deal. On average, a booster got busted once a month. Nine times in ten, he was out the next day. "That's the system, you understand," Stoney said. "We don't kill nobody, we don't mess with the messer, so we don't do no time. Every five dollars we take, we put one aside for expenses, like a road toll, and all the rest be gravy."

At the end of a half hour, Rickey O came in, more baleful than ever. His fur hat was off, revealing a shaven skull, and his milk-white eye glared sightless, a basilisk. The Japanese had tricked him. Rickey O had got the wallet, no problem, but it contained no cash, no credit cards, nothing but a lock of coarse white hair and a snapshot of an aged man drinking soup, beaming vacantly behind steel-rimmed glasses.

Nothing to do but start afresh. Refugio and Sinbad set off to ride another ferry, the others scattered; Sasha Zim returned to his Checker. "Got to go hurt me somebody," said Rickey O. Then he too was gone, head down into the wind, with his Russian hat pulled low, a red bandanna over his mouth, like a masked avenger.

Stoney remained.

It was ten past eleven: "The bar be open," he said.

He led me down Broadway, swung me through an alleyway, and we were back at the Killarney Rose. By daylight, the place was transformed, a great bustling rialto, full of stenos and junior brokers, off-duty moneymen. Stoney drank Grand Marnier, a 7UP on the side. His gaze grew solemn. "So what do you think?" he asked. "Should I get ordained?"

It was in his blood. Bisonettes had preached for generations, his father and his father's father, his Great-Uncle Hubert, and all of them were younger sons, just like Stoney himself. "God-entitled mouths," he said.

Among the devout, they were a Carolina institution—"not famous, you understand, just reputed." It was true they had never thrived in Rocky Mount itself, but they were known throughout the backcountry, the dirt roads and piney woods. For fifty years and upwards, Bisonettes had preached in tents and sanctified tin shacks, by mud holes for instant baptisms; at crossroads. And they were respected for it. Saved women honored them, love children favored them. But something was lacking. "All those long, hard years of believing," Stoney said, "they never figured out what they be believin' *in*."

He had inherited the curse. As long as he could remember, he had been driven to testify. Not just urged but consumed, a blood-deep hunger to rise up and speak what he knew. But what did he know? He didn't know.

It was a confusion; his brief history was filled with confusions. His father, the licensed man of God, had been shot dead while robbing a liquor store. Stoney was seven years old, a seventh son, Martin Luther Bisonette, but his mother could no longer afford him, so he was packed off north to New York City, to go live with his Aunt Clara on the Upper West Side, Ninety-eighth Street, a block off Broadway.

Today, that would be a chic address, aswarm with Upwardly Mobiles. But times were different then. Back in the early seventies, the neighborhood was as scabrous as any in the city. Aunt Clara's block was strictly SRO, single room occupancy, which was sweetmouth for Dump City.

Clara herself was a junkie who hooked to support her habit. She meant no harm, had always treated him friendly. But she had no space for him. When she wasn't hustling, she was partying. Either way, Stoney waited out in the hallway.

Many times she left home, was gone for days on end. Then Stoney would sit in her room with the TV on, an old black-and-white Panasonic. The only other furnishings were a sofa bed, a fridge full of spoiled milk and half-eaten Hershey bars with the almonds left out, and an altar put together by Aunt Clara's last live-in boyfriend, Humberto. This featured a 3-D picture of Christ crowned with thorns, the drops of blood so fat and real that Stoney kept wanting to reach out and crush them, like ticks, between his thumb and forefinger. Also, there were candles, glasses full of different-colored water, a necklace made out of animal teeth, hanks of hair, a sequined crucifix, and one spent bullet, all ringed by festoons of fairy lights.

After nightfall, Stoney would switch these lights on, turn out the naked bulb that hung down over the Panasonic but leave the set itself on, and in this flickering dimness, he spoke in tongues.

He'd had no message, even then. All he did was imitate, try to echo the same sounds he'd heard his father make and that he now heard Sunday mornings on gospel TV. Most times it was just play acting, to help time pass; but sometimes the spirit would burst out inside him for real, bear him away, so that he fell down on the floor, out of his body, out of his own self.

It was not a thing you could explain. Though he was only gabbling, making noises at random, sometimes words would come together, as if of their own accord, and for a moment they almost made sense. But he never could quite catch them, hold them down. When the rapture left him, so did the words.

After he testified, he'd fall asleep on the floor, a dead spent slumber that lasted until morning or until Aunt Clara came home. When she didn't return at all, he went out on the streets, taught himself how to pick pockets.

Right from the first time, he loved it. Loved everything about it, the ritual as much as the reward. First the eye contact, the zoom when you saw a score and knew it was for you; then the casing and the circling, zoning in so natural and easy you didn't seem to move; and suddenly you were there, the mark seemed to sit up begging, saying, "Now, right now." Then all you had to do was reach out, let it fall into your hand, it was yours. "Like ripe fruit, or a woman. But better," Stoney said. "Less mess."

It was a gift, God-granted. Stoney called it *allure*. Serious thieves—*cannons, whizzes, kick-reefers*—did not have greedy hands, and they never chased. All they did was make themselves available. Then they had only to wait, and the score would come to them.

Their whole skill lay in jumping on the right thing, passing by the wrong. "*Patience* and *recognition; recognition* and *pa-*

tience," he said, mantralike. "The picking itself, any fool can do that. Just leave it to the good-hands people, and the poke is history."

Under pressure, he admitted that the fancy words were not his own. He owed them to a player named Aaron Harris, who used to hang out at juvenile court and later became his tutor, his personal larceny school.

Aaron was much older, maybe twenty-five when Stoney was turning ten. A skinny Hasid out of Mount Vernon, he had been a cannon himself, and a good one for many years—called himself Sol Sharkey—till he got caught trespassing on the wrong people's turf, and the wrong people broke his hands, so now he could only watch.

Watch he did. Every time that Stoney was brought up for arraignment, Aaron Harris would be seen to be sitting in the exact same seat, three rows from the back, right on the aisle. Finally, he introduced himself. "Why get caught?" he asked.

Good question. Stoney could not read his own name, still sucked his thumb, and already he was a three-time loser. If he'd had proper papers, he would have been locked up. But Aunt Clara had seen to that. On his first night on Ninety-eighth Street, she had given him her best and only advice. "Don't give your right name," she'd said, and helped him burn up all his documents, feed them to the candles. She had sprinkled his forehead with black water that smelled like a dead animal; given him a hunk of rubber to hold, to symbolize his own erasure. Then she'd shown him the door.

Officially, this meant that he did not exist. Haled into court, he would be shuffled off from one city agency to another, but none would have any part of him. In the end, there was nothing to do, just kick him back on the streets, pretend he had never occurred.

So he had a free ride. Still he kept on getting busted. And for why? Mulishness; a perverse pride. Instead of just making his score, then vanishing, he had to stick around and showboat.

Unless he flaunted, stuck his tongue out, it seemed he could not be satisfied. "Which is garbage," Aaron Harris now told him. "Talent like yours, you oughta be a shame."

To some, their meeting might sound suspicious, a grown man taking up with a ten-year-old. But they were two artists, was all: "Same shapes, just different sizes."

Like a cross between Fagin and one of those all-wise Zen masters in the kung-fu films, Aaron took Stoney in hand, became his street demonstrator. Polished him, taught him to read and how to handle himself, how to stay by himself and like it: "I'm a tellya, the man was a kingship," Stoney said. "Man could walk and chew gum, man could talk for ten. What I'm saying, if the man laid down the law, the law stayed laid."

Aaron Harris lived in a cellar on East 111th, right in the heart of the barrio; and when he got Stoney down in that cellar, he got to talking, and he talked, and he kept on talking still. And when he talked theft, that was where the Zen came in. To Aaron, picking pockets was an art, a most high discipline. *Dipping*, he called it—an antique term that he loved to savor—and dressed it up in rhetoric, all kinds of fortune-cookie sayings: "Dipping is not taking, just consenting to receive," he'd intone. Or again, Stoney's own favorite: "To catch the thief, first conceive the thievee."

So deep in love with larceny, Stoney had small time or wish for the rapture. Even so, there would come moments without warning when he rose up signifying, talking out of his head. Just walking down the street sometime, or drinking Aaron's homemade kosher wine, deep in the midnight hour, spirit words would catch him by his throat and fling him down headfirst, prostrated in the dirt.

Then the Lord spoke, direct.

Stoney was trawling in La Marqueta, on the fringe of the barrio. It was his best loved place, a great sprawling street market, all of the colors, sounds, and stinks in creation flung together, with stalls that peddled everything from ceramic saints to plantains, botanica spells, knocked-off Reeboks, salsa records, *bacalaitos* and *rellenos de papa*, plastic seat covers, yams. Hot idle afternoons, Stoney loved to cruise the lanes, "not serious whizzing, understand, just flexing my fingers, keeping in shape. Anyways. There was this one stall in particular, it specialized in little girls' bridesmaid dresses, and I don't know why for a fact, it just always pleasured me. Tucked away in the shade, right next to the record store, and the speakers be blaring Tito Puente and all that good Latin shit, and those cute little girls in their lace dresses, white and cream and powder blue, cotton-candy pink, all those bows and frills, starch petticoats, the works, and the heat burning down on everyone else, but me, in my corner, I was cool. So then. So then one time, I don't know why, I just reached out my hand to touch. To fan that cool, crisp lace and let it go away with me. Last thing in the world I'm wanting, a fool bridesmaid dress. But what I'm saying, I had the need. Anyways. So my hand snake out, like of its own accord. And I'm just about to fork. And then," said Stoney, "the Lord speaks."

And there the story ended. Sitting sipping in the Killarney Rose, looking back down the years, Stoney made no attempt at a punch line, just left the tale dangling, myself along with it. "So what did He say?" I demanded.

"I don't know," Stoney said. "I couldn't catch it."

"Then how d'you know it was Him?"

"It was His voice." He seemed put out by the question, as if I'd doubted him. "I'd know Him anywhere. But we must of had a bad connection. Or maybe the wires was crossed. So I heard His call, but I could not grasp His word." He called for another round. "It was the rapture, was all."

Afterwards, it was hard to say why, he began to drift apart from Aaron Harris. Somehow the act got old, too much Zen talk, too much talk altogether. But Stoney still bore him gratitude, and always would. "Man was a gentleman thief and an actor," he said.

The actor had sprung ready-made from the thief. After his hands got wrecked, Aaron had joined a community theater group, studied mime and jazz dance. Then he'd turned street performer. Stripped to the waist, in Turkish pantaloons and a yarmulke, he used to swallow fire outside Broadway theaters. The Great Mephisto, he called himself: "Was known, was reputed. I'm a tellya, the man was *certified*."

His speciality was mutation. He had the gift of turning himself into any person he so desired. All he had to do was study them for a few seconds, then catch them unawares, *front* them, face to face, and he'd be them. Or rather, he would be their twisted reflection. The postures and expressions, all the gestures were photo-perfect. But something beneath the skin made the models squeal, jump back: "Like they touched live wire," Stoney said. "Or they looked in a crazyhouse mirror, they seen their worst nightmare, and it was they own selves."

In that moment, Aaron believed, they were his, completely under his power. If he'd been in love with evil, he could have raped and killed on a free license. But he came from a kinder school. So he just dipped.

The key to the whole trick was anonymity—a face like a magic slate, on which the actor could scrawl anybody he wished, then wipe them off without trace—and Stoney proved a born blackboard. So he became Aaron's disciple, and in time his superior. By fifteen, he was out on his own, and that's the way he stayed, a loner, till he fell in with the Liberty Boosters.

And Aaron Harris? "I heard somebody deceased him," Stoney said. "Some failure to communicate, what I heard, and they blew his shit away." At the thought he looked pensive, drank deep. "I wouldn't swear he dead. But I know for a fact he ain't living."

In street years, Stoney was now a grizzled veteran. These last months, since he'd run with the Liberty Boosters, he had a room by himself on Avenue A, but mostly he stuck around Broadway, slept or sat up in all-night coffee shops, and listened to his soul growing old. Two days a week he still worked, and the rest of the time he lay low. Fifteen hundred dollars was a good week, five hundred was bad, but it was not just the money that drove him, he was still hooked on the act, the *allure*. He was twenty-three years old.

Along the bar at the Killarney Rose, five empty Grand Marniers stood in line with five 7UPs, and Stoney called for a sixth. He raised his glass in salutation, his face as bland as the moon's backside. Just before he drank, he treated himself to the smallest tight smile. "Well?" he asked. "Did I break your fuckin' heart?"

It was way past lunchtime. When we went outdoors, the morning freeze had given way to a soft rain, melancholic as Irish mist. Together we walked out of the side streets, back towards the Battery. "So what about the rapture?" I asked.

"I still got it. Believe me, it's in me yet," Stoney said. But he didn't look too sure. "Course, it's been gathering rust. Years on the shelf, it's only natural, it could do with dusting down and a taste of fresh paint, a little bit fine tuning. Rapture be like a race car, time to time it needs a lube job. But that doesn't mean it can't run no more. It can," he said. "And kick ass, too."

Strolling through Battery Park, we passed Refugio and Sinbad. They looked glum, but gave no sign of recognition. Outside the South Ferry subway station, Indio gnawed at a pretzel, studiously bored. He had come from Nicaragua, down out of the mountains, with high cheekbones and jet black hair, eyes so black and deadly that Stoney had renamed him Cholo, after Roberto Duran.

Along the embankment, another shift of derelicts began to gather, shuffling into place. In the meat of the day, the cops kept them moving, to save the tourists distress. But now the afternoon was running down, already the streetlamps were on. With darkness, the nightstalkers would be free to come creeping back, repossess their cardboard boxes. "They claim in New York City you can't tell the homeless from the rats, but that's not a fact, you can," Stoney said. "The rats be fat."

for Manhattan where we sat. Twenty years afterwards, Peter Stuyvesant had bowled down ninepins on the same ground. George Washington had lived right up the street at the McComb House, 39 Broadway. And Adriaen Block, the Dutch sea captain, had built the island's first four huts at 45. At Cape's Tavern, the triumphant Revolutionary army had ended their victory parade. A few yards on, sick of Broadway's climate, Alexander Hamilton and Thomas Jefferson had determined to move America's capital south. Lord Cornbury, the English governor, had flaunted himself in drag here. There Captain Kidd, the pirate, had press-ganged his volunteers. Nathan Hale and Benedict Arnold, Washington Irving and Benjamin Franklin, John Jacob Astor, DeWitt Clinton, Commodore Vanderbilt—Bowling Green had known them all. Now, on the bench next to us, sat a woman covered in pigeons.

She was feeding them bits of stale wedding cake, and they sat clustered on her shoulders and feet and knees, even perched on her scarfed head. Her name was Ellen Fogarty; she weighed ninety pounds; she was sixty-three years old: "Half a lady on my mother's side," she said. "But the Dad was County Mayo."

She came here two, three times a week and the rest of her life she spent by herself in a house with nine rooms, four baths, and a conservatory in Tottenville, Staten Island. Over there she was Ellen Parisi, a widow. But Parisi was not her right name, and Staten Island wasn't the place she belonged.

Where she belonged was Broadway. That's what she had come from, what she understood, and all that she cared to remember. Not just Broadway itself but the whole of Lower Manhattan in its velvet days—Wall Street and Trinity Place, the Aquarium, the Fulton Fish Market; above all, Bowling Green itself.

Her father had worked here. Christopher Cornelius Fogarty. Christy. All through her childhood and teens, his office had been right across the street, 25 Broadway, which was now reduced to a U.S. Post Office but once had been the Cunard

who for first time is witnessing Broadway at place of its beginnings,
Sasha Zim intoned, his voice flat and dead. *Thrill of first glimpse
of great street curving on way uptown in bobsled run of skyscraper-
high steel and concrete, once-in-lifetime sensation.*

Broadway proper starts at Bowling Green. On a mild, rainy
morning, Sasha shared my park bench. Spume cut the buildings
off at the knees, seemed to coat all things in slime. This made
me hunger to get moving, but Sasha Zim wouldn't hear of it,
not till he was done mumbling through his guidebooks.

Spectacular sightlines, he read. Dutiful, I gazed where directed and it was true, they were. Other city vistas might be
more poetical, but in sheer weight and force of stone, Lower
Broadway gave no quarter. Behind us sat the Custom House, a
beaux arts colossus; before us, like an urban Stonehenge, mega-
liths moderne and Gothic, space age, mock-baroque; and at our
feet, this tiny patch of garden: *Grandeur overhead emphasized
by flat speck of Bowling Green, which, like teardrop lake in some
mountain watershed enveloped by heaven-bent range of stony
architecture, gives birth to mighty river.*

History penned us in with concrete clamps. Half of New
York's whole epic, it seemed, had unfolded within sight. In
1626, Peter Minuit had paid the Algonquins twenty-four dollars

As the ferry neared land, Stoney took up position tight against Baines's chest but facing outward, showing only the back of his neck; and slowly he began to inflate. Like a flat tire getting pumped, he swelled and rounded. His color deepened, his flesh grew taut and shiny. By the end of a minute, his whole head looked gorged, a blood clot about to explode. That's when he swung on his heel, jumped in the equestrian's face. And Maynard Baines met his twin.

Baines shied; he reared back. Stumbling, he tripped on his own feet and almost tumbled into the stairwell. Luckily, Indio was right there to catch him.

On Broadway and Fifty-fourth there was an Irish pub, McGee's, resplendent with quasi-classical murals, gods and goddesses at sport. The bartender, a purist, refused to serve Grand Marnier with 7UP, so Stoney made do with Pernod and black currant juice. Before he'd finished his second, Indio loomed up in the backbar mirror, framed by Pan and assorted nymphs. His face was a well-kept grave.

The partners took a turn around the block. When he returned, alone, Stoney tried to look inscrutable. But grins kept busting out on him; he was dimpled like a tan Liberace. Though he would not specify the haul, his eyes held a dreamy look.

For the longest while he kept silence, then he shook himself all over, like a dog emerging from bottomless waters. "So what do you think?" he asked. "Should I get ordained?"

The last Liberty ferry was loading, and he came to a snap decision. Normally, it was against his policy to work twice on the same day. "Familiarity breeds arrest," was his rule. But on this day, turned reckless by confession, he would make an exception.

At dusk, we cast off again. Floodlit, Liberty looked less like a muse than ever, and more like a gargantuan neon logo: MEAT-O-MAT BEEF PATTIES, writ in flame. On deck, huddled against the rain, the tourists had lost all the Pollyanna glow of the morning. The tired and the hungry, bellies full with sights, they herded together like kine. Instantly, Stoney was one of them.

Hard to define how he altered. It was nothing to do with disguises. Neither clothes nor features were touched; he even moved the same. Yet somehow he'd ceased to be Stoney, turned into Martin Luther Bisonette.

It was all in the eyes. Of a sudden, instead of streetwise wariness, they showed only innocence, trust. One glance, and you could tell this boy was country, always would be. Young Carolina pitchforked into the Big Apple, he was out of his league, overwhelmed. So he gazed on Liberty as a stranger, some rube who thought the lady was very big and real impressive, he wished he'd had a camera, but at the same time his feet hurt, rain kept dripping down the back of his neck, and the one thought that haunted him was he would kill for an ice-cold Dr Pepper.

For the trip back to Manhattan, Indio was positioned near the top of the companionway, black eyes downcast, apparently half-asleep. And next to him was a conventioneer, a man in a seersucker suit, with a nametag that read MAYNARD BAINES and underneath, in smaller letters, EQUESTRIAN ORDER OF THE HOLY SEPULCHRE OF JERUSALEM.

He was a bladder of a man, with purpled cheeks and tom-turkey wattles, the overstuffed look of an alchoholic blood-pressure case. Stick him with a hatpin, you felt, and he'd squitter away like a pricked balloon.

Building, back when New York was the world's great port and
Cunard its great steamship line. The *Queen Mary* was a Cunard
boat, and her father went aboard it any time he liked. That was
his job, to welcome it when it docked, wave it good-bye when
it shipped. It paid him a living wage. He even got to wear a
uniform.

Two uniforms, to be exact. The first was white and shiny
with brass buttons, and he wore it only for special, the times
when she wasn't allowed to go with him or even touch. But the
second was for everyday, a dark-blue serge, so dark it seemed
black, bog-thick and rough against her face. And the smells it
held, the Paddy whiskey he drank, the bay rum he slapped his
face with, the shag tobacco he smoked, and the aniseed balls
he was always chewing—those smells defined him, and so defined herself.

What was he like? "The Dad? A big red man with a big red
face," Ellen said. Not fat, never porky, more like a side of raw
beef. "What he was, he was a man," she said.

She was a hushed woman. Everything about her seemed to
carry the whiff of suppression, of too many years spent biting
her tongue and knuckles and nails. Her woollen scarf was faded
oatmeal, her coat a pale heather mixture, washed out to match
her eyes. She spoke in a dead monotone.

Only the legs showed life. Trim-ankled, still sprung upon
high arches, she showed them off in brown lisle stockings neatly
rolled. They gave her a childlike look; and this was fitting, for
childhood was the time she clung to, truly lived in. "The school
I went to, Holy Angels of Mercy, was right off Broadway," she
said. "My mother was too much half a lady to go walking. So
my father had to take me everywhere. He'd deliver me at school
in the cold dark winter mornings and, when we were let out
afternoons, it would be dark again but never seemed so cold.
And he'd be standing waiting across the street, in the doorway
of the pastry store, Bertoni's. Mrs. Angelo Bertoni & Five Sons,
it was called. All the mothers and the fathers would be waiting

in one group together, but the Dad stood apart, on his own. Course, he had a uniform."

They lived on Washington Street off Rector, two minutes' slow stroll from here. In the twenties and thirties, even after Hitler's War, the neighborhood had been a sort of casbah, teeming of Syrians and Armenians and Turks. Lost between the skyscrapers had stood low wooden tenements built in Eastern style, with courtyards and exterior stairways, carved balustrades, painted eaves, the smell of incense everywhere. Two doors down from Ellen's own home was a shop like Ali Baba's cave, jammed floor to ceiling with halvah and Turkish delight, hubble-bubble pipes, great swathes of bright silks, Persian rugs, brass bowls, carved scimitars, sequined slippers, beads. There was even a one-eyed black cat in the window. "You think I'm lying, you could look it up," Ellen said. "The Arabian Nights wasn't in it."

The Fogartys were the only Irish on their block, a family so alien that their neighbors couldn't understand them enough to hate them. Ellen's father chose to live there because it lay close to work and also because he was in love with magic: "Would have been a conjurer, only his big red hands, his fingers were fat as sausages. But he did tricks. They never worked, but he did them."

All Manhattan had been like that once, a magical land. They'd called it City of Wonders, and so it was. Now people, when she tried to tell them, they looked at her sideways down their noses. On her own street in Tottenville, she'd see the white-lace curtains twitch and flinch, like whisperers, when she walked past. "People think I'm lost in mind," she said. "I'm not."

As if to prove it, she rose up off her bench, tugged me behind her to 25 Broadway. "Look up. Just look up," she commanded. So I did, and there above me was a sixty-five-foot rotunda, gold and silver and deep sea blue, ablaze with frescoes of great ocean voyages down the ages. Sea gods and goddesses stood guard over the portals, ancient sailing ships were carved in the stone walls. "A Taj Mahal," Ellen called it. "Now they use it for losing letters."

The Cunard Building was just one example. In the days of its pomp, the Port of New York had been its own kingdom, and Lower Broadway lined with its palaces. The Custom House, whose grandeur seemed today so overblown, irrelevant, had been a maritime senate, the center of a universe. One Broadway, now a Citibank, was the United States Lines; 9–11, now a Radio Shack, had housed the French: "The might of empires," Ellen said.

She was transfigured. The wraith that inhabited the present, this forlorn old biddy awash on a park bench, fell away. Borne back to Xanadu, she was reborn, flesh and blood. "You want to walk up Broadway the way it's become, first you have to know the way it was," she said. "Wasn't always a cesspool, a pit of hell and jesusbedamn. Heroes used to walk here. The masters of the Seven Seas. Great men. The greatest in the world."

Best of all had been the ticker-tape parades. They'd used to be reserved for real-life heroes, not rock bands or New Jersey football teams, most certainly not blacks. The Dad would take Ellen up in his office, then stick her out of the window and let her dangle, upside down and swaying, a hundred feet above the pit, with all the people yelling, the brass bands playing, the confetti flying past her head like snowflakes, in her eyes, clinging to her skin, and the hero himself, a general, a great explorer, a president even, like a cardboard cutout, propped rigid in the back of the open charabanc, his smile stuck on with paste. And she would be screaming, of course, like you scream on a roller coaster, dread and thrill mixed all together, the street rushing up to claim her from below and above, when he swung her round, the Dad: "I was safe then," she said.

Across the park, outside a coffee shop, a drunken derelict stood begging. He was a grotesque, all scabs and strings of drool, and as adhesive as birdlime. Anyone who blundered within lunging distance was not merely accosted but instantly grappled tight to his bosom, clutched and clung to with such an octopus tenacity that twenty-five cents for ransom seemed cheap at half the price.

An altercation sprang up. An unwary STAB (suit, tie, and briefcase), emerging from breakfast, found himself first cornered, then passionately embraced. When he tried to bust loose, the embrace turned into a full-body tackle. The beggar's face thrust close to his own. The toothless maw breathed out, a dragon's reek; then breathed back in, and seemed to swallow him whole.

For an instant the STAB was lost. Then a frenzy of pure panic surged up out of his bowels, and he managed to wrestle half-free, bull his way across the sidewalk. For two or three yards, he dragged the beggar along bodily, a humanoid ball and chain. Then, pivoting, his briefcase swung wide for balance, he kicked him in the groin with his tasseled right loafer.

Guccis were not designed for putting in the boot. Though the tassels danced like tiny flags of war, the thud of impact was mushy, the drunk not much discomfited. If anything, the blow recharged his batteries. Spinning blind, exultant, he flung himself on the next passerby.

It was a cop.

From the fastness of the Green, Ellen Fogarty had followed this mime with relish, a certain preening smugness, as though it was staged for her private savoring. By the time that the panhandler had been frog-marched away, she was almost smacking her lips. "Lindbergh. Grover Whalen. General MacArthur," she mused. "Now there were men."

"Were also great pigs," Sasha said.

This was his cue to dematerialize. He needed a fat day in the taxi, a windfall, so that he could pay back a loan from Alexei Alexandrovich and rescue his drums from the bath, where they'd sat hostage too long. "Is farce. Is total stupidity absolutely," he said. "I cannot play, and Alexei can't wash, and starving children everywhere."

Already a pattern was forming. Each day he would set me afloat upon a different pond, then leave me to sail it or sink. If I made safe harbor, well and good. If not, it was not in his contract to stick around and fish me out.

Watching him depart, trailing guidebooks and bumf, Ellen sucked down hard on her gums, which set her dentures clicking like castanets. "Is that the class of person you'd call an émigré, or did he just wash up with the tide?" she enquired.

"Bit of both, I imagine."

"The Dad was neither."

"Then what was he?"

"Required," Ellen said.

The necessary man. All week he would toil, the first on board each great liner as it docked, first to shake the captain's hand, first to hoist the welcoming glass. Weekends he rested and took his daughter on treats.

Mostly they just walked. In those years, Lower Manhattan was still self-contained; Uptown was another land. From City Hall southwards, Friday evening to Monday morning, not a bar or restaurant was open along Broadway, not a body stirred on the side streets. Father and daughter had the run of the entire neighborhood, their personal secret city. "A cathedral," Ellen called it. "You'd walk for a mile and hear no sound, just the echo of your footsteps. And the streets so narrow and dark, the skyscrapers up to heaven, it felt as if you were treading the ocean bed. Way deep down in a bottomless pit. So then, when you came out at last in the open, the light would blind you, you were stunned. Bedazzled."

What thrilled her every time was when they emerged from the chasms into Battery Park and suddenly there was the sea, the great port itself, a thousand different boats all shapes and sizes, tugs and pleasure trippers, barges and freighters and tramp steamers, motorboats riding the waves like bucking broncos, the old-style ferryboats with their dirty brasswork and stubby little funnels belching black smoke, the ocean liners sheer and towering as moving skyscrapers, and then the yachts with their bright sails unfurled, reaching clear out to the horizon, to infinity, it seemed. In stormy weather, the waters would turn a deep bottle-green, almost black, and the wind's howling like a lion's roar sent her clinging in the depths of her father's coat, drowning out her dreads in the warm frowst of aniseed and bay rum and shag. But on calm days, blue days, the slapping and the kissing of the waves against the harbor wall seemed the sweetest song.

At South Ferry, she'd never forget it, there used to be a placard advertising some kind of tonic or vitamin booster, the name itself escaped her now but the poster was bright yellow and down along the bottom, in flowery red lettering, was the slogan DON'T GROW OLD—GROW UP.

On Broadway itself, you could stand right where we were sitting now and look directly uptown, past Trinity Church, as far as the Woolworth Building, and if you saw another citizen living, you'd think they were trespassing, it felt like a sacrilege. "Because this was our private place, you see. Before they raped it," Ellen said.

"Who raped it?"

"Robert Moses, who else? The man destroyed New York."

"How destroyed it?"

"He broke up the Aquarium."

It had been housed in Battery Park, just over our left shoulders, buried in the dungeons of a mock-medieval fortress. In history, Fort Clinton had been a genuine stronghold. American Independents had built it to fight off the Redcoats; men had borne arms and been prepared to die in its defense. But it did not look genuine. Tarted up and renamed Castle Clinton to sound more imposing, it seemed to come straight out of a storybook—a white-stucco fantasia, spilling over with turrets and fake battlements, rows of flags fluttering.

To reach the Aquarium itself, you first had to pass through a grim stone portal, twenty feet high, studded with iron bolts. Then you were plunged underwater, into a sea-green Atlantis.

More than fifty years on, Ellen could still reel off the inhabitants: groupers, toadfish, spotted morays, seals; Japanese veiltails, calico popeyes; x-ray fish, translucent as stained glass; golden dartfish; guppies no bigger than your little finger; and jewfish so hideous, with their big curved snouts and fat blubber lips, their predatory stares, that the Hebrews of Manhattan petitioned to have the name changed to junefish. And all of this was swathed in mysterious half-light, a clinging greenish mist, reminiscent of a funfair Ghost Train. "To this day, any time I dream I died and went to heaven, paradise is that same off-green color," Ellen said. "God punches my ticket, and I go walking among bright fish."

And Robert Moses had ripped the Aquarium down. He was a builder, a maker of highways and state parks and later housing projects, also Lincoln Center. But roads were the heart of his empire, in the age when automobiles still ruled America unchallenged; and through them he built up such omnipotence that for decades he was New York's unofficial boss, its one unchanging power. La Guardia and Lindsay and Wagner, Alfred Smith and the Rockefellers—all came and went. Moses seemed forever.

He was the nastiest piece of work—vainglorious, megalomaniac, the style of man who made lesser men wax fat just for calling him Master Builder or Mighty Mover of Mud. And his vengeances were terrible. His goal, which he saw as his legacy for the ages, was simply that New York should boast more numerous and more humongous autoroutes than any place else in creation. It didn't need them, indeed could not contain them. But Robert Moses required them for his greater glory, so the city must somehow endure them.

To this end he razed neighborhoods, evicted hundreds of thousands of tenants, turned whole communities into outcasts forever. Ellen had spoken no more than the truth—he was indeed the man who'd destroyed her New York. And almost nobody had dared fight him. He was too wealthy, much too strong, both in resources and will. He could bring down mayors and city councils, smash boards of estimate, banks, entire administrations on whim. For thirty years, he held the whole city in pawn. For his reward, Fordham University gave him an honorary degree, called him Doctor of Human Betterment.

But all that lay in the future. In 1941, when he trashed the Aquarium, neither his viciousness nor his reach was yet public knowledge. It was his first open act of vandalism, his great unmasking. Afterwards, he stood revealed—"Genghis Khan in a white suit."

He'd only done it for spite. Moses had long been planning to vault a mammoth overhead roadway directly through the Battery. This would have ravaged both port and parkland, poisoned the whole of Lower Manhattan. A pretty show of strength, indeed. But the Master Builder had shown his hand too early, too cavalierly. His say-so was not yet automatic, and just for once he found himself opposed. Eleanor Roosevelt and others clubbed together to outflank him. Moses' plans were rejected.

Destroying the Aquarium had given him his revenge. Striking deep in the night, when no city board could stop him, he'd packaged up the bright fish and moved them to the far Bronx, where Ellen Fogarty could not reach them. Instead of sea-green Atlantis, he left only a roofless pit, scattered hillocks of black mud, broken stones, shattered glass.

Half a century later, it did not sound like much. But Ellen believed to her soul that, with the first fish dispossessed, something in New York had been changed forever, something irreplaceable lost: "The people," she said. "Ever since, they haven't counted. What they think, how they feel, it's not been worth a jesusbedamn."

She spoke without surface rage. Her voice remained the same suppressed undertone, a metronome, as if she were merely intoning responses. "I don't have a screaming mouth. Never had," she said. "Sometimes I wish I did."

She would fall silent for minutes on end, staring slack-mouthed at the cracked concrete slab between her feet. But whatever flickering or guttering fires she might see in its fissures, she was not saying. She smoked Camels; she fussed with her hair. At moments she appeared to be dozing. Then, out of nowhere, her shoulders would straighten, her headscarf rock back, and that changeless rippling murmur would start up anew. "Nineteen thirty-eight," she said. "And in forty-three I met my husband, Dom, and in forty-five we got married; in forty-six we moved to Staten Island."

"And the Dad?"

"He'd gone before."

"Gone where?"

"He drowned."

When her father departed Broadway, so did she. Already the Fogartys had been uprooted from the casbah, driven out by the three-hundred-pound Turk down the hallway, who favored little boys. "Didn't bother me," said Ellen. "But the Dad did not believe in it."

"What did he believe in?"

"The Dad."

It was a plain fact. Though her mother dragged her sick self to Mass both morning and evening and three times Sunday, her father had always treated religion with indifference, a breezy condescension, which he'd passed on to her. So when he was taken from her, she could not turn to Mother Mary. All she could do was dance.

She was sixteen, could pass for twenty, and she was a dancing fool. Her mother had moved her to the East Village, where they practiced hating each other, the two of them spitting snakes across a single room, Fourteenth Street and Avenue A. Down at the corner drugstore, Ellen kissed the boys behind the magazines. When her mother found out, she was kicked out of the house entirely and moved uptown, to fresher air. On West Forty-fifth, she took refuge in a theatrical boardinghouse filled with musicians and magicians, songwriters, acrobats, freaks.

A bearded lady lived upstairs. They took tea together, and the lady read Ellen's palm. Her fortune promised pain, and she couldn't pay the rent, so she took work in a Times Square dance hall. The Carioca or the Casablanca, some such name: "Right off Broadway," she added slyly, knowing it would please me.

She was a taxi dancer, two feet for hire, ten cents a dance, and that's where she met Dom Parisi.

One slow Friday after midnight, he came in blind drunk. He was too far gone to stand up straight but strangely not to dance. At the table, he slumped, stupefied, his head kept falling in his drink. But out on the floor he moved free and superb; she'd never known a dancer like him, so smooth, so light: "A bird. The man was a flyaway bird," she said.

So they got married.

Right from that first meeting, they did not talk, they just clung, and to Ellen this seemed only proper. Talking she'd done with her father. With her lover, she danced.

Dom was in the building trade; he worked with his father, Carmine, who had his own construction company in Brooklyn, in Canarsie. What was ironic—you'd have to cry if you forgot to laugh—was that he'd done business with Robert Moses, and it was Moses who'd made him rich. On her wedding night, courtesy of that Mighty Mover of Mud, Carmine threw a gala reception for three hundred guests in the Sons of Italy Social Club, Flatbush. Fuzzy Campese's All-Stars played requests, and Dom danced with Ellen the whole night long, every single number. Out on that dance floor they'd been married for real, made one. Then they drove off on their honeymoon, four days in Atlantic City, and never danced again.

Instead, they moved to Staten Island, where they remained together for thirty-nine years, four months. At the end of Year 32, Dom bought into Tottenville, high on a hillside, at the end of an oak-lined avenue; and there he built his house of dreams.

All his working life he'd been a lousy builder but well connected. This had made him wealthy, respected—everything but happy. And that was Ellen's fault, for she'd failed to bear him sons.

It spoiled everything. Without sons, Dom Parisi's whole lifework—the contracts and the kickbacks, the civil wars, the fat cars and fatter cigars, the respect—lost its meaning. He was a big man, *capo forte*, but he had no inheritors, no living monuments to his glory, so he was nothing.

He sulked; he festered. He died.

First his blood went bad, then his heart. Before he passed away, however, he finished the big house down to the tiniest detail, complete with swimming pool, a billiards room, a sauna, and a solarium; and he gave it four extra rooms, which stood empty, for the four sons he'd craved and Ellen had failed to deliver.

The day the last nail was in place, he smashed a bottle of French champagne across the front door. Three weeks later, he fell down choking on his blood and left Ellen alone in his house to rattle.

Even this she told without drama, as though it was a tale that everyone knew already and so wasn't worth embellishing. "He was a made man and prideful, a take-care man, and you must never cross him," she simply said. "I crossed him."

At the end of thirty-nine years, four months, it was her only summation, the one thing speakable. Now Dom was dead, and only his house remained. For weeks and months after the funeral, Ellen had stayed inside it, immured, and could not stop herself from shaking. Then one Wednesday in November, don't ask her why, she rose up out of her bed at first light, drove herself across the island to the ferry, and she came back here to Bowling Green: "To set," she said.

That was four years ago; four years and two months. "The first time back, I threw up. I stood outside 25 Broadway and rained my guts in the gutter," she said. "Four days later, I was here again."

She had not missed a week since. One of her neighbors, who worked in a pastry shop, supplied her with bags of old wedding cake, and the pigeons did the rest.

So she thought about the Dad. And she thought about Dom Parisi. The thing he'd hated worst, second only to having no heirs, was when his buildings fell down. It caused scenes and harsh words, lawsuits, every manner of aggravation. Dark men in dark suits would come to his house late at night, talk with Dom behind closed doors, and when they went away again, he'd be so mad, he looked like he should go kill someone.

One night in particular, she'd never forget it, he woke her up at three in the morning and insisted on taking her out for a drive. They rode the darkness in silence, down to his newest construction site. He'd only just laid the foundations and already there was trouble. And when they reached the site, Dom rolled down his car window, and he stared for a long, long time. All you could see was mud and cement, and the cement was still half-wet, glinting in the headlights. The black night, the muck and mire, the cement. And Dom said just one thing. *Wet cement is sorry stuff*, he said. *And sorrier still when you're buried beneath.*

At the time, she was so taken aback she couldn't speak. Later on, nothing seemed worth the trouble of saying. "It wasn't what I was used to. Not what I once knew," was all that she murmured now. And she went on feeding the pigeons.

base, so I moved into a walk-up hotel in the West Forties, hard
by Times Square. In the next room lived a girl so beautiful it
hurt. Her name of choice was Lush Life, but on her welfare
checks it said Geraldo Cruz.

Sasha Zim saw her first. Or she saw him. When we pulled
up in his Checker, Lush Life was slouched on the hotel stoop
painting her fingernails Passion Pink. She wore a yellow silk
dress with embroidered dragons rampant, skintight and slit high
on the thigh, a look pirated from Susie Wong. But her face—
high Spanish cheekbones, black cannibal eyes, blue-black hair
swirling wild, as sleek as a raven's wing—was strictly Ava Gard-
ner. And her legs were Cyd Charisse.

Sasha was sunk on sight. Before he could even climb out of
the cab, Lush Life had laid aside her paintpot, hula-hooped her
hips across the street. Putting her red mouth in at his open
window, she breathed on him just once, a scent of cinnamon
and cloves. "Wanna get fresh?" she asked.

Ten minutes later, Sasha Zim came back alone, the scimitar
birthmark on his cheek so incandescent, it looked about to burst
into flames, spontaneously combust. "Nice ride?" I inquired.

"*Yob tvoyu mat!* Is revisionist," he hissed. And chucking

my belongings wholesale on the sidewalk, he drove off with no good-bye.

The hotel was run by two Greek brothers, Mike and Petros Kassimatis. Both were short, wide and bald, fire hydrants with feet, in the style of Two-ton Tony Galento, and what hair they lacked on top, they more than made up elsewhere. Impenetrable black jungles sprouted at their wrists and throats, escaped their sweatshirts at the waist, even curled up vinelike from under their trouser cuffs. Mike wore glasses and many gold chains; Petros had a wart on his nose. Otherwise, they might have come off a conveyor belt: "Two piss in a pot," in Sasha's phrase.

Checking me in, Mike looked me up, looked me down, and spat on the tiled floor. But when he saw my typewriter, a battered Adler portable, he shied like Count Dracula zapped by a cross. "You a writer? You gonna write about this place?" he growled.

I grunted, noncommittal.

"You write about this place, you better not write nothing bad. You write something bad, you gonna be writing with busted hands."

"No, he won't. Won't be writing with no busted hands," Petros corrected him. "Won't have no hands left to bust."

By neighborhood standards, they ran a tight ship. There were washbasins and blankets in every room, the towels were changed weekly, crack-smoking was discretionary, and any guest who spray-painted graffiti in the hallways was requested to leave feet first. Five floors held twenty-eight rooms and one telephone: INTIMATE ACCOMMODATIONS FOR THE DISCERNING FEW, read the faded notice, cyclostyled, tacked up inside my door.

My room was a cell, ten feet by eight, but not ungracious. Beneath the naked lightbulb, there were flowers. Nosegays of blue and pink roses bloomed on the wallpaper, and marigolds peeped coyly through the stains on the coverlet. It was true that my window faced an airshaft, a concrete wall, metal pipes. But if I stuck my head out far enough, then craned my neck and twisted, I could see sky.

In Times Square mythology, this place was known as the Hotel Moose. Nobody knew the reason, except that there was also a Hotel Elk, out beyond Eighth Avenue: "And this ain't it."

My first night alone, I sat reading *Struggles and Triumphs*, the autobiography of P. T. Barnum. He was Broadway's spiritual father, and his story, stuck in the fifty-cent rack at Isaac Mendoza, had seemed the perfect *vade mecum*.

It proved a sore disappointment. As a writer, Barnum's prime gift was for transmuting gold into dross. Still I persevered. By midnight, I'd reached the passage where General Tom Thumb is presented to Queen Victoria. He is twenty-five inches tall, advertised as eleven years old and fifteen pounds seven ounces, and Barnum drives him to Buckingham Palace in a carriage drawn by four snow-white dwarf horses. Dressed in a brown silk-velvet cutaway coat and matching britches, the general deports himself with gravity and poise, scores a thwacking success. For a full hour, he keeps the court entertained with songs, dances, and his imitation of Napoleon. Then he takes his leave.

As etiquette demands, he exits backwards. And he has almost covered the long gallery, reached shelter, when he is set on by the queen's pet poodle. Using his cane as an épée, the general defends himself with vigor. But the beast is too huge, too fierce, and he is overwhelmed. The poodle towers above him. A massive paw descends, blocking out the light. Queen, court, and palace all vanish; the poodle roars: "Don't ask," said Lush Life. "Just don't ask."

She had come to borrow my eyebrow tweezers. When I had none to give her, she did not act shocked. One glance at my beard and hat and Buster Brown boots, my thrift-store Donegal overcoat, and she'd guessed that I did not vogue. "Doesn't make you a bad person," she said.

Up close, she looked quite different. Outside in the street by daylight, she had given off mere glamour, a secondhand

Hollywood glitz. In this room, in the glare of its white light, she made me want to cry out.

It was the nakedness. In my life, I had never seen flesh so fine grained. Backlit, it seemed almost translucent, as if half the layers of skin had been stripped off. She wore a kimono, two sizes too big and loosely tied by a sash-cord. It was studded with rips and cigarette burns. Some greedy claw had torn off an arm at the elbow and left great rents in the back and breast; had left her without camouflage. When she stood over me where I lay, sprawled out across the marigolds, I felt I was looking clean through, kimono and flesh and all, every bone laid bare, every flinch of muscle and nerve. "Turn out the light, why don't you?" Lush Life said, shivering. "Do you want me to burn up?"

She was waiting for her girlfriend, Denise Denise. But her girlfriend was late, or maybe she wasn't coming. Lush Life had bought herself a pint of Night Train; already she was half-cut, softly slurring. The bottle, what was left of it, dangled from one hand; with the other, butterfingered, she tried to light a candle. "Night Train, it's good," she said. "Thunderbird is not so good. But Night Train, it's better." She reached out the dregs towards me, proffering. She beckoned me in. "Have a drink. Do you good. No, it won't," she said, and she snatched back her hand, drained off the last drops herself.

The candle kept guttering. It was coated in some black filth that choked it and stank like a slaughterhouse. "Burning dead bodies in your room. It isn't proper. Not *camelfort*," Lush Life said. "Not on your very first night."

For compromise, we sat in the dark with the door open. Out in the hallway, the bloods were smoking crack, mumbling. "Lush Life, Lush Life," somebody unknown kept keening, half-singing it.

In the dimness, the highlights on her cheek and bare shoulder, the hollow of her throat, seemed filtered through stained glass: "Ladybeard, I am so sickly," she said. "Encore de Night Train, why not?"

I bought it, she drank it; Denise Denise still did not come. The voice out in the hallway kept repeating Lush Life, Lush Life. "I won't talk," she said, and she talked.

Geraldo Cruz had come out of Bayonne, New Jersey, one mean town. His father had packaged dead chickens, and his mother sewed skirts in a sweatshop. Afternoons, after Geraldo got out of school, he used to care for his kid sister, Paloma. Together they'd play house and try on his mother's clothes, even though they were kind of dowdy, no bright colors and the most dated styles, strictly from Rent-a-Frump.

The shoes were worse. His mother had the saddest feet; she was a martyr to her bunions her whole life, so she could not tolerate pumps, only sandals and flats. Dresses looked silly that way, even nylons lost their flair. The best you could do was take a pair of Chinese-style satin slippers and restyle them, fake a heel with papier-mâché and bottlenecks. Which was exactly what Geraldo was doing the day his father got laid off work, came home early to get blind drunk, and found his son in a garter belt.

This father was one tough Dominican. All the time, every day of his life, he'd be bragging and cursing, doing that macho strut. But now, face-to-face with Geraldo, he did not say a mumbling word, just crossed the room to the whiskey and climbed on board, slugging straight out of the bottle. Then he sat down bump on the floorboards, staring into the cracks. Still he didn't start to yell; he spoke real soft. "You sick. You need help," he started out.

"Fuck help," Geraldo told him. "I need heels." And he walked out of that house; he did not ever go back.

He was fourteen going on fifteen. He had a dollar he'd taken out of his mother's purse. It got him downtown and into the bus terminal, and there he'd met such a nice old man, and he told this man the saddest story, how he'd traveled out to Bayonne from New York to visit his best friend in the hospital, only somehow he'd lost all his money and now he was stranded, he couldn't get home again. So you see. So the old man staked him to his fare and in return he asked for nothing, almost nothing, just to cop a feel. So Geraldo let him, what the hell? But afterwards he was crying; he was all upset. He started to make noise and the old man freaked, he was shaking and sweating blood, and he gave Geraldo fifty bucks, or it could have been a hundred, to keep his mouth shut. So he did. He rode the next bus into Manhattan, and when he climbed down on the New York sidewalks, the first thing he did, double-quick, he hauled ass to the nearest clothing store. At first the young lady serving looked at him kinda sideways, but then she saw he had a knife. So you see. So she smiled. His arms were piled up high with nylons and silk negligees, Maidenforms, satin panties, teddies, the works. He took them all in the changing room. Or part of him did. Geraldo Cruz went in, Lush Life came out. So you see.

There the story left off. Whatever had happened since, she was not about to tell. Geraldo Cruz had been some other body, a person she had once known. So his story remained just that— history. Retelling it meant nothing more to her than telling a movie script or some story she'd read in the paper. But herself, Lush Life, that was something else again. She had her pride, her privacy. She might go fuck with a stranger. That didn't mean she would tell him stuff.

It was two o'clock. Out in the hallway, a subway rhythm, I could hear the slapping of heads and bodies against the walls. The Brothers Kassimatis were making their goodnight rounds, chasing demons. I closed the door, shut them out, shut us in. Somewhere close above me I could hear a slithering and hushing of silk, the kimono fluttering. Lush Life was shivering still. So we held hands in the dark.

false spring, which lasted one day. For a full week it had been
storming and sleeting nonstop, such blizzards that we'd scarcely
ventured outside the Plum Blossom. Then one morning it was
sixty degrees, and everything seemed made new.

Lower Broadway was abandoned. At first light, the avenue
looked like a film set, one of those Armageddon 2000, post-
nuclear-holocaust jobs, when all humanity has been reduced to
little brown puddles and only the garbage lives on.

Walking uptown, we could track New York's progress year
by year, decade by decade. For as long as Manhattan had been
settled, Broadway had been its hub, the main drag. It had been
born as an Algonquin warpath; now it stretched far into the
Bronx, twenty-one miles away. *Story line of Broadway goes from
rags to riches*, Sasha quoted. *Set on which it plays runs from
harborside to hillside. Very name needs no elaboration. Is not
called street, avenue, boulevard, parkway, alley, terrace, drive. Is
Broadway and who would not know what that means?* He sucked
in sunlight through his nostrils, hollowed and deepened his voice
for extra solemnity. *Is spine of New York and each intersection
with another avenue . . . sparks different interaction. Each of
sparks generates own brilliance, which may flare briefly or leng-
thily, may fade or may burn once again. Broadway, in all euphoria,*

is Yellow Brick Road, one that seductively promises, but doesn't guarantee, Emerald City at road's end.

He scratched his skull. Then he scratched it again. "What hell is meaning?" he asked. The scuffing of his steel-capped heels on the sidewalk rang hollow, a dead canyon echo that made one look up for circling buzzards. "Quiet," he said. "Too quiet."

Not for long. As we passed the Wall Street subway, a single figure appeared in the mouth of the uptown stairwell. It belonged to a bookish little man in an army-surplus duffel coat and prehistoric sneakers, with his possessions in a Big Mac bag. Gray-faced and shrunken, he looked an ill man, climbed the steps with painful labor, holding on tight to the rail. When he hit the light, he ducked his head, as if the brightness hurt.

At the top, poised between Broadway and the pit, he stopped to rest. Half a block away, a large swaddled woman was setting up a fruit stand. In the current fashion, it featured all manner of exotica. Not just apples and oranges, but mangoes and papayas, strawberries big as golfballs, California peaches, and many, many kiwis.

The bookish man looked at them blankly, as though he'd never seen such stuff. "Well?" said the woman, snappish, but he did not answer, just stood gawping and, as he gawped, he was hit.

There was no warning. One moment he stood alone, the next he'd been ploughed under. As if at a secret signal, the morning's first wave of workers was unleashed out of darkness, came pouring up the steps in a flood tide. The man in the duffel coat was sunk without trace. Then the wave had passed over, and he was left stranded. "Well?" the fruit woman repeated.

"I could tolerate a kumquat," the man replied.

Between the first wave and the second, there was a brief gap, one minute, maybe two. After that the onslaught came nonstop. Swept away, we were flushed down Wall Street, plunged into regions of perpetual murk. The financial district was a maze of single-lane defiles. In New Amsterdam, they had been cowpaths. Now, oversoared by skyscrapers, they were abysms.

Cliffs of fall frightful, sheer, no-man-fathomed—when I looked up, the perpendiculars seemed pleated like an accordion, the lines converging as they fell, a dizzying plunge of stone and concrete and glass that dropped the entire gross tonnage upon the base of the skull, plumb on the pressure point. Perhaps that was why everyone seemed to walk tilted forward, necks bent and shoulders sagging, as if toting sacks of cement.

Borne along by the crush, we swirled through the tube at random, washed up outside the New York Stock Exchange. It was a Roman Renaissance temple, its entrance framed by six massive Corinthian columns. On the pediment, in bas-relief, were allegorical figures of Agriculture, Mining, Motive Power, and Design. Their centerpiece, all powerful, was a goddess of infinite bounty.

This goddess was named Integrity.

The men in suits who entered her shrine passed us by with canceled faces. The elders favored neutrality, the impenetrable blandness of the poker player. The young preferred frozen rage.

For both, the keynote was self-absorption, an unblinking android fixity. In money wars, this was called the Game Face, and it caught us unprepared. From recent TV and press coverage, we had been expecting a slaughterhouse, awash in human wreckage. "Bloody Monday. Death of Eighties. Good-bye good-riddance to gold age of greed. Kinder, gentler greetings from recession," Sasha summarized. But no bodies flew out of windows; no gunshots echoed, off. On the contrary, the NYSE seemed exultant, *en fête*.

From the visitors' gallery, where we looked down from a great height, the trading floor was like a football field viewed from the bleachers. Recession or no, the arena teemed with straining bodies, scurrying back and forth in the choppy, speeded-up rhythms of Keystone Kops. We could see them flailing their arms, sense their bellowing. The pace never flagged. Still the point remained obscure. "Fun game, I think," Sasha said, "but how touchdowns are scoring?"

Back on the streets, the hating faces rammed hard into our own, would not be denied. They carried energy but no vitality, hunger but no appetite. Overmatched, we backtracked.

In Trinity Churchyard, where Wall Street returned to Broadway, we sat down among ancient graves. It was a seventeenth-century boneyard, the oldest in the city. Alexander Hamilton lay there, so did Robert Fulton and the Captain James Lawrence who died crying "Don't Give Up the Ship." Now the walkways were littered with ticker tape and rolls of toilet paper, hangovers from some parade, and Barney, the Wicked Messenger, was sleeping it off beneath the west wall.

It was the most consoling spot. When New York was in its infancy, Trinity had been in its anchor, the one stable point in its insatiable growth and shifting. Always it had hushed, had reassured. And its function was not changed. The church itself, rebuilt in the nineteenth century, might be a blackened urchin thing, all spire. But an organist was practicing Bach, the Toccata and Fugue in D Minor; and in the graveyard the day oozed by, sweet-soft and sticky as saltwater taffy. "Tonight, tonight, I get my drums for sure," Sasha said, easing away, and soon I slept.

When I reopened my eyes, I was being closely inspected by a man who looked like an antique black jockey. "You looking to get yourself robbed?" he enquired.

"Not right now."

"You could have fooled me."

His name was Lucius; he came from New Orleans. For forty-some years, he had shined the shoes of senior partners, CEOs, great tycoons: "And little bitty dirtbags, too."

Onyxing the Oxfords, he called it. In the days when fine work was still valued, it had been considered a craft. He'd even had his own business cards printed up. LUCIUS HAVENS, SHINIST, they read, CATERING TO THE CREAM OF MANLY FOOTWEAR. But of late he'd let them lapse. Wall Street man was too busy hustling to notice the niceties. His customers today, they didn't know his name, didn't look him in his face when they paid. What with all the French and Italian imports, the footwear itself was stylish enough but often neglected, ill used. "One true thing I have learned," said Lucius. "You can't judge the mens by the shoes that's wearing them."

He was a tubular piece of work, some five feet two of bumpy road, all angles and odd twists. He had arthritis, he said, and was cutting back on his work load. At seventy-four, all the stooping and the crouching that the shinist's art required took its toll. But he still came in to Wall Street. It was the place he knew.

There was a sandwich shop on Trinity Place that employed him part time. "Sometimes I delivers, sometimes I just spreads," he said. "Sometimes I don't feel right and I start in to miss my woman. My sweet wife Marie, I should say. She home in Brooklyn, Crown Heights, a long hour ride on the subway car, still I gotta go see her. I'm hard, y'understand. I'm so hard it hurts. Maybe it's just morningtime, I still gotta take my easement. What else a man gonna do? When he so hard he hurts?"

He pronounced it *so hoard he hoyts*; sucked on the phrase like a jujube, squeezing out the tang. When he laughed, which was often, he would wrap both arms tight about his skimpy child's belly, as if to hold the entrails in. This laugh, a keening trainwhistle moan, made me shiver. But Lucius said it relieved him. "Hoyts so good," he said, "I could kindly enjoy to die."

On the stroke of 4:00, the market closed; at 4:01, the morning stampede reversed itself. Only this time the charge was in slow motion, an army in retreat, battered, not quite broken. Near the uptown subway entrance, the fruit stall was all out of black grapes and pomegranates. This was a sign, said Lucius, that the Dow Jones was up.

He went east; I went west. On the far side of the churchyard, across a narrow wrought-iron bridge, was an upstairs pub called

Michael's I, a space as neutral as a doctor's waiting room. "And how was your day?" the barman enquired.

"Oh, God," said Liquor Jack.

His given name was Jack Young. In his pomp, he had been a financier, a home-run hitter, but now his role was reduced. "Short-term trading," he said. "I bunt."

At fifty-seven he was a man of flesh and many tangled tales. With wattles at droop and eyes like yesterday's fried eggs, slimy side up, he looked like an elderly coonhound that had lost the scent. Still he had pedigree, panache.

Thirty years back, there had been no sprightlier blade extant. The name alone, Liquor Jack, had been a code word for all things louche, unspeakable, irresistible. He had defined *boulevardier*, that magic word, and there were generations of debutantes, many now grandmothers, who still squeaked and colored at his mention.

A battered grace survived. Sweat-stained armpits or no, he bore himself as a man apart, *chosen*. In these last years, Wall Street had been overrun by barbarians, a plague of swine. The old style and values were gone forever. Jack Young was left over.

He had begun in Louisville. His mother's family, the Siminons, were prime Kentucky bloodstock. They had been there as long as the state itself, and they had thrived. By the 1930s, they owned much of Mockingbird Valley and Indian Hills, and they lived in a prototype Tara, complete with crystal chandeliers, a sweeping stairway, and one cow. Then had come Thatcher Young, Jack's father, to foul everything.

A beautiful ne'er-do-well, his son called him. He had ranked ninety-eighth nationally at skeet and trap, worn his jodhpurs like one of God's elect, but his notion of big fun was to sit alone at the center table of the Bachelor's Cotillion in the Louisville Country Club with a dozen White Castle hamburgers and throw them, one by one, into the overhead fan. And when he went slumming in the bars downtown, picked up some girl from a meat-packing plant, and left her with child, that was bigger fun yet.

Here was an awkwardness. The girl had to be pacified and sent away, the child brought up by Seminon grandparents, and Thatcher Young himself palmed off as the boy's elder brother. Jack was schooled to ride a good seat, observe his knives and forks. He was a privileged person. When he was six years old, his grandparents were off on a trip somewhere, Thatcher was nowhere around, and Jack's mother showed up, just appeared in the driveway and took him away in a pickup truck.

She was a mountain woman, a classical Appalachian, gaunt and bloodless, emaciated to the point of being spavined. She lived in a fall-down, tin-roof shack somewhere way out in the backwoods, with a numberless tribe of relatives. Total strangers kept pawing Jack, hugging on him and kissing wet. It was the most peculiar sensation, not unsavory exactly but foreign, a thing that was not done. To escape, he spent his days throwing a hard rubber ball up onto the tin roof, then waiting till it rolled down again. His mother sat in the doorway; she watched but did not speak. When the dogs ran away with his ball, she brought him a replacement. It was their one connection.

On the fifth day, the Seminons came and took him back, and Jack did not see his mother again. Fifty years afterwards, he could not remember her face or the name of her homeplace or any one detail about her. All that remained was the fat *plock* of the ball on the tin roof, like a stone dropped into deep waters, and the waiting till it reappeared, rolled back down to his hand.

I submit to you, he said, *I was not firmly rooted.* He had grown up a gentleman, yes, but restless, volatile, always a tad unsteady. At sixteen, in lieu of just running away, he faked his age and enlisted in the navy. By the time he got out again, two years later, Thatcher had gobbled huge chunks from his inheritance. A mere $1.3 million survived.

What to do? *I submit to you, I was startled.* But not for long.

Turning the entire pot into cash, a spending wad, he took it to New York.

What did all this have to do with Wall Street, with Broadway? In that era, quite a bit. Manhattan in the early fifties was full of such histories. It was the prime time of Cafe Society—*Caff Sosh*, in Liquor Jack's shorthand; of the Stork Club, the Copa, El Morocco. People had names like Rollo and Beau and Slim, and their vocation was behaving badly with style, just wild enough to be amusing but not to be threatening. They had family and freedom, unlimited time, and they didn't give a damn, not one.

It was not easy now, slumped over his oars in Michael's I, to conjure up just how it had felt. There had been such an ease, such utter certainty. In the whole of Western history, had any time and place been more confident? He thought not. America ruled the world, New York was the center of the universe, and thus it would always remain. And you, yourself, were immune. Impervious to age, damage, loss, all pain. Nothing bad could happen, not really *bad*. Nothing that could not be fixed.

Morals had no office here. They were not distasteful, just irrelevant. Only a goddamn Communist would suggest that elitism was not a birthright, or that flaunting privilege was ungodly. In Caff Sosh, such questions were not taboo—they simply did not arise.

You'd had to be there. Rehashed at this dry distance, it sounded tawdry, a touch absurd. Perhaps it really had been. But fun, Lord knows; so much fun. In eighteen months flat, Jack had run through his fortune, the entire $1.3 million, and he did not regret one cent.

What had it gone on? "Things. Just things. Attractive people and their foolish schemes. And bar bills, of course," he said. "Oblivion."

He went downtown to Wall Street, *The Street*, and got a job at City Bank. He was in love with adventure. "Action," he said now. "I didn't care what shape it took, or what it cost, just so long as it kept coming. And the market was action guaranteed. It was legalized gambling, and the wagering was no-limit."

It was also the most marvellous humbug. Not to offend the conventions, one must pretend to be truly at work, a small earnest cog in a mighty and God-blessed economy, when all the while one was hanging by his bootstraps, living and dying with every turn of the ticker tape, as hellbound a gamester as any back-alley crapshooter.

At least the blind tigers were commodious here. The Wall Street of that era was a fastness, a giant fraternity house, as consoling to the backside as a split-log fire. It had its quota of cads and bounders, thieves and financial hoodlums, just as it always had and ever would; but it knew how to tie its bow ties.

Liquor Jack, a clubbable man, fit right in. "My credentials? I was a funny fellow, I suppose. In those days a degree from Harvard Business School was not necessarily perceived as a plus. If anything, it was a black mark, made you look a little pushy, a show-off. The real plus was simply to be a right person, known to other right persons."

Two gangs ruled The Street, locked in uneasy alliance: Dusty Money, the great WASP merchant houses; and Our Crowd, the German Jews. Between them, they set the modes and mores of the whole financial world.

It was a benign dictatorship, structured around a series of unwritten, immutable laws. Prime among them was the assumption, true or false, that business was a compact among gentlemen. Friendly competition was fine, guerrilla warfare was not. In the boardrooms of the Great, all mahogany and wrought iron, nothing essential had changed since the nineteenth century. Handshakes were still binding; ticker tape was the ultimate software. Above all, most sacred tenet of all: "A man's word was his bond," Jack said, "if there were witnesses."

Given hindsight, he could see that the whole Byzantine edifice had hung on a single given—the innate blessedness of tradition, its divine right to command. But nobody questioned the franchise then, *nobody but nobodies.* One played by the rules, or one simply did not play.

He found a model, a mentor. Paul Shields was an old man who drove a canary-colored Rolls with midnight trim, dated the model Suzy Parker, and kept her in rubber sheets: "D'Artagnan with a swizzle stick; an authentic giant of the Street, worthy of the name *financier.* When he was seventy-two, he got busted with two hookers, one white, one black, and the *Daily News* ran the headline 'Two Gals in an Antique Bed.' It was his proudest moment."

But not his greatest achievement. In between escapades, Shields & Co. had helped create the block-trading boom, floating deals worth hundreds of millions: "And all done with mirrors. His own total capital was $15 million, barely a drop in the bucket, and here he was spawning these blockbuster trades, life-and-death gambles, as if they were bagatelles."

Nothing that came after could hope to equal that first rush: "Oh, we felt like God's own. As if we had a secret knowledge, and nothing and no one could bring us to earth. We were," Jack said, "the Premium Select."

There I left him. And found him again next day. In between, I bumped into Lucius Havens on the street, his arms full of sandwich bags, laughing hard. When I mentioned Paul Shields, he laughed still harder. "A gentleman and a sport," he said. "I use to onyx his Oxfords, oh, a many, a many a time. He never broke a ten-dollar bill and never forgot to pass on a good thing to those less apropos. One Christian sinner, Mister Shields. And that Mister Jack Young."

"What about him?"

"Hoo-weeh!"

D'Artagnan with a swizzle stick—Jack had used the phrase for Paul Shields, but it could have been himself. Already there'd been the fracas in the Village, outside the San Remo, when he'd punched an off-duty cop, got shot in the leg, and spent three months in Bellevue's prison ward. Then there was the battle royal with six waiters in the Stork Club; "Sore Patron a Bear in Cub Room," the headline had read.

"Situation fatal but not serious," said Jack. In those years, it didn't seem to matter what atrocities he committed, he was always invited back. On one North Shore estate, asked to tea by some Dusty Money, he'd gorged himself on sticky cakes and finger sandwiches, then proceeded to push Grandmother's grand piano into the swimming pool. The next week, he was asked to dinner. "I would submit to you that I was a scoundrel; *a whoreson, flap-eared knave*," he mused. "But a young knave, don't you see, of impeccable lineage."

And then, quite suddenly, he was not so young anymore. He could never work out quite when or how it had happened, only that it had, and that it spoiled his sport utterly. Somehow, in a fit of absentmindedness, he seemed to have mislaid twenty years. Now he was plumped down blindly into the eighties, and all the rules were changed. Strange young men with Brooklyn accents and Nintendo eyes kept rushing past, shrieking. They were not Dusty Money, not Our Crowd, just brats, a pack of baby-faced killers.

Orderly ascent, the art of gentlemanly accumulation, meant nothing here. These people were bomb-throwers, financial terrorists, who thought in billions, and billions *now*, and they were constrained by absolutely no limits. "It's a whole new ballgame," they brayed. So it was.

What was left was the morning after, a hangover for the ages. With vague surprise, Jack noticed that he had been married and divorced; that he had acquired a second wife, assorted offspring and obligations, all the trappings of the Real World; and that he could pay for none of them. So he changed jobs and made more money. Then he changed again, made even more. Still he couldn't seem to equalize, and still he was not young again. "Embarrassed?" he said. "One was mortified."

What had happened here? Abstractions and analyses were

not Jack's style. But his friend Michael Thomas took a grave-digger's view. Quite simply, a world had died. And why? For the same reason that all worlds die. The old order was exhausted. The Street was America in miniature, and the American century was over. It had taken three things for granted—its primacy in morality, in war, and in wealth. On these three struts had been built its whole sense of mastery, of innate superiority. But the disasters of the seventies, *its triple hegemonic cataclysms*, had mortally wounded all three. Watergate had shot down its moral certainties, Vietnam its military, OPEC its economic. Religion had already bitten the dust. So had the cult of discipline.

Ergo, anarchy. Before 1974, there'd been no such thing as a hostile takeover. But in the new order, nothing counted but the moment, and the will to win, which was polite parlance for the hunger to kill.

This was no climate for kumquats. Where were they all, Jack Young's contemporaries, his peers? Elsewhere. Those who had triumphed were either retired or out of sight, unreachable in their chauffeured Oldsmobiles, in their Park Avenue condos and Hamptons beachfronts. They were on boards, they hosted charity balls; they were everywhere but around. As for those who'd failed, they were long since dead of cirrhosis or, worse, at pasture on Long Island.

Clearly, Jack had missed a turn somewhere. In the glow of his infatuation, one basic truth about The Street had eluded him. People came here to get rich.

How come he hadn't noticed? "Too busy having fun. Too contrary, too much in love with the game for the game's own sake," he said. "And then, of course, my jackass ego. I said 'bullshit' to the witch doctor, and the good doctor shrank me."

Too busy having fun. It was an epitaph. In the days of his ascendancy, he could have cashed in easily, secured himself at a word. But the word had slipped his mind, and now what was left? "Picking flyshit out of pepper."

The Game Faces had inherited the earth. Across Broadway,

a few blocks to the south, was Harry's at Hanover Square, where the bond traders retired to swap war stories. It sat in the basement of The India House, a fine nineteenth-century merchant house, foursquare and discreet. But the discretion quit on entry. Standing in ranks around the rectangular bar, the bondsmen drank on the hoof, sweating men with wet mouths and ties all askew, and they howled.

A few young women were also present, seated at tables along the low windows. The men called them gals, and they wore a generic look of trimness, crispness, like freshly washed romaines. "Tight," said my next-door neighbor, Louis, who had once bonded junk at Drexel Burnham. "Tight, tight, tight."

It was the female catchword this year, the ideal. Tightness of limb, tightness of mind; tightness of smile and soul. "It works, too," Louis said. "The tighter they get, the sharper they feel. The sharper they feel, the more they kick ass. And the more they kick ass, the more they want to kick some more."

"What for?"

"What are we here for, my friend?"

His own ass-kicking statistics, however, were mired in a deep slump. Five years back, he had stood five feet six, weighed 280 pounds, and been worth $11 million. To celebrate reaching eight figures, he'd bought a sailboat and voyaged to Martha's Vineyard. On his second day out, he had a heart attack. The doctor told him to diet or die. So now he weighed 162, 163, and he was worth loose change. But he stood almost five feet seven: "Which just goes to show," Louis said.

Reverses did not dismay him. "The ebb tides of fate," he called them. Empty bags of skin hung off him in folds, made him look like a balding bloodhound, and he puffed at a dead corona that he was forbidden to light. Still he felt strong; he felt good. "I have seen the future," he said, "and it's me, very rich."

Harry's was among the last refuges of the entitled drinker. The current crusade against liquor had swept Wall Street with a withering blast, laying waste a century's proud tradition. In Jack Young's heyday, booze had been the market's Esperanto. A personage like Joseph Thomas, Michael's father, when he was CEO of Lehman Brothers, would conduct his operations from a steam room, stretched naked on a massage table, with a lit cigar in one hand and a vodka martini in the other, the *Daily Racing Form* spread out on his paunch and, for his emphysema, two clear plastic tubes running from his nostrils to an oxygen tank. As fashion statements went, it had seemed bold but not outrageous. Now alcophobia was run amok. The merest whiff of merriment on the breath after lunch and you were cast into outer darkness, a pariah.

Even at Harry's, the revelries were dimmed. For every bull-horn bourbon tosspot, there were two joggers on white-wine spritzers. As for Louis himself, it was true that he swilled J & B. But he was also in AA: "For the action."

It was the Street's latest brotherhood. In this dry season, AA was fast replacing the men's club as *sanctum sanctori*, the prime place to wheel and deal. Each morning before the market opened, and each evening after it closed, the smart money would gather in a basement on Trinity Place and work the floor, swapping tips and hatching plots, exchanging true confessions. It was cheaper than buying a round, Louis said: "And the sex is out of sight."

Liquor Jack was not amused. Of all the fads that had combined to render Wall Street hideous, good health stank foulest. His second wife, *my incumbent Duchess*, had once dared to speak of it in his connection. But only once. "Cast off the antic crutch of sin?" he'd said. "I rather fancy not."

These days he occupied a desk at Smith & Co. The Smiths were two brothers, John and James, out of Brooklyn. Their father had been Jewish, their mother Irish; the brothers themselves mixed cunning with combativeness: "Tire-iron street fighters," said Jack, "but tire-iron fighters with *direction*."

John Smith, the kingpin, sat in the middle of a long table

like a conveyor belt. Flanked by his hirelings, he presided like Prince John in the banqueting scene of Errol Flynn's *Adventures of Robin Hood*, with short-term traders standing in for courtiers and computer printouts for the chicken bones, flung recklessly about the festive board. But this was no smoothie-chops Claude Rains, all pout and purr. On the contrary, he was wound tight as a steel tourniquet. In his early forties, dandified but deadly in striped shirt and canary suspenders, he wore his hair cropped close, rarely smiled, but cracked his knuckles constantly. All his motions were fastidious, spare, and his stare indifferent, yet he gave an impression of furious energy—rage, just barely reined in.

The image did not offend him. It was true, he said, he was a human timebomb. To defuse himself, he had to run eight miles a day, pump iron till he hit the wall. Otherwise, his systems would overload: "Which would be counterproductive," he said.

His satellites seemed less controlled. Sweaty youths, they hunched squinting over computer screens, bawled into phones and thin air. What exactly they did was mysterious. But it seemed a lot to do with anal sex. Apparently, the world was full of fucking assholes, all looking to fuck each other up the fucking ass, and the only fucking way to survive was to fuck them up the fucking ass before they fucked you. No shit.

Crouched low in a separate cubicle, like a sniper in a foxhole, Liquor Jack placed orders and collected tips, counted down to four o'clock. His phone manner was hushed, conspiratorial. Sparse hairs lay like mist across his pink scalp. From time to time, when negotiations bogged down, he would reach up absently, wearily, to smooth them.

Somewhere else in the room, out of sight, a shrill voice lashed out, reflexive. "Fuck him!" it shrieked. "He can stick his fucking tongue up my fucking asshole!"

"I could," said Liquor Jack, "use a drink."

At Michael's I, right next door to the AA basement, he was safe. It was a bolthole, a place where he and like renegades could gather unseen, *in search of surcease of sorrow*, and drink themselves into quietude. Because it reminded him of an airport lounge, Jack called it the Terminal Bar: "And I mean that sincerely," he said.

His drink was vodka tonic with no fruit, his best game remembrance. As the evening drew on, and discontents deepened, his drawl grew more Louisville. Kentucky speech rhythms, lazy and arching, worked just fine for indifference, hauteur, but were not so hot for humility: "I would submit to you, it is no crime," he murmured, "to be conscious of who you have been, and who you are."

The murmur was a trademark. Now that he had joined the Seniors' Tour, he'd traded in the sozzled war whoop for the wry grimace, the smile at the foot of the scaffold.

What would set him to whooping again? It was hard to say. Once he had wanted more; now he just wanted out. If somehow he made a killing, he'd back up a station wagon to the bank, take out every cent and just start driving. Or forget the killing. All he wanted was a moiety, one used four-wheel vehicle and a road to anywhere.

On the bar lay a ten-dollar bill. When the time came to pick it up and go home, Liquor Jack let it slip through his fingers. It fell between his feet, and he bent to pick it up. Then he changed his mind; let it lie.

friend called Velma whose square name was Joe Wojcik, a short-
order cook. Before slinging hash, she had been a truck driver,
a stevedore, a security guard, and before all of that, she'd been
dead.

The greasy spoon where she worked lay neatly in my path,
a few blocks north of Wall Street. Lush Life suggested that I
stop off, get acquainted. "Ladybeard, you'll love her," she promised. "She is nothing but a lady."

"So how come she died?"

"Crazy Eddie done it."

The reference was to commercials. For fifteen years or more,
before bankruptcy nailed him, Crazy Eddie had been a New
York institution. Who the real Eddie was, hardly anyone knew
or cared. Some Syrian recluse who'd made and lost a fortune
selling discount stereos and videos, electronic toys. But his TV
alter ego was everywhere, a chubby balding actor with a mouth
big, wide, and bottomless as the abyss, who peddled software
in bug-eyed frenzy, a wail like a police siren. "Crazy Eddie
cannot, shall not, positively will not ever be undersold," he'd
shriek. "His prices are *insaaanne.*"

What was this to do with Joe Wojcik's dying? "Don't ask,"
said Lush Life. "It doesn't become you."

I did not argue. The hiatus was welcome, for Broadway was going through a bloated patch, pigged out on too much allegory. In the half-mile since Bowling Green, I'd passed enough Romanesque statues, Grecian columns, and mythological bronze reliefs to surfeit Caesar's Palace. Where they fronted major corporations, they'd had a certain pompous splendor. But hereabouts they stood guard over warrens of one-room offices, filled with private eyes and divorce lawyers, patent healers and defrocked chiropractors.

The sidewalks were frenzied here. Though there seemed nothing worth racing for, everybody raced regardless. Perhaps it was just force of habit. For this had ever been striver's row. "The great fighting ground of the city," Richard Harding Davis had called it. And James D. McCabe, in his 1879 *Lights and Shadows of New York Life*, wrote: "Every class, every shade of nationality and characters, is represented here."

McCabe had been Broadway's greatest chronicler. A Virginian Confederate and war journalist, he only came north when he was already dying. But his final years were spent tramping Manhattan, ten hours every day. He was not a fine stylist but his eye was sharp, his curiosity boundless. He saw New York and Broadway, not as platforms for distant reflection, but simply as astonishments, a magical and inexhaustible bazaar, through which he swam dazzled, appalled, above all in love.

His canvas was all-embracing. He wrote of Wall Street and Fifth Avenue, the Bowery, the Five Points, the Port; of newsboys and pawnbrokers, bulls and bears, street musicians, private eyes, flower girls, engravers on wood and steel, dealers in cheap watches, agents in indecent publications, gold beaters, fruit persons, bummers, bishops, the lost sisterhood, the heathen Chinee, and lawmen, fair and foul.

Ever and again, he was drawn back to Broadway. "It is the world within itself," he wrote, anticipating Jon Bradshaw. "High and low, rich and poor pass along at a rate of speed peculiar to New York, and positively bewildering to a stranger. Fine gentlemen in broadcloth, ladies in silk and jewels, and beggars in squalid rags are mingled in true Republican confusion. From early morn till after midnight the throng pours on."

Only the trademarks had changed. Now gilded Mercuries flew out of pizza parlors, Knowledge and Experience stood watch over OTBs. I met Lush Life at the AT&T Building, a wedding cake built of nine mock-Parthenons, one on top of another, and she showed up as Audrey Hepburn in *Breakfast at Tiffany's*—pink Capri pants and pink ballet slippers, bare midriff and knotted white shirt. She dragged at a cigarette holder like a poison-dart blowpipe, blew smoke in my face. "Quel rat," she said.

It was snowing, a gray sleet that turned to slush on contact, and the sidewalk was ankle-deep in ooze. But Lush Life could not afford a trench coat, and any other coat would have ruined the look. So she stood shivering, her Cleopatra eyes smeared all over her cheekbones, while a man with a sandwich board paraded on the curb, extolling Le Club Hot-Stuff. With her dark glasses off, she looked fifteen.

Joe Wojcik worked just opposite, in a defile off Nassau Street. The place was run by Israelis; travel posters for Tel Aviv and the Red Sea adorned the walls, and the menu mentioned gefilte fish; but the smell said "Eats." Behind a stainless-steel counter, Joe griddled eggs over easy, hash browns, stacks. A man somewhere past thirty and not yet fifty, he stood foursquare, his bare arms and throat covered in a fine brown fur like babyfuzz. A fat pink scar like a lightning bolt zigzagged across his scalp. Around it, he was almost bald.

When he saw Lush Life, he did not clap his fingers to his mouth and screech like some other girls, but reached across the counter and shook her firmly by her hand. His knuckles were bloated, deformed, and his eyebrows tortured by scars. "Girl boxed pro," Lush Life explained.

They went back a long way. When Lush Life first stepped out into New York, she had known nobody, nothing, but some of the girls who worked Port Authority had sent her to Sally's Hideaway on West Forty-third Street, which called itself Transvestite Capital of the World. There Velma had saved her life.

By now we had an unspoken deal: I would ask no questions, she would tell me lies. Nights in my cell at the Hotel Moose, Lush Life would sit cross-legged on the marigold coverlet and do her nails and spill herself till daylight. But only on her own terms. I must not pump, never try to pin her down. At the first query, she'd cut off dead and the face she turned on me then was a Medusa snakeshead. "I hate spies," she said.

So now, waiting for Joe to finish his shift, we sat at a corner table, I kept my mouth shut tight and Lush Life studied her horoscope. "Don't ask," she said. "A meeting with an intriguing stranger promises romantic complications. Follow your heart but exercise care." She puckered her brows, she pondered. "What if you have a careless heart?" she enquired.

Sally's Hideaway had been a long, dark room behind a tiny, dark window. For her first night, she wore a white shirtwaister with matching white pumps, her hair cropped short as a Marine's, sort of a tomboy look, like Jean Seberg in *Saint Joan*, only Joan of Arc did not wear pink satin panties with an inset purple heart. The whole dark room was jammed solid like a rush-hour subway train, and Grace Jones was blaring on the jukebox, *I Need a Man*, and this big black girl, she must have weighed two hundred pounds, in a red sequin dress and an Ann-Margret wig, she threw Lush Life up against the wall and ripped her dress off. And all the other girls watched. So you see. Lush Life begged the girl to hit her, hurt her, only please not to ruin her outfit. And the girl, some *girl*, the only way she'd see forty again was on a NO SPEEDING sign and her arms were as thick as Lush Life's waist, all bloated and sagging, they made you think of rotting hams; anyhow, the bitch did hit and hurt her, then she ruined her outfit as well. She stripped Lush Life to her skin, out back by the john, where everyone could see and know the truth, that she'd had no silicone implants, no hormone shots, she didn't even shave her legs. *Plucked chicken*, the woman called her. "I could of died," said Lush Life.

Maybe she would have, only then another girl came, all squat and bandy in a spandex microskirt, and she didn't hardly reach to the black girl's chests, but she hit her one left hook and starched her stiff as Nancy Reagan's smile. And this girl was Velma. She carried Lush Life inside the john and stuck her clothes back on with Band-Aids and safety pins, she took her home and made her hot chocolate and put her to bed, and the whole time she said just one thing, *Shut up, bitch*.

In the morning there was no Velma, just Joe, a regular guy in a string undershirt and baggy pants, chugging beer in front of the TV. If it wasn't for the lipstick and the silver-sparkle fingernails, he might have been some other person.

This was a rarity. Most dressers, when they'd dug this deep into the Life, stayed *femme* night and day. But Velma and Joe split shifts. They'd been together twenty years, ever since Joe was in the navy, and sharing had become their second nature. They were like an old married couple, Lush Life thought. Each had their set role, their routine. They even looked alike.

In the course of her recitation, she had slipped out of character. Now she remembered Holly Golightly, *top banana in the shock stakes*, and she went back into hiding behind her dark glasses, she practiced blowing smoke rings. "Where do you stand on enemas?" she asked.

When Joe got off work and came across to our table, he seemed to have stepped out of the 1940s. He wore a double-breasted blue suit with cuffs, corespondent shoes, a porkpie hat with a feather in the band. The uniform made him look even squatter and squarer, a Danny De Vito with silver-sparkle nails. "Hello, Life," he said, a flat nasal voice, muffled by crushed cartilage. "You wanted me?"

"I always want you, chérie."

"How much?"

"You know how it is, so many places to do and people to

be, *La Vie en Rose* to die for, and all so simply madly gay it makes you sick, you get old."

"A Jackson? A Franklin?"

"If you don't pay the piper, you don't pay the rent," said Lush Life. "But chérie, I tell you, his prices are insaaanne."

Out of his back pants pocket, Joe produced a billfold as fat as that and peeled off five Hamiltons. But when he pushed the money towards Lush Life, she stayed him. Her child's hand fell on his wrist, bitten nails almost lost in tangled brown fur, and she gave him a look that had no one name, tenderness and mockery and challenge all mixed, a mirror look. "Velma," she said.

"Shut up, bitch," said Joe.

Lush Life kissed his mouth, took his cash. Her wet clothes clung to her body, and she was shivering again. "Quel prince," she said, then she was gone. A small puddle marked where she'd sat.

With his hat on, and the pink scar hid, Joe looked more deadpan than ever. He had the classic face of the opponent— scattered nose and conch-shell ears, eyes tunneled deep behind cliff-hanging brows. He even talked in boxing rhythms, staccato flurries like combinations, that never stopped and started quite where you'd expect. "Three and eleven. But," he said, "I was robbed."

Three wins and eleven losses, and not one had ended in a clean knockout. "A lot. Of pushing and shoving, a whole lot of. Hurt. But I never did kiss canvas," Joe said. The flat voice met questions the same way he must have met fighters, head on, without fuss or feint. "What I was best at," he said, "I knew how to soak. Up punishment."

His room was on Ann Street, just around the corner, at the top of five flights of stairs. The street was a survival from an earlier Broadway, when its people had still lived in houses. Hemmed in by monsters was a single row of redbricks, walk-ups, complete with broken windows and iron fire escapes. Isaac Mendoza Book Co., the city's oldest booksellers, huddled here. So did Adult Books & Peeps, XXX.

In the 1840s, this had been the most glamorous spot on Broadway. Within fifty yards had stood the Astor House, the first of New York's great hotels, built by John Jacob Astor at a cost of $1 million; Mathew Brady's daguerreotype studio, where Abraham Lincoln, James Fenimore Cooper, and Edgar Allan Poe sat stiffly for frozen portraits; the offices of Horace Greeley's New York *Tribune* and James Gordon Bennett's New York *Herald*; and right at Broadway and Ann, most glorious of all, P. T. Barnum's first American Museum.

It must, in 1841, have been a staggering sight. According to Irving Wallace's *The Fabulous Showman*: "One morning it was a hulking, drab, marble building, and lo, the next, it was a breathtaking rainbow, a kaleidoscope of color and curiosity." Outlandish oil paintings of birds, beasts, and creeping things covered the fourth story; illuminated glasses, boiling and bubbling like primitive neon, halted the night traffic. In its own moment, much like the Statue of Liberty or the Empire State Building later on, it was the one New York spectacular that no visitor dared miss.

Joe Wojcik lived facing a defunct pawnbroker, at the top of five flights of stairs.

The room itself was just a garret with a skylight. There were plastic geraniums in a window box, blue and yellow towels drying on a line, a metal-frame bed and a flowered china washbowl, and maybe a dozen sea lockers, piled high against the wall or ranged like stations of the cross at intervals across the floor. Obliterate the TV and the whole set could have played *La Bohème*.

Faintly from Isaac Mendoza's came the musty scent of caged books. Seven hats—homburgs, trilbies, stingy brims—hung on an ornate wooden rack. Above them, framed, was Joe's honorable discharge from the navy. "Fourteen years. I'm here and still not. Unpacked," he said, indicating the trunks. "But what? The hey?"

Fishing a six-pack of lukewarm Colt 45s out of a copper coal scuttle, he perched himself on the bed, made me hunker down on a locker. Thus set above me, he had control, was free to speak what he chose. "In the first place, I'm out. Of Brooklyn, Troy Avenue. In Crown Heights," he began. "My old man was a cop."

"What about Crazy Eddie?"

"Wait," said Joe. "Just wait."

Before he died, he had lived. For twenty-eight years and change, he had been one of the crowd: "Your average transvestite. Altarboy prizefighter son of," he said, "a Polack cop."

The altarboy had come first. That was the start of everything. Sometime around his eleventh birthday, Father Cavanaugh had called him into the dark and touched him. Father Theosophus Tone Cavanaugh. It had felt just fine, relaxing, not strange at all. The only thing was, it made him see stuff.

What kind of stuff? That was the problem. The things he saw had no titles. There was nothing defined, no one thing he could pick out and say *Gotcha*, cut and dried, like *I saw a garden, I saw God, I saw ice cream, I saw up my own asshole*. Instead, there was a whirl of colors and shapes that never stopped shifting and breaking up and reforming. Like looking into a kaleidoscope, only different. It was hard to define, and he never was any good with words, they never seemed to say what he thought they did. But, well, these colors and shapes, they were beautiful, the most beautiful things you'd ever see but they were scary also, unholy. So that you knew you shouldn't fall in among them. Only deep down you wanted to. And any time you thought you had them nailed, and one certain image was just about to surface, the whole pack would be reshuffled, everything would just slipslide away, and you'd be right back where you started, locked out. And all this, of course, in real life, it was just a flash, a few seconds at most. But inside your own self it went on forever.

As he talked, he kept glugging beer. He had the most seamless technique, would tilt his head back and open up his throat and pour down an entire can in a single swig. Stray suds ran down his chin and hung there, like raindrops on a wire. "What would you call that? A vision? A dream?" he asked, idly belching. "I called it losing. My mind."

Whatever it was, it came on its own calling, not his. After Father Cavanaugh, a whole year went by undisturbed, maybe two. Then he was at some football game, he couldn't remember what game now, but it was nearly over and his team was driving for the win. There was a big play. He jumped up on his feet. And he saw stuff again.

To make a long. Story short. Over the years, these attacks, visitations, whatever you'd care to call them, kept recurring. And after he started boxing, they started to come more often. He felt good in himself; he had no problems that he knew of. His only curse was blushing. In every other respect, he was a hard case; a loner, who could not abide effeminates. Crimes against nature, *weird stuff*, made him sick. But every so often he'd be sparring, or just standing staring on some street corner, and he'd get this weird buzzing and numbness inside his skull, sort of like a tuning fork vibrating, and suddenly the colors and shapes would flood him, wash him away. Like nothing. On earth.

Now the point. Though he could never get the frame to freeze, never isolate any one detail, certain patterns kept repeating. There were curves and billows, sudden swells like sails or backyard washing in the wind, swoops like birds, soft, fat moons. Most familiar of all, there was a black hole that kept growing and shrinking, flexing and sucking, like a mouth or asshole or maybe just space, a void.

And one day he was unwinding after training, drinking a few beers and watching the Mets on TV. The commercials came on, and suddenly, out of nowhere, there was the same black hole, selling discount TVs. It was the mouth of Crazy Eddie.

Velma was still new then. She had made her debut when Joe was in the service. On her first night, she had performed a striptease to "Diamonds Are a Girl's Best Friend" at his ship's Christmas party. But she was not really a party girl. For a long time, she was a mousy little girl who could not stand to be loved, didn't dare go outside her own room. Her evenings were spent in washing and mending her clothes, demure mail-order outfits, all drabs and beiges and fawns, with white collars and sensible flat-heeled shoes. She cut out coupons, saved travel brochures. No strange colors or shapes troubled *her*.

But Joe could not escape them. By the time he retired from boxing, they were coming so hard and fast, they almost seemed routine. "You might say we'd took up. Housekeeping," he said.

From where I sat squatted below him, my sightline took in a furry ankle, one brown-and-white wing-tipped shoe, a tattered edge of yellow towel, half a geranium, and an oblong of purpling sky. "So then came the big," Joe said. "Equalizer."

In his last fight, six rounds with some Panamanian kid, Maurizio Mendez he thought the name was, at the old Sunnyside Gardens he took his first real whipping. The kid was not schooled but he was strong, full of sap, and he could hit like a kicking mule. Joe did not go down but he was busted up good, and the ref stopped it after five. So that was it. He was twenty-four, an old man.

So all right. So he goes back in his dressing room, the doc fixes him up, the promoter pays him off, his trainer takes his cut and runs, he gets showered and changed, and off he heads. For home. He walks out of the Gardens down underneath the el. The subway is roaring through right above him and then it's gone. But the roaring is still there, inside his head. And all the colors and shapes fly in at once, fill him up. Too tight. He can't contain them all, hold them in. Too much pressure. One more twist, and his skull will burst. And then, right then, out of the whirlpool comes the black mouth. Sucking in, sucking in. And this time it gets him, he has no choice, he falls. Right. In.

When he came to, he was in the hospital, and they told him that he'd died, his heart had stopped and he was gone, twenty minutes or more, before they pulled him back.

So then he knew Death by her right name.

Crazy Eddie.

And that was the last of the colors and shapes. After he got out of the hospital, he took this room. The building was tied up in litigation then, still was, else it would have been pulled down or sold long ago. So he clung on by default. "Every day is borrowed. Time," he said.

All of this had taught him sufferance. Nothing sickened him now, not weird stuff, not any stuff on earth but cruelty. So here he sat and roosted, and drank his Colt 45s. "Joe Wojcik lives. A boring life," he said. "But what? The hey?"

And Velma? She thrived. As Joe had slowed down, drawn in on himself, so she had taken wing. She started to go out nights, strut her stuff in Sally's Hideaway, and her whole attitude turned around. No more the meek and dowdy housegirl, she was cut loose: "A natural woman," Lush Life said.

Her one consuming passion was clothes. She did not flirt, didn't sleep around, didn't care to get involved. On every other subject, she made no fuss and no demands. But clothes, that was something else. Each week she must have a new outfit, sometimes two. If she didn't get them, blood flowed.

"What can? You do?" Joe said. Truth was, not a lot. It took him every minute of his working life to earn enough, keep her satisfied. But he did not begrudge her. They were partners, after all; her happiness was his own.

Outdoors, it had grown dark. Rain flurried on the skylight, and Joe climbed down off the bed. Back on my own level, he shrank, became again a short bald man with silver-sparkle nails. Floor space was tight, and when I got up from the sea locker, we brushed together, my shoulder against his hip. He shied as if I'd struck him.

Beyond the drying towels, out of sight, was a walk-in closet. Inside was Velma's wardrobe. "Would you? Care to?" Joe asked, not meeting my eye.

"We wouldn't take the same size."

"To look. I meant just. Look."

Rose-madder blushes mottled his forehead and neck. With face averted, he ushered me through a faded taffeta curtain. On the other side, lantern-lit, was an Aladdin's cave.

It was filled with colors and shapes.

the horse was New Day Dawning, and out at Aqueduct, it has
probably finished by now. In the Park Place OTB, I tore my
betting stub three times lengthwise, three times across, then
scattered the confetti. The stout party with the flushed face and
the black suspenders to my left regarded me sourly. "New Day
Dawning? What kind of fool bet was that?" he said. His stomach
growled. "What you get for backing a reformer," he said.

The party's name was Matthew Joseph Troy; Matty Troy.
In the sixties and early seventies, he had been both a city coun-
cillor and the Democratic chairman of Queens County: "The
biggest liar and most honest man in New York politics," wrote
Richard Reeves in a *New York* magazine profile. Soon afterwards, Troy went to jail.

At his peak, nobody elected had cut a wider swathe. There
was hardly a day, it seemed, when his mugshot wasn't splattered
all over the *Daily News*. He went charging through the city like
a wounded bull elephant, with his minions and pet scribes at
his elbow, TV crews and photographers in panic pursuit, and
as he rampaged, spooling out quotes like a ticker tape, flinging
insults and shooting lines, he did not give one good tinker's fart
what was said, or what dread power was offended, just so long
as the press kept spelling his name right.

The quotes were verbal firebombs. "The media is 99 percent of a political career in this town. You get them by being controversial. You've got to tell them the truth, but it helps to embellish it a little," Troy believed. "Lying is an essential part of the political process."

It wasn't these home truths themselves that shocked. Everybody who could read and most who couldn't already knew them. What made Matty Troy unique was simply that he spoke them out loud. Shouted them, in fact. "Only egomaniacs are in politics," he'd snap in his belly-deep rasp. "I love the guys who talk about serving the public. This business is about men kissing your ass and girls who screw."

The man in the OTB parlor, sweating over his form sheets, was twenty years older, a tad less incendiary. He now worked for the Long Island Gasoline Retailers Association as a publicist and lobbyist. Mostly he worked out by Roosevelt Racetrack, but his duties also took him to Albany and Washington, to the World Trade Center, and, sometimes, back to City Hall, just a stretch-run up Broadway from the betting shop. He'd used to have his own office there; these days he required an appointment. For the first few years, the comedown had distressed him, but no longer. He was sixty; he had a hernia. No more grandstand plays for Matty Troy, and no more grief: "Suits me," he said.

The truth was, he had no choice. Power, once lost, was not refundable. So here he stood, figurating, a hulking and rumpled figure of the type once called Black Irish. In this equine bucket-shop, he cast no shadow, drew no stares. To one side of him was Juan Rosario, a messenger on his break; to the other, Eula Mae Beales, an off-duty cleaner at the Woolworth Building. Post time for the fourth race was eight minutes off and counting. "So who do you like?" Matty asked.

Nobody seemed sure. Juan Rosario was chasing the Pick Six, Eula Mae leaned towards a Trifecta, I myself was flat busted. Matty liked Buckshot Behave. He also fancied Just Be Just, but that was sentiment speaking: "Reminds me of my father," he said, and he backed Buckshot Behave.

His father had been a special sessions judge. Before that, he'd been Fiorello La Guardia's personal attorney. Matthew Troy, Sr., whom no man ever called Matty. There were people who still remembered him, his gentleness and grace, his chivalry, his toughness at root. He was a West Meath man who'd settled in Bay Ridge, in the parish of Our Lady of Perpetual Hope, and his ruling passion was Irish unification. In Matty's childhood, his home was always full of Fenian activists planning campaigns, raising funds. Paul O'Dwyer, the dean of New York Nationalists, was a household fixture. Then the movement was taken over by Sinn Fein and the IRA, the bombings started, the murders of women and children, and Judge Troy didn't speak of One Ireland again.

In New York, judges were elected. Each county leader had a certain number of judgeships tucked in his back pocket. Some were purchased with bribes, some with favors; just a few were earned on merit. Matthew Troy was one of these last, a political maverick, neither Democrat or Republican, who ran for Brooklyn borough president and Brooklyn County Court on a Fusion ticket and lost both races handily. Afterwards, he retired from active politics, confined himself to the Ancient Order of Hibernians. But by then it was too late: Matty, aged twelve, had been fatally infected.

What hooked him first was scurrility. In that pre-computer age, votes were still cast at the push of a lever. A well-greased election inspector could spike it by sticking gum or wax or a toothpick to the underside. Or else, the standard dodge, he'd simply slip a sliver of lead beneath his thumbnail and shift the Xs to the line where his money lay. When Matty spotted this, and the Xs did not line up next to *Troy*, he started punching heads.

His first arrest followed.

Eula Mae Beales, hearing this, pantomimed dismay: "Only just a baby and already in jail," she said. "And your poor momma, too, just conceive how you make her grieve."

"My mother? She beat the living hell out of me. My father, till his dying day, he never once laid his hand on me. But my mother, God rest her, she wore out the strap." Matty shook his head, pleasantly borne back. "Wore out the strap," he said.

Not that it bothered him. Getting whaled on was *action*, getting into fights was action, and action, any action, always made his motor purr. He was a pistol, a brawling, big-mouth Harp with solid-brass balls. Mouth flapping, fists flying, he roared his way out of Brooklyn into Queens County, through two years in the army, then through Georgetown and Fordham Law School, and when he surfaced at the far bank, miraculously intact, he found himself a career politician.

In the army, he'd gone through basic training in the bunk next to Edward Kennedy. The apprenticeship was not in combat alone: "Teddy's like me. A put-on artist. He knows it's all bullshit. His father fixed it up so that we would both be assigned to NATO Headquarters in Paris. Then we took our physicals and I lost out because I was an inch under six feet. I spent a week trying to stretch myself with braces and racks and hanging upside down from the horizontal bars but I just couldn't make it. So I went off to Korea, and Teddy went to the Crazy Horse."

That was all the practical politics he needed to know. Demobilized and back in New York, he joined the Queens Village Democratic Club, worked his way up to campaign manager, and by 1964, aged thirty-five, he was city councilman for the Sixteenth District. His best friend and first lieutenant was Donald Manes, who would, some thirty years afterwards, be exposed as a massive bribe-taker and fixer, Mr. Big, and thus set off the worst municipal scandal to hit the city since Mayor William O'Dwyer in the late forties.

Buckshot Behave came in nowhere. Kissing off the OTB, we crossed Broadway into City Hall Park. It was the lunch hour;

the pathways and benches were jammed. Under the trees, a string quartet was playing Schubert for the sandwich crowd, but the only spots free for Matty and myself were over towards the Brooklyn Bridge, among the derelicts. Matty sat down heavily, eyes dull. Two men wrapped in newspapers lay rolled up beneath the bench. Behind our heads, the quartet switched to Smetana.

We stared out on the gridlocked traffic inching out of Manhattan. "I have to eat," Matty said. Absentminded, he belched. "Gas," he said. "It kills you."

He hardly looked a demagogue. Passing him by, one would have guessed Irish cop, retired. Nassau Street, right across from us, was full of private eyes, stolid and weary men with paunches and high blood pressure, who had traded in their badges for licenses and now played out their string in tracing missing persons and twenty-four-hour surveillance, parked outside hot-mattress motels. Matty Troy, burping, fitted in seamlessly.

It was not ever thus. When he looked behind him at City Hall, he started laughing, a serious belly laugh, deep and ripe as rolling thunder. "The numbers we did. The scams we pulled," he rumbled. But the small eyes in the big face did not laugh along. "You wouldn't believe," he said, "the numbers we did back then."

He seemed to speak of a bygone age. And he did. New York politics in the 1960s, more or less, had been the New York politics of the 1880s. Its constituency might have grown more polyglot, its leaders a little more polished, and there had been a few new cant phrases to master, *civil rights, the Great Society, Afro-American, freedom.* Otherwise, the system had survived untouched.

It had its own secret bible. In 1905, a Tammany Hall ward boss from the West Side, name of George Washington Plunkitt, had sat in his office, Graziano's bootblack stand in the old County Courthouse, and dictated *A Series of Very Plain Talks on Very Practical Politics.* His conclusions? "Honesty doesn't matter; efficiency doesn't matter; progressive vision doesn't matter. What matters is the chance of a better job, a better price for wheat, better business conditions."

Plunkitt's musings boiled down to a single deathless phrase, "I seen my opportunities and I took 'em." In his view, city government was about one thing only, and that thing was looking after those who looked after you. To do so, you walked the tightrope between opportunism and illegality: "Honest graft and dishonest graft," he wrote. "Every good man looks after his friends, and any man who doesn't isn't likely to be popular."

It was very much a Hibernian world, and why not? "The Irish was born to rule, and they're the honestest people in the world. Show me the Irishman that would steal a roof off an almhouse! He don't exist. Of course, if an Irishman had the political pull and the roof was much worn, he might get the city authorities to put on a new one and get the contract for it himself, and buy the old roof at a bargain—but that's honest graft. It's going about the thing like a gentleman."

By 1964, it was true, Tammany Hall itself was defunct. In its latter years, Jews and Italians had been let in to rub shoulders with the old-guard Irish. The last high sachem was Carmine DeSapio: "A gentleman, a fashion plate, and absolutely lethal," said Matty Troy. "The kind of political surgeon that would slit your throat with a smile, and you wouldn't even know it till you turned around and your head fell off in your lap."

When DeSapio went to jail for a construction fraud, Tammany Hall fell with him. But the Democratic clubhouse continued to dispense the spoils of the city—contracts, favors, patronage—howsoever it thought fit. Reform movements rose up, reform movements sank: "Morning glories," George Washington Plunkitt had called them. "Looked lovely in the mornin' and withered up in a short time, while the regular machines went on flourishin' forever, like fine old oaks."

Matty Troy might have been Plunkitt's second coming. Gasconading into the Queens Village clubhouse, he found a roomful of old men, *the geriatric irregulars*, content to play pinochle and organize dinner dances. He also found a tutor, Lew Wallach, the Democratic leader for Glen Oaks: "You could call him my sponsor," Matty said. "Or maybe my wet nurse."

Temperamentally, Wallach was Troy's polar opposite—a born chess player, close-mouthed and canny, who always saw five moves ahead: "A master of the game." Under his tutelage, Matty learned how to work a room, build up a power base. Within a few years, he'd made the Queens Village machine his own.

Already Donald Manes was his closest friend and ally. "No two brothers were ever closer," Matty said. It was as if they were the two halves of a pantomime horse, Matty the head and Donnie the back legs. Donnie's father had committed suicide, had gone down in his basement and put a gun in his mouth. Donnie was a child then, he'd come home from school and found him dead. Afterwards, for the rest of his life, he'd never dared descend an unlit stairway. Someone always had to precede him, light the way. "I guess," said Matty, "I held the damn light."

Back then, he had wattage to spare: "I'm not saying I was a knight in shining armor, which I wasn't. It was just I saw a lot of things that needed doing, and I was the one had the balls to get them done. Back then, I did."

Things that needed doing did not include social upheaval. Irish pols had never been bothered by an overview. They dealt strictly in particulars. And Matty Troy, above all things, was an Irish pol. "Compromise and *quid pro quo* were the bulwarks of my thought. I'm not an opinionated man, I swing with the tide," he growled. But he spat on double-talk and evasions, *dishonest graft*. "I might be a liar myself. At least I admitted it," he said. "What I couldn't stand was the mealymouths and muckety-mucks, the creeping Jesuses, the *smooth* men."

His platform then was built on seeming candor, *the voter's right to know*. In its name, he declared war on hugger-mugger and conspiracy, clandestine deals sealed in backroom booths. Matty too made deals, but openly, his enemies said wantonly. In 1971, for instance, he had traded three State Supreme Court judgeships to the Republicans in return for two judgeships, a district attorney, a counsel to the public administrator, and a state investigation commissioner to be named later. Not only that, but he put it in writing and wanted Nelson Rockefeller to sign it.

All of this caused sorrow, grave concern. "He was a rolling hand grenade, the Bugsy Siegel of New York politics, and as such he had to go," wrote Sidney Zion.

Hand grenade or no, by the seventies he was a major populist leader, carrying 85 percent in his own Queens district, Our Lady of Lourdes, and widely tipped as a future mayor. He himself had his eye on becoming a senator, so that he might eventually be reunited with Teddy Kennedy. To that end, in his national debut, he went out campaigning with George McGovern: "A sweet, sweet man, and absolutely hopeless."

And his policies? What policies? "The way I worked out where I stood on any question, I'd find out where John Lindsay stood, then take the opposite," he said. "Some of my positions I believed in, too."

What he understood, first and last, was the formula for turning waverers into voters. "You can't be patriotic on a wage that just keeps the wolf from the door," George Washington Plunkitt had said. "Any man who pretends he can will bear watchin'. Keep your hand on your watch and your pocketbook when he's around. But, when a man has a good fat salary, he finds himself hummin' *Hail Columbia*, all unconscious and he fancies, when he's ridin' in a trolley car, that the wheels are always sayin' *Yankee Doodle Came to Town*."

In this grand tradition, Matty Troy found no ploy too demeaning, no chore too small. He took care of jury notices, had wayward trees trimmed, paid off fines for garbage violations,

fixed potholes. He was strong on patronage jobs, on schools
and affordable housing. He also had Mayor Lindsay's doorman
arrested for walking his dog unleashed. "Isn't there any level
you wouldn't sink to?" Lindsay demanded.

"Absolutely not. There's nothing I wouldn't do."

"That's a double negative."

"Well, you've been a double negative to the city ever since
you took office," Matty would snap back, with a roll of drums
in back, a vaudeville clarinet bleat, and then he'd be off again,
on another crazed tear around the town, Chairman Matt, seven
functions a night, six nights a week, with his half-blind driver
Charlie Gilvary, and his red face sweating, his paunch belled
out ahead of him like a foresail before a fair wind, Jimmy Breslin
to the left of him, Pete Hamill to the right, and Donald Manes,
always Donnie, half a step to his rear.

He'd thought himself untouchable. All the people around
him, he'd made them, they owed him. "Oh, I was full of it. Full
of it. I acted like I had a full house, when I was holding a couple
of deuces," he said now, coughing hard. "My hat got away from
my head."

In skimming his Plunkitt, he'd overlooked one critical passage: "The men who rule have practiced keepin' their tongues
still, not exercisin' them. So you want to drop the orator act
unless you mean to go into politics just to perform the skyrocket
act." And this oversight proved fatal.

His fall was sudden, very steep. In 1973, Matty backed the
wrong horse for mayor, got boondoggled by his own man, and
wound up running afoul of Abe Beame, the new incumbent.
Richard Reeves's *New York* article that March proved the
clincher. "I worked all my life to get into a position of power
and I'm not about to play it down," Matty was quoted. "The
one thing more important than power is fear of power. I get
things because people are afraid of what I might do. I lived for
weeks off a picture of me on the front page of the *Daily News*

with McGovern and Ted Kennedy at the airport. What no one knows is that all I said to them that day is, 'The car's over here.'"

And: "One of my problems with the other [county] leaders—the four gravediggers—is they take themselves so damn seriously. . . . When we get together, you'd think a grand jury was after us with everyone whispering and looking over his shoulder. The first thing we always do is make a pledge that no one will speak to the press. Then, when it's over, we all race like hell for the nearest telephone to call reporters and get our side in first."

And: "Patronage is why people love me so much."

And: "Making deals is what a leader does."

And: "I've learned that you can get away with anything with bluff and saber-rattling."

Only this time the bluff was called. Every line, so sweet in the speaking, so juicy to savor in print, came back on him redoubled. Within months, Abe Beame had contrived his ouster as Queens County leader and placed Donald Manes in his stead.

It was a classical betrayal. In all their years together, Donnie was the one person he'd ever taken for granted. "Of course, it was my own dumb fault. In politics, you don't trust *anyone*. If you do, you got no gripe coming," Matty said. Even so, his temper had frayed as he watched Donnie rise: borough president, the king of Queens, unofficial mayor in waiting.

"As for me, I didn't do so hot," he said. At a stroke, stripped of his power base, he'd lost all heft, was reduced to a sound effect. "Wind outta burst balloon. I dropped so fast I was dizzy," he said. The indictments followed.

There was a grand larceny concerning an estate his law firm had handled. There was tax evasion and perjury. He served fifty-six days on the first, twenty-six weekends at Riker's Island on the second, but beat the perjury rap. He said that he had known nothing of these matters, that the whole thing had happened in his absence. It was possible. But the responsibility was his, just the same. So he did the time, was disbarred from his law practice: "As for politics, of course, I was dead meat."

Since his release, he had lived quietly with his wife and ten children, not far from Belmont Racetrack. His father had suffered a stroke, just shortly before the arrest, and had never known of his son's disgrace. That was one good thing, Matty said. A blessing, he called it. But his voice was as flat as Johnnie Ray.

For himself, he'd come to terms long ago. Leastways, if he hadn't, he must be fooling himself. The way he felt, he was better off. New York politics had no need of one more old man.

In the park behind us, lunch hour was over, the string quartet packed up and gone. Slow and heavy, as if we'd eaten too much, we walked towards City Hall. "So that's the story," Matty said. "Or the fable, I should say."

City Hall itself was a marbled palace built in 1811. Designed by a Frenchman and a Scot, it was a perverse but pleasing bastard, part Georgian, part Palladian and part French Renaissance, ostentatiously elegant, and wholly artificial. In this city where politics had always been muck and bullets, devoutly soiled, the Council Chamber was a thing of mahogany panels and fluted wainscoting, and the people's elected sat at slanting eighteenth-century desks arranged in a semicircle in front of a dais draped in flags. Overhead, its details picked out in gold, was a mural of *New York Receiving the Tribute of the Nations*; below, stuck to the undersides of the councillors' desks, was wedged the rocklike chewed gum of the ages. "I had fun in that place," said Matty Troy.

His own office had been in the basement, the West Wing. There he'd sit playing cards with the boys from Queens Boulevard, while upstairs the mayor and all his men would be sweating blood to balance the budget. After hours, Matty would slip across Broadway to the Longchamps. That had been the city pols' bar then, and after he'd had a few pops, he would hit the street running, back on the circuit with Charlie Gilvary, poor

bat-eyed Charlie, bouncing off buses, shunting through fences
and over back lawns, more often on the sidewalk than out in
the road, a dinner dance in Flushing, a fundraiser in Mineola,
a wedding reception, a wake, a firemen's ball, and everybody
gladhanding him, slapping him on the back, all of the Clubhouse
chiefs, the boys, because it still was a man's world, and it was
all laughs, a lotta laughs, so many laughs.

Where Longchamps had been, there was now a Plymouth
Shop, selling chainstore women's clothing. Politicians did not
drink now, not where they could be seen. So the City Hall place
these days was Ellen's Coffee Shop, run by Ellen Sturm. She
had once been a Miss Subway System, and the outside windows
were plastered with glossies of other Miss Subways. Inside was
diet soda and lots of fatless fiber. So that was the difference,
right there. At Longchamps, your dinner was six large whiskeys,
and here it was skimmed milk.

Fun was the word he kept returning to. There had been so
much of it around, and today there seemed none at all. "Sometimes you read the papers, you watch TV, you talk to the
people," Matty said, "and all you keep hearing, over and over,
is 'What in hell happened here?' "

"Lots of stuff," was the short answer. Watergate, for one.
Tapped phones, for another. TV, because on the screen the
people could see your smile freeze while your face melted when
you were caught in a barefaced lie, you couldn't get some aide
to cover your ass, the way you could with the press. And then,
of course, there was 1975. "What happened here?" New York
went bankrupt, that's what.

The change had already started creeping in before the default, but the longer Matty looked back, he had to say a whole
world had ended right here. Tammany Hall and the Clubhouse
and the rest of the machine, they had all stood on one basic
given, that the city thrived, always would thrive, and, however
much of the pie you cut up, there would be plenty left.

Of course there had been the depression, when all construction work had been frozen and the city was full of half-built skyscrapers, stairways that led to nothing, the blank stare of glassless windows. Dreadful times, and Matty's father had often recalled them. In Bay Ridge, the people would wait at the garbage dump, and every time a new load was delivered, they'd dive right in, digging with their bare hands for any stray scraps of food. There were soup kitchens right on Broadway, doled out from the back of army trucks, and the breadline, *the worm that walks like a man.*

But that was a special case, the whole damn country was in shambles, not just New York. And even then, you didn't see too many pols in the breadlines, their tin cups in their hands. The machine kept ticking over. Believe it. When Fiorello La Guardia, the Little Flower, when they made him mayor in 1933, and he went running up the steps to City Hall on his Inauguration Day, shaking his fist at the marble walls and hollering *E finita la cuccagna!* No more free lunch! Death to Graft!, it sounded good, it looked great in the morning papers, but truly it was just wind. The machine kept ticking. Believe it. And when La Guardia was dead, ploughed under, there was still free lunch in the Clubhouse, more savory and fattening than ever.

So when the city's bankruptcy blew up, it hit like a thunderbolt. "I had people come to me and say they can't believe it, this isn't fair. Not fair," Matty snapped. "They've been ripping off the city for twenty, thirty years and suddenly the ride is over and all they can say is *Not fair.* And most of them really believed it."

One tale told it all. Back when he'd first gotten involved with the Queens Village Democratic Club, there had been six younger guys to the fore, all of them bright, tough, ambitious; and this Gang of Six—himself and Donald Manes, Nick Ferrara, Sy Thaler, Gene Mastropieri, and Jack Bronson—had formed an alliance. In the short term, their idea was simply to build up a power base; in the long, they dreamed of a whole machine, a network so strong that no New York politico, not even the mayor, would be able to function without its say-so.

The first part had worked. In short order, the six had become chairmen and state senators, judges, district attorneys. And how had they finished? Himself in jail, Donald Manes indicted and a suicide, Nick Ferrara dead, Sy Thaler indicted and dead, Gene Mastropieri indicted, Jack Bronson indicted. "Batted a thousand," Matty said. "Not a man jack left standing."

Of a sudden, people stopped speaking out loud. At meetings, everybody sat deadpan and passed notes. The phones were all tapped or, if they weren't, you thought they were, which worked out as the same thing. Special prosecutors went riffling through your garbage, searching for stray dirt. Shredders got real popular in a hurry. So did the street-corner conference. And the strain was something fierce. In the City Council, Dominick Corso, out of Brooklyn, got so maddened by the nagging and the dread, the reformers busting his chops, that he clean forgot his party lines: "You think it takes guts to stand up for what's right?" he railed. "That doesn't take guts. What takes guts is to stand up for what you know is wrong, day after day, year after year."

The fear didn't stop the stealing. It just took away the fun. Practical politics became a nonstop round of cold sweats and antacid pills: "But the funny thing was," Matty said, "the bigger the odds of getting nailed, the stronger the pull to mess around." We turned away from Ellen's, walked back towards the park. "What's the word I want?" Matty asked. "Something to do with lemons. . . ."

"Lemmings?"

"That was us."

Round the back of City Hall, the marble ran out, and the walls were a dowdy brownstone. When the building went up, it had stood at Manhattan's northern limit. Further expansion was deemed unlikely, and there had seemed no point in spending extra on a back view that would never be seen. So the city politic had remained, quite literally, a façade: "And that's on its best day," Matty said.

What I had to understand, he said, was that New York was not governed by its elected governors, never had been. Look closely at its history—every major change had been dictated, not by pols, but by bankers, by realtors and Wall Street men, people you never saw and never would, most times you didn't even know their names. Reformers called them the "permanent government." And they were in a whole other league. Working stiffs of councilmen could spend their entire lifetimes slogging and scheming away, and still they'd be nothing, the driest drop in the deepest bucket, compared to the big leaguers.

It gave pause for thought. Once you grasped exactly how many billions were in the pot, and how little difference your own abstention made, it was hard not to come down with sticky finger. "Lookit," Matty said. "Whatever people tell you, I myself never took. Money just never bothered me that much. And anyhow, like I told Dick Reeves, *There are so many legitimate ways to make money in politics that I can never understand why anyone steals.*" But then, he always had been eccentric.

We had come full circle, back into the park. On the patches of mud that had once been grass, great stacks of police barricades were piled, on hold for demonstrations. Bull-buttocked cops strolled, watchful, on the cobblestones beyond, their back pockets bulging with blackjacks and/or flashlights, handcuffs, citation books, walkie-talkies. But a chill wind had come up. It was still February, and no fit season for protest. Matty was due back on the Island.

A few minutes more, we sat on a bench close by Broadway, overhung by leafless branches and pigeons of deadly aim. At this off-hour, our only companions were drug dealers. A heavy man with heavy jowls, Matthew Troy turned up his coat collar for protection, stared dead ahead. "You really don't miss it?" he was asked.

"That was another Broadway," Matty said.

He kept thinking of Donald Manes, of the scandal that had brought him low and killed him. "Go figure," Matty said. "When we started out, I would of believed Donnie before I believed myself, which wasn't saying a helluva lot, God knows, but still, we were partners, a team. He would of sworn on his mother, and so would I. That he never would take a bribe. And even after he knifed me, which he did, God rest him, even then I couldn't hate him. I felt badly; I didn't understand. But hate him? In my heart, I couldn't do that."

They had met again when Lew Wallach died. Both Matty and Donnie had known him and owed him from way, way back. "So I go to the funeral and I listen to the eulogy, and then I feel a hand on my shoulder, it's Donnie and he's crying, he says *I feel terrible, I feel just terrible for what happened, I just want you to know I love you.* So then, of course, I'm thinking, *If you feel so bad, how come you did it? And are you saying you wouldn't do it again? In a New York minute?* But it's Louie's funeral, and Donnie's crying, his big fat face all twisted up and sweating, and I have my soft side—I like to make out I'm a tough guy, gruff talking, a terrible temper when I blow up, which is the truth, God knows, I just go crazy. But I can be sentimental, too. So anyhow, he's crying, and I'm crying, and his wife is crying, and he's saying *I love you* and I say *I love you, too,* and the usher comes up to us, he says *You're making an exhibition of yourselves, you better go in the other room,* so we do, and we have a drink, we say *I love you* some more, and then we say good-night, we go home to sleep it off. And the next thing I know, it's in the morning papers, Donnie's told the press, about him and me, I mean us crying and everything, at Louie Wallach's funeral, and I think, *strange.* That's all I think, *very strange.*"

They did not grow close again. From time to time, Matty would see Donald Manes at some function or a dinner dance, or he would be somewhere lobbying for the gas retailers and Manes would pass him by, smiling, with his fat hand out. He always looked very nervous, he was always pouring sweat and chewing on his lips, he looked an ill man, physically, in his head, both. "But I didn't say nothing, it wasn't none of my business, I just nodded," Matty said. "And then the whole thing breaks wide open, the scandal, the payoffs and all, and Donnie tries to kill himself, and Donnie's in the hospital, he's going to be indicted, then he *is* indicted, and then he does kill himself, he's dead."

Up and down Broadway, the office workers came piling out at day's end. Bundled deep into his overcoat, Matty fell silent. He took another antacid pill. He burped. "So then what?" he was prompted.

"So shock," he replied. "I mean, it surprised the hell out of me. I couldn't figure it out, none of it, and I'm sitting in front of the TV, sort of watching but thinking at the same time, too, and all I keep thinking is *used to be*. I mean, *We really used to be*."

And that was all. Before one more question could catch him, he stood up straight, he buttoned his coat. His stomach growled. "Gas," said Matty Troy.

"USED TO BE,
used to be. So sick I am of used to be," Sasha said. "Is just old
men in their hasbeens, breaking wind on water, passing water
into wind."

To him, Broadway's histories had all been directed towards
a single crowning moment, St. Patrick's Day, 1982, the day he
first set foot on it. "Was raining, was sky falling down," he
recalled. "I am coming up from deep dark earth, Times Square
subway. Was Monday night, was corner of Nathan's Famous,
Forty-third Street, only then I don't know it, all I'm seeing is
Broadway, Great White Way. *Baseball, Mom, Apple Pie, and
Chevrolet. Levi Jeans, Lee Jeans, Jordache Jeans, Wrangler Jeans.
Come Alive with Pepsi.* Oh, brudder. *Nothing Comes between
Me and My Calvins. If You Got Time, We Got Beer.* Forgeddaboudit. *Takes Two Hands to Handle Whopper; Melts in Mouth
Not in Hand.* What to tell you? Is pissing down rain black like
devil's asshole, crazypersons everyplace shouting, screaming,
one man trying to save my soul, one man trying to rob my wallet,
one man with plan, and one man with gun. Hookers, hustlers,
bad cocaine. *Is Real Thing, Coke.* Bluelights, redlights, silver,
gold. *Have You Ever Seen Grown Man Cry?* And I'm running
out in middle street, staring up, every crazyman going crazy,
honking horns, yelling, cursing 'Geddoudagoddamway, stupid

slavets.' Raspizdyai srany, filthy genital person. But what hell? I'm crying, I can't be moved. *You've Come Long Way, Baby.* Most beautiful sight in whole damn world."

Seven years later, his passion remained unquestioning, insatiable. He was not blinded to New York's faults in general. Park Avenue and the South Bronx alike would send him raging back into Russian, spewing forth wild cataracts of lamentation and obscenity, *tampon talk*. Only on Broadway, he still found the America of his imaginings: *"Dollar and Dream,"* he said.

In the first weeks of our walk, he'd mostly been marking time. These somber glades we'd been trudging through—Bowling Green, Wall Street, City Hall—might belong to the cartologist's Broadway, but not to his. Fretful as a tap dancer in traction, he itched to hit his spots, bust loose. TriBeCa gave him his chance.

It was a wasteland turned playground. For decades, it had been almost uninhabited, an area of warehouses and wholesale outlets, greasy spoons, skid-row bars. But the outlandish rents charged by Nosferatu landlords uptown had revived it. From the late seventies on, a steady stream of artists and musicians, punk designers, drug dealers and their caravans had sought shelter in its cellars and lofts. The Mudd Club thrived; downtown was reborn as Downtown. Then the landlords caught up and TriBeCa—the Triangle Below Canal—turned chic. The pioneers scattered to the East Village, Hoboken, Long Island City, and were replaced by a second wave, less cold in hand: illustrators and fashion photographers, journalists, French restaurateurs, and actresses, lots of actresses.

Some of these last, when not waiting tables, gave shelter to stray Sovericans. And it was fortunate that they did. One evening, shortly after we'd crossed Maiden Lane, Sasha had returned to Alexei Alexandrovich's to find his drums stacked in the hallway. Since then they had commuted between his taxi and a series of soubrettes' sublets.

Currently, they reposed beneath the high brass bed of a

former Tennessee beauty queen, a third runner-up for Miss Wonder Bread 1980, now turned dancer, painter, performance artist. Her professional name was EmCee Marie.

We approached her late one fine and breezy Friday afternoon, rising up from Lower Broadway like surfacing pearl divers. Having toiled so long and deep in darkness, the first flash of sun and open space stopped us dead.

From the churchyard of St. Paul's Chapel, we could at last see trees, grass, sky. Most dazzling of all, we could gaze on Cass Gilbert's Woolworth Building, towering above us like some great upflung fist of freedom.

It was a Gothic castle straight out of *Jack and the Beanstalk*. Outside, it exalted merchant majesty. But its true glory lay within, where the atmosphere turned devout. One step beyond the revolving doors, and we were plunged into a realm of cathedral half-light. Through the dimness loomed a stupendous marble stairway, granite walls thick as medieval tombs, elevator doors of hammered and sculpted copper, cartouches, sconces, illuminated tableaux, hanging lamps like censers.

Cocktails were served in the crypt. Across the navelike lobby, Liquor Jack Young came sailing through the pillars, fully furled, like a square-rigged galleon. At sight of us, he tacked, hove to. "Have you seen a young lady pass, twenty-five, twenty-six years of age, five feet seven, 118 pounds, blond, blue eyes, full figure, small skull and crossbones tattooed on buttock?" he demanded.

"Which buttock?" Sasha asked.

Across the street was Park Row, which had once been Printing House Square, home to half the New York newspapers. Most of the offices had long since vanished, but the old *Times* Building survived, more or less, as a part of Pace University. "When I'm first coming here, I have girlfriend, forgetername, she's taking classes in money. So I'm waiting in this park for her every night, right here," Sasha said. "Is hot, hot summer days, everything burning up, and crazyman is playing Max Roach drums. Right here, on Broadway."

"What crazyman?"

"Robert Blue. Little bit stick of body, not man or meat, but he's beating sweet holy hell out of drums, believe it, is putting on whipping but good." His birthmark glowed. "Is beautiful. Is all."

Blue had worked the lunch crowd, backing himself with tapes of John Coltrane, Pharoah Sanders, Sun Ra, and his battles with the string quartets across the lawn were legend, a bloodless race war. Sasha had become his lone white foot soldier. In time, he'd even been entrusted with passing the hat. Then the summer faded and the cops came, took Blue away in a paddywagon. Possession of stolen goods, the charge was. To whit, silver plate and candlesticks, a pearl choker, assorted jade: "Taste was superb, sentence was eighteen months," Sasha said, "and Zim is getting Max Roach drums."

It was hereabouts that Broadway's push north had first gathered steam, begun to acquire real purpose. In its infancy, when its population was under a thousand, New York had ended in a stockade fence at Wall Street. Only Broadway had reached beyond. Adventuring, scouting like an advance guard, it kept driving up the island, setting up series of base camps. At each in turn it paused, consolidated its gains, just long enough for the rest of the city to catch up. Then it ploughed ahead once again.

We followed it by City Hall Park. Beyond Chambers Street, the perspective shrank, turned intimate again. In the 1850s, this had been Upper Broadway, the heart of high fashion. A. T. Stewart's department store, the Bloomingdale's of its moment, had stood where Ellen's now primped, and from there had flowed the nightly parade of carriages and curricles, broughams, cabriolets, promenaders, back and forth to Union Square.

It was this ritual that had first made Broadway synonymous with the Night. Thumbing through a nineteenth-century anthology, Sasha had come upon a story from *Harper's New Monthly Magazine*, circa 1878: *In carriages we discover opera and ball dresses, while men on sidewalk move along saunteringly, nearly every one with cigar in his mouth, and crimson tips of weeds glow in air like so many setting suns,* he read. *These are Men who make World.*

Nowadays, the tone was less highflown. When fashion moved on, these blocks had turned into the Dry-Goods District. After that, they'd become a midden of sweatshops and wholesale outlets. The buildings were mostly cast-iron manufactures, their windows garish with chintz and cotton and gold lamé, and the night's cavalcade was of wage slaves running to the subway. But the basic equation was unchanged: *Though well-dressed people preponderate,* Sasha read, *workmen in fustian and poverty-stricken workgirls appear in stream, besides threadbare adventurers and abject devotees of gutter.*

Workmen in fustian, threadbare adventurers, abject devotees of the gutter—we had these three covered. All that was lacking were the poverty-stricken workgirls, and Sasha knew just where to find them. Leaving Broadway, he went gusting down side streets, past neon-sculpture shops and charcuterie takeouts, designer ice-creameries, slimming salons. At a corner, behind blank windows, was the Baby Doll Topless.

It was more neighborhood saloon than fleshpot. Warehouse workers and messengers, salesmen from Canal Street, and truckers fresh out of the Holland Tunnel commingled at the bar, their backs turned to the stage. If they peered into the backbar mirror, they could see women dancing with no clothes on. But not many made the effort. Baseball spring training had just begun, and the talk was all of phenoms, trades, rotator cuffs.

EmCee Marie was a ChiSox fan.

She sat brooding over a boilermaker, a dark and muscular presence in a bomber jacket, with thick, black hair sheared short in a Brillo-pad shag and eyes very fierce, unblinking. On her right wrist were tattooed the word *Pudge* and a scarlet heart pierced by a whaling harpoon. "Only three things are forever," she said. "Death, taxes, and Carlton Fisk."

The voice was startling. The softest Tennessee drawl, it didn't match the leathers or the eyes. Nor did the body compute. Lushly curved, it belonged to a Vargas calendar girl. But access was barred by studs, steel chains.

Nights, she worked topless uptown. She rarely got home before dawn, and when she did, she could not seem to sleep. Sometimes she worked at her paintings, or she played solitaire. More often, she hit the bars: "To get tired. To get some rest," she said.

She was twenty-eight, had been in New York six years. Before that, she'd been married with kids in Knoxville, where her husband had owned bodyshops and a muffler franchise. When Marie was pregnant the third time, she miscarried. It was a sign, she believed, and she came north with a bluegrass band. Through summer and fall, she shacked up with the mandolinist, toured up and down the Northeast. Then it turned cold in Trenton, New Jersey, and the mandolinist took homesick. The morning after, Marie turned in her wedding ring for art supplies, caught a bus into Manhattan.

At Port Authority, she asked directions to the nearest cabaret. It had proved to be Show World, a sexual supermarket near Times Square. There she'd won a job as a Real Live Woman, who sat behind a plate-glass window in an open negligee and performed whatever lonely acts men commanded. A phone connected her fishtank with their booth, and they paid a quarter a minute. More often than not, they just wanted to watch her fingers move. But there were others who liked to talk, and the stuff that ran from their mouths had seared, was vitriol: "Can't wash out the stain like cum," said EmCee Marie. "Won't wash out, period."

Sasha had returned to his taxi. In his absence, Marie ordered up more boilermakers, and many more after those. Sometime between six and midnight, when her next work shift began, we wound up back in her studio, above a Broadway button factory.

Her room was as spacious, airy, and impersonal as a high-school gym. Canvases hung along the walls, but all were covered with dustsheets; even her easel was disguised. Apart from Sasha's drums, peeping coyly out from behind a nest of shoe-boxes and carrier bags, the only private touches were the brass bed itself, which had belonged to a great-aunt, and an outsize autographed picture of Carlton Fisk.

"He's the best. Just the best," said EmCee Marie. She'd loved him since she was in eighth grade and he was a rookie catcher with Boston. Now he was the oldest position player in the Major Leagues, a patriarch, the calm and all-wise image of the father that should be and never was. He was always going down with horrendous injuries, his face smashed in, his knees ripped to shreds. Yet he kept coming back, the same stoic, rocklike Pudge: "Rip out his heart, and he'd still hit two-eighty, drive in seventy-five," she said. She poured herself a drink. "He's just the best," she said.

Sprawled on an overstuffed beanbag, she had shed the bomber jacket, wore only jeans and a ChiSox T-shirt. The body revealed was so opulent, it looked almost cartoonish. But the snapping-turtle eyes, the hedgehog quills of black hair, did not encourage liberties. Nor did the raw whiskey mouth. "Why're you here?" she demanded.

"You asked me."

"Quiet," said Marie. "I'm drinking."

Across the studio was a small side room, which she called her gallery. Its door was padlocked; the key hung on a chain from her throat, squeezed tight between her breasts, like a cru-cifix. "I won't show you," she said. "Don't even think of think-ing I will."

"You don't have to."

"I won't." She rose up a little unsteady, touched the brass bed for balance. Her scent, up close, was of pine and damp peat. "Why EmCee?" I asked.

"Masked Cocksucker," Marie replied. "What else?"

On a small bookstand beside the brass bed sat the *Baseball*

Encyclopedia, a Gideon Bible, novels by Faulkner and Dashiell Hammett, the *Collected Stories of Flannery O'Connor*, and Ashley Montagu's *The Elephant Man*.

Picking up this last, Marie went searching for a quote. "The best. It's just the best," she said, softslurring, and she read out loud: "As a specimen of humanity, Merrick was ignoble and repulsive; but the spirit of Merrick, if it could be seen in the form of the living, would assume the figure of an upstanding and heroic man, smooth browed and clean of limb, with eyes that flashed undaunted courage."

When we came here, we'd carried a pint of I. W. Harper. Now it was three parts empty, and Marie threw the book against the wall. "First drawing I ever did. The Elephant Man," she said. "I read that passage, it was the middle of the night, of course I didn't have any drawing paper or anything like that, I just stripped a page out of the phonebook, the first thing that came to my hand, and I drew it in one line." She poured the last drink but did not down it. She turned the glass in her hand, as if studying its light. "All I saw," she said, "it was just a line."

Her gallery proved to be a small, square box, eight feet by eight. On the far wall was a glass box, its contents blacked out, and in front of it a swivel chair, on which I now sat. Marie shut off the overhead light, shut the door, and left me alone in darkness. Then the glass box lit up from within, presenting a series of slides.

They showed variations on famous paintings. Mantegna's *Agony in the Garden* came first, then Rembrandt's *The Night Watch*, then a Courbet studio scene, a Van Dyke cavalier. After that, the exact sequence blurred, but it included Matisses and Manets, a Watteau, a Franz Hals. The single common denominator, at least to my own eye, was that all were dominated by central male figures.

The style was De Mille Realist. What Marie had done was take the originals, copy them faithfully, then filter them through a Technicolor nightmare, so that they took on the tones of lobby

cards or depression postcards. The result was a world of Old
Testament sunsets, scarlet eyes, purple blood, and spun-gold
tears.

There was more. To each scene, the figure of Marie herself
had been added, black-masked and nude, crouching at the feet
of the leading male and delicately, chastely, performing fellatio.
The male organs projected stark white, just the tip of the glans
swallowed up, and their owners stood with fists clenched,
heads flung back, in attitudes of torment and abandon, a terrible
helplessness. As for EmCee Marie, who could say? Her mask
hid all.

The Elephant Man came last. It was smaller than the rest,
not the line drawing she had described, but an ink wash. John
Merrick stood in shadow, his silhouette barely suggested. Only
his massive head and his cock caught the light. On Marie's right
ring finger, gently cushioning his balls, was a small circular
mirror.

Trapped in the dark, I sat very still, I started counting. At
fifty-six the slide shut off and the light overhead returned. Back
in the studio, the I. W. Harper was all gone, and Marie was
zipping up her bomber jacket, preening herself for work.

She looked like a woman with no clothes on under her
clothes. "My maiden name was Carbone. Anna Maria Carbone,"
she said. "My mother was a strong woman."

A weight lifter lived in the room above. Sharp at eleven,
tonight and every other night, he began to clean and jerk. After
each failed lift, the crash of tumbling barbells shook the building
like a wrecker's ball. EmCee Marie, making up in a wicker-
framed mirror, found that the glass would not keep still. At
every thump, her image lurched and twisted, veered out of
control. But she did not show irritation. She just reached out
and held the glass flat, in place. "My mother had five daughters;
she raised them all herself," said Marie. "She was just the best."

"And your father?"

"Get out of my house."

Her hand was steady; her voice quite clear. The alcohol, it seemed, had killed its own effect. "I don't want you here. I don't want you here," she said. At her doorway, she stood rubbing the Pudge Fisk tattoo on her wrist. Her black hair bristled, stiff and angry, but her eyes were merely dulled, out of sync. "Are you a fool?" Marie asked.

"Of course."

"Oh, well," she said. "It's a living."

9 / ON FRANKLIN STREET,
as she left Peggy Doyle's Restaurant, a woman was run into by two black youths. One of them knocked her off-balance, the other snatched at her purse. But the woman, though she was not young, refused to let go. She was a small but elegant package, impeccably wrapped in a dove-gray suit with matching picture hat, knee-length snakeskin boots. Her purse was dove-gray also, studded with gold fittings, with a gold-link chain that she wrapped around her wrist, and she swung it like a loaded sling-shot, skulling the youths with calm expertise, till they scuttled off up Broadway.

As soon as they were safely gone, a uniformed cop came by and began to batter the woman with questions. How were the youths dressed? Could she describe them? Would she recognize them again? "Know them anywhere," the woman declared.

"How can you be so sure?"

"They're my clients."

The woman was Enid Gerlin, Attorney-at-Law, and she was on her way to 100 Centre Street, the Criminal Courts Building. Much like the theaters uptown, the courthouse was of Broadway but not on it. A massive art deco mausoleum, it sat lowering across Foley Square, the image of dread and all abandoned hope.

In its moment, 1933, this place had been much celebrated.

It went up on the site of the Collect, the city's eighteenth-century garbage dump. Its architect, Harvey Wiley Corbett, was the high panjandrum of moderne, as deco was then called, and 100 Centre was hailed as his life's masterwork—not just another courthouse, but the New Age incarnate, a paean to Justice, *The Awful Awe of the Law*. What that boiled down to was a railway station without trains.

Monumental it was, gun-metal gray, with vaulting doorways and dim empyrean ceilings, adamantine pillars, sculpted brass. Back in the age of the shoe, its marble floors must have echoed superbly, a symphony of grave and measured treads. In the sneaker age, they just squeaked.

Across the vast frozen steppe of the lobby, an army of dark youths came gliding, shaking and baking, a moveable A–Z of basketball struts and strides: "You'd think this was a playground," Enid Gerlin said. "And you'd be right."

In the cafeteria, Shaquille Cleamons, nineteen, munched on a sugar roll. One of Enid's past clients, he went six feet six, 170 pounds, a praying mantis in sky-blue-and-yellow Nikes, gray sweats, a black bandanna: "We only be hangin'," he said. "It was an accident."

"From the beginning," said Enid Gerlin.

"An accident was all."

"You were hanging out?"

"Shootin' hoops. In the yard. We just be chillin', shootin' hoops." He bobbed and weaved in his seat, pantomiming a spin move, a jumper, a dunk. "Then the gun go off."

He was out of East New York, the Linden Houses on Stanley Avenue, right across the street from Gershwin Junior High. Down the block from Gershwin was the yard, "like a park, just no grass." It featured a basketball half-court, a wire cage, one hoop, two floodlights on a pole. On summer nights, it was always full of action till late, one, two o'clock in the morning, but most nights in winter it was deserted.

Last night had been an exception. One of the Jacks from

the projects, Leavell Robinson, had showed up sporting a brand-new pair of Air Jordans. How he came by them, don't enquire. But, of course, he needed to strut them. So he went out in the park, it must have been round midnight, in the cold and drizzling rain, and his homeboys with him—Tyrone, Kenny, K-mart, Shaquille Cleamons—to keep him company.

Shaquille's skull was lopsided, the work of a drunken obstetrician. Burn scars puckered his left cheek, drawing up the eye into a permanent squint. "So you were hanging in the yard?" Enid Gerlin said. "So what then?"

"DOA."

The trouble started around one. Leavell and his homeboys, they called themselves the LHCs, the Linden Houses Crew, and they were tight. Gershwin was their yard, their turf. Then three others came by. Shaquille had seen them around, they used to hang on Van Siclen, just down from Key Food, but he didn't know them to speak to. One of them, he thought, was called Money. The others he couldn't say. Anyhow, they came by and they took one look at Leavell's Air Jordans, they started laughing. Then the one they called Money, he went in the cage, he was moving across the yard with his hand reached out, his middle finger curled way back and beckoning. But Leavell stood him off. He had a temper, Leavell, he'd jump in any fool's face. So the two of them, they came together. No punches were thrown, not that Shaquille could see, just a lot of grabbing and shoving, a lot of language. Then Money swung something blunt and dark, it had a dull sheen, could have been some kind of metal. It hit someplace upside Leavell's head, and it made a sound like pulping, like when you burst a ripe fruit. Leavell sort of stumbled, then he turned to run, but Money grabbed him back. Money had a gun. He had Leavell around the throat; Leavell was struggling to bust loose, but Money was too strong. Shaquille shut his eyes. There was one shot. Then everybody started running.

"So what then?" Enid Gerlin asked.

"I was running, then I stopped," said Shaquille. Icing sugar smeared the inside of his loose lower lip, stark white against raw pink. "I went back to look."

"How long after the shot?"

"Two minutes, three." The squint made him look like a child with an old man's eye. "Everybody was back inside the cage."

"Was Leavell dead?"

"Didn't have no shoes on."

Police came, then the ambulance. From the far end of the yard, underneath the hoop where the floodlights were, Shaquille could not see much, just the medics crouched down with torches and Leavell's feet. He wore white athletic socks. "So what then?"

"They call the morgue."

By now a crowd had gathered, people were pushing and yelling, trying to get a better view. Leavell's mother came down, she started to scream. Everybody was all excited. But there was nothing left to look at. Shaquille stayed close by K-mart and Tyrone, down under the hoop. The basketball was just lying there. So Tyrone picked it up and flipped it in the air. Then he took a shot, sort of a fallaway hook, and K-mart rebounded. Then someone else took a shot, and someone else. "Did you?" Enid asked.

"Didn't shoot. Just played D," Shaquille told her, sucking on his sugared lip. The morgue wagon came, Leavell's body was removed, the crowd began to break up. "So what then?"

"We played half-court."

The cops broke up the game. Detectives started stalking the cage, asking questions, taking names. "They ax me where I been, ax me what I seen," Shaquille said.

"So what did you tell them?"

"Said I wasn't there." His wizened eye stared down at his hands, idly flexing in his lap. The fingers were long and supple as a cellist's, with pale-blue cuticles, almost silver. This was strange, for blue cuticles were normally a symptom of recent electrocution. "I didn't see nothing," Shaquille mumbled. "Was an accident, anyways."

"But you saw Money. You saw Money with a gun."

"I guess."

"So how was it an accident?"

Shaquille shrugged. "We only be hangin'," he said.

The cafeteria was hot and fetid, as airless as a holding pen. Creaseless in her dove-gray suit, her matching hat, Enid sipped gray coffee from a plastic cup, fanned herself with the *Daily News.* "So why are you here?" she asked.

"Mistake-A-DNT."

His brother Darnell was on trial for armed robbery, some stuff about a gold chain and a crackpipe, and their mother couldn't attend in person, she was busy working in the beauty salon, so Shaquille had been sent to substitute. He did not complain, he would perform his family duty. But he was not thrilled: "Sugar roll be stale," he said.

When he left, Enid bought herself a red apple, began to peel it in one continuous loop. "Same old story," she said. "Only the names and the shoe brands change."

All about us, sweat dripped off chins, oozed down the backs of necks. Stocky, square-built, Enid was a woman who did not tell her age, and she was afflicted by a trembling, which made her fight to control her movements. The joints on her fingers, heavy with rings, were swollen, out of true. Still, she looked like a lady who lunched.

A few yards away was Judge Solomon's court, AR–1, in which arraignments were processed and Enid served as a court-appointed counsel at forty dollars an hour. It was a large, high room, a seat of majesty, with mahogany paneling and more fine echoes. In its well, yawning clerks shuffled papers and guards chewed gum, lawyers scratched where it itched, Judge Solomon practiced patience and the prisoners sat waiting, waiting, ranged in line along one wall. IN GOD WE TRUST, said the sign.

The procedure was simple. Each prisoner, brought forth from the holding pens, would consult briefly with counsel, then stand up before Judge Solomon, a youngish man already marked by a look of ageless sufferance. Charges ranged from vagrancy to homicide, and they could either plead guilty and be sentenced on the spot, or elect to go to trial. Five times in six, they chose the former. It was less fuss.

I'd first heard of this court from Stoney Bisonette, for whom AR–1 had long been a second home. There was no sign of him or the Liberty Boosters this day. Even without them, however, the caseload was gargantuan.

Anyone who could not afford his or her own lawyer qualified. The favorite crime seemed to be drug dealing. But this, Enid said, was deceptive: "They're just junkies. They go stumbling round the night streets, too strung out to watch themselves, and the cops pick them up with a pooper-scooper, claim that they're big-time dealers. That way they bolster the arrest slates and look good, too. I mean, you bust a street junkie and it sounds picayune. But you bust a druglord, and you're a prince of the city."

The first five names called were Jesus Gutierrez, Robert Mandela Smith, Al Gross, Jamaal Chatman, Shinique Star Wilson. On average, their cases took up two minutes, twenty-three seconds.

Mercedes Purissima Vargas sat third from the right. Her lank black hair, shoulder-length, was streaked orange and blue and green, and she sat folded double from the waist, so that the hair fell sheer in a curtain. From time to time, she would gather herself to a convulsive effort, straighten up. Then the curtain would fly back to reveal a face of wax, a death mask, yellow-white and guttering.

She was here for possession of heroin with intent to distribute. Also, for selling her baby. At two in the morning, strapped for a fix, she'd been picked up in a doorway on Eighth Street near Avenue A, attempting to auction off her year-old daughter,

Dynasty, who lay uncovered in her baby carriage. On being charged, she had said, "I could not sleep."

She still couldn't. Every time that she tried, a female guard would shake her, force her to sit up. Then again the scrim of her hair would be torn away and the death mask exposed, staring sightless at the white light. This was her forty-third arrest.

Mercedes wore Nikes. So did Son Johnson, twenty-two, whose case came to Enid. A security guard at Food City, he was accused of boosting five cases of canned cling peaches in syrup, a charge he denied, though he had been caught in the act. "Racism! Police brutality! *Amandla!*" he kept crying out, regardless of the question. "I have no right to be here."

"Me, too," said Enid Gerlin.

She had been working this building for thirty-five years. She'd made herself a lawyer in an age when women attorneys were widely viewed as freaks against nature. She had defended gays before Stonewall, sweet-talked torpedoes, been jailed for talking back to judges, and pilloried for pleading in floral hats. Now she looked along the row of metal chairs, at Mercedes Purissima Vargas and Son Johnson, at Jesus Gutierrez and Shinique Star Wilson and Robert Mandela Smith, at the Nikes and Converses and Pumas, the Pump Reeboks and the scuffed Pro-Keds: "I'd rather be in Philadelphia," she said.

Her father had been a toy manufacturer, the creator of Sleepy Head and the Flapper Doll, and in her childhood she'd been as pampered as a doll herself, so cosseted and protected that New York's realities never touched her. When she grew up, and they did, all she wanted was out. She traveled, she took a business degree in Ohio, she went to work in air-traffic control. When she felt ripe, she came back to Brooklyn Law School.

She wanted newness, challenge, risk. "I was not a person who was ever much afraid," she said. "I was brought up to fight my own battles. To be a lady always, except when I was not."

This taste for combat had been richly gratified. In her first years at 100 Centre, threatened males stood in line to test her, try to break her: "I got knocked down so many times, I couldn't count the ways. My revenge was to buy more hats."

Her hats had made her famous. One judge, a Justice Irving Saypol, had called them offensive and tried to ban them from his court. In a written opinion, he bemoaned a "grotesque hat situation, some kind of flamboyant turban with the many colors of Joseph's coat, misplaced in any courtroom" and another "large picture hat, more appropriate for a lawn party or some such social, like Eliza Doolittle's in the second act of *My Fair Lady*, depicting her at the Ascot Races." When Enid failed to kowtow, he cited her for contempt, and the *Post* headlined the story "Judge Blows His Top Over Lady Lawyer's Lids."

The harassment had helped shape her practice. In the early sixties, gay sex was still illegal, gays routinely framed and entrapped. Established lawyers ran shy of such cases, gay lawyers shyest of all. Enid, who had nothing to lose and wouldn't have cared if she had, filled the vacuum.

Her tactic was simply to drown cant in absurdity. Police assigned to the gay detail, known as the Flying Fag Squad, kept the world safe from perversion by twin maneuvers, either picking up men in bars or spying on them in public bathrooms. On the first dodge, Enid would cross-examine in minute and excruciating physical detail—whose hand was where, what did it touch, how big was it, did it then get bigger, how much bigger, would the officer care to show the court?—till the cop either fainted or cried mercy. On the latter, she'd have a model toilet constructed and the cubicle wheeled into court, then make the wretched lawman crawl inside and try to spy what he claimed to have spied, a physical contortion, she knew, that would have defeated Houdini: "I had them standing on their heads, climbing up the cistern, knee-deep in the pan. And once I had them going, I wouldn't quit till the judge pulled me off them, stopped the fight."

Those were heroic years. Her record was one long string of TKOs, and she ran a big office right across from the courthouse, secretaries and flunkeys on twenty-four-hour call, thirty new clients a week, supplicants waiting in line. Every Christmas, she sent out four thousand cards: "I was bouncing with judges and cops, with gays and hustlers, every kind of highlife and lowlife, and I never even paid bribes. Lots of judges would make a contract, take money for a quick dismissal, but I didn't believe in paying. I was too aggressive, too feisty, I guess too honest. I had too much chutzpah for my own good. Just say I had too many laughs." Then she fell in love.

Romance was never her strength. "There was something out of whack somewhere." She was a woman so constructed that she must always spurn the men who pursued and adored her, crave only those who caused her pain. "Same with food, same with love," she said. "If it wasn't bad for me, I couldn't stomach it."

The man she chose to love was a furniture salesman turned limousine driver. Her mother took one look at him and said, "He's gorgeous, and he's not for you." So Enid was hooked. For fourteen years, she lived with him, in him, through him, till he had consumed her utterly. When he left, there was not enough left of her to rekindle, "not even to strike a match on."

By then, 1975, consenting adults had finally been licensed: "So the bottom dropped out of the gay trade." She had to start over, and she couldn't. She was tired of socializing, tired of the bars and the cocktail parties, tired of running, and tireder still of dancing. Love and Broadway had used her up: "Destroyed my femininity. Left me short somehow," she said.

She found herself taking cases of violence, homicides and armed robberies, sick and ugly and just plain filthy things. Formerly, she wouldn't have touched them with a hatstand. "Sex was one thing, evil another." But what choice did she have? "Sex had stopped paying the bills."

So evil it was. She still handled private cases that stemmed from her gay contacts. Just the year before, she'd defended an

Irish-German boy, very cute, well spoken, and polite, who was accused of stabbing his Hispanic boyfriend to death. They had been walking to the subway in Jackson Heights, Queens, when an argument broke out. Before it was resolved, the boyfriend had been stabbed seventeen times. But he had been high on cocaine, and cocaine may promote violence. So Enid had argued self-defense and the Irish-German boy, very cute, well spoken, and polite, was acquitted in ninety minutes: "A sound upbringing, a liberal education," she mused. "You just can't beat good breeding."

That had been a rare treat. Much more frequently, her cases were repulsive, the rewards minimal. When she went to visit her clients in jail, she was afraid to enter their cells. Enid Gerlin, who was never afraid of anything. But that had been in another world: "Before it became a garbage barge," she said, "there used to be a city here."

Used to be, used to be—the chorus never changed. "We had a system. We had corruption, perjury, prejudice, stupidity, but we had rules. Now the system is, there is no system," she said. "You have judges on the bench don't know the law, still less the street. You have prosecutors, all they know are arrests and convictions, forget procedure, forget the citizen's rights, don't even mention Justice. And the defenders, they put more people in jail than the government. You have college boys and girls playing games, you have both the cops and the DA's department unscrupulous, unethical, barefaced liars. People dying out there every minute, the whole metropolis up in flames, and the law just watches and warms its hands, time to time gives the ashes a poke. And you ask me how I'm feeling. Ask me about my health." She paused for breath; she twisted her painted mouth. "A lady does not expectorate. But she sure as hell can spit."

Outside in the hallways, lunch recess served merely to back up the traffic. The great soaring spaces of the lobby were clogged with straining flesh. Only the dark youths strutting seemed re-

laxed. They were the plaintiffs, the accused, yet they traveled
100 Centre as if on their home turf, while the white men in suits,
their accusers, walked on eggshells.

White men in suits, but not Enid Gerlin. A sawed-off shotgun, she might tremble but she did not quail. With jaw outthrust,
she cut a swathe dead-center through the crush and any dark
youth that pimp-rolled in her alley was blown away, impaled
on the spikes of her snakeskin boots.

Back in the well of AR–1, she leaned close above a twitching
body loosely wrapped in rags. Its name, no lie, was Justice;
Lionel Ward Justice. "What happened?" Enid demanded.

"I took sick."

"Sick? How sick?"

The rags jerked and jumped, but the wizened brown face
above them was perfectly still. It sported a toothbrush moustache, the remnants of a quiff, three teeth. "Just sick," it said.

According to the charge sheet, Lionel Ward Justice, while
under the influence of a controlled substance, had taken a crow-
bar and used it to smash up a parked Lincoln Continental,
inflicting damage estimated at some fifteen thousand dollars.
He had then resisted arrest, assaulted an officer. On his way to
jail, he had also attempted to harm himself with a corded length
of string. "Why?" Enid persisted.

"I was lonesome."

He would say no more. When his case was called, the rags
jerked again, but the body remained inanimate. Limp and shape-
less, propped up between two guards, it was bundled like a
coalsack before Judge Solomon. When its name was read out,
there was forced laughter in court. But Lionel Ward Justice
seemed not to hear. Indeed, he seemed oblivious to the whole
proceeding. Only, on his remand, a leprous hand sneaked out
from a burlap sleeve, plucked weakly at Enid's wrist.

"Did the Knicks win?" Justice asked.

Sasha and I would end up where we'd started, back at the Plum
Blossom, to wallow in more duck soup. It soothed, it satisfied;
it was an elixir. At our lowest ebb we need only plunge in its
sour-sweet depths and all weariness, hurt, heartsickness washed
away.

Canal Street was a sewer; always had been. In the eighteenth
century, when the Collect was Manhattan's trashcan, Canal had
been its drainage ditch, and somehow the habit had stuck. So
now it was synonymous with all things soiled. Spilled across its
sidewalks was a sprawling, blaring bazaar—fake Rolexes and
fake Cartiers, cut-price electronics, plated gold, New York souvenirs and posters, hardware, unmarked firearms and unregis-
tered ammo, military surplus. For decades, Meatballs had
disputed the turf with Guineas, Krauts with Kikes. But this was
the Year of the Snake.

Chinatown, three blocks west, had burst its bounds. As if
scattered by firebombs, its refuse had helter-skeltered down the
hill and washed up, suppurating, in the pit of Broadway. Overnight, it seemed, stalls and arcades bulged with paper dragons
and shot-silk fans. Upstairs, through steel doors, were floor upon
floor of sweatshops. Signs announced Wong Choy Fashion and
Sing Lei Sportswear, Kong Wing Kee Fast Food, Ken Cheng

Construction. In the Pearl River, racks overflowed with Darkie Toothpaste.

The riot raged all day. Then came dark, and everything shut down dead: "Like curfew in plaguetown," Sasha said. Only the Plum Blossom did not close.

Midnight to dawn was the graveyard shift. From time to time, another taxi driver would stop off for coffee and an egg roll, or a drunk would come tapping on the plate-glass windows, supplicating for alms. Otherwise, we had the place to ourselves. Impersonal as it was, with its Formica and blank walls, its stale reek of disinfectant, it made me think of hospitals. But Sasha loved it. "Is hell. But clean, bright hell," he said.

From our table beside the window, we commanded the whole block between Broadway and Lafayette, spread out before us like a stage set. In these chill hours, few live bodies dared the sidewalks, but dark shapes loomed in the doorways of the Pearl River. They belonged to Gum Lan, the Vietnamese youth gang whose American name was BTK—Born to Kill.

They were newly raised to stardom. Only three months before, right in the middle of an evening rush hour, they had waged war with the Flying Dragons on this same block. The battle had lasted thirty seconds, maybe less. But when the gunfire ceased, two Flying Dragons had been shot dead, the remainder routed.

It was an epic victory. The Flying Dragons were the enforcement arm of Hip Sing, the oldest and richest tong in Chinatown or all of Chinese America. No other gang, not the Tung On or the Fu Ching, not even the Ghost Shadows, had ever bested them. And Gum Lan were not even ranked contenders. They were sixteen years old, sometimes younger— shaggy-headed runts in black leather jackets. But they were possessed of a blind and lunatic passion. While the Dragons had grown slack from lack of challenge, and merely massacred by rote, the BTKs killed in blood exaltation. Now they held Canal Street from here to the Hudson River, and any gang member who impinged must pay them forfeit. Translated, their motto was *Eat Shit or Eat Steel*.

It could not last. Some night the Flying Dragons would come roaring back to reclaim their turf. Right of might, sheer weight of numbers and artillery, would prevail, and Gum Lan would be exterminated. No matter. All that Sasha requested was a grandstand seat when the showdown came.

"Novokuznetskaya," he said.

The whole of his last Moscow winter, every dusk after school, he had sat in the Baikal, a white-tiled cafeteria on Novokuz and Arbat, glued to just such a plate-glass window, awaiting just such a massacre.

Only the titles were changed. In Moscow, the youth gangs that counted had all been named after English pop groups of the sixties, the more obscure the cooler. Wimp suburbanites chose the Beatles and Rolling Stones; inner-city stylists preferred the Yardbirds or Them. On Novokuz, which must always be hippest of all, prime icons included John's Children, the Action, the Troggs.

Sasha himself had been a Fruit Eating Bear, but they were fragile goods and shattered at the first contact with the Pretty Things, who were the neighborhood kingpins. The Things had the deadliest weapons, the sharpest clothes; they looked the most Western. Only the Hi-Numbers dared challenge them.

To rule Novokuznetskaya was great glory. It was the city's rebel heart, the last quarter that clung to its identity, its own fierce soul. All other districts had been rendered interchangeable—mile upon mile of Lego-brick apartments, concrete wastelands. But here you could still tell the houses apart. Lurking among the autoblocks were alleys and courtyards and secret gardens. Street stalls sold *kvass*, twenty-two kopeks a glass; in the cafeterias you could watch soccer games on TV and get vodka-blind for a ruble. Criminals were admired, warriors idolized.

This was the turf that the Things and the Numbers disputed,

and the Things would kill to prevail. Other gangs stuck to fists and cudgels, brass knuckles. Sasha and the Fruit Eating Bears were quite content to throw snowballs. But the Things had outgrown such stuff. They were ripe for blood, and blood meant knives.

These were not hard to find. Novokuz was black-market heaven, half the price of Gorky Street, twice the authenticity. At an hour's notice, you could lay greasy hands on any thing your lust required. So Boris Starkhov, Borka, the Pretty Thing's leader, picked up a joblot of straight-edge razors, Wilkinson Swords. Then he split the stock in two and dumped the blunter half outside the Hi-Numbers' clubhouse, a bunker out back of a bakeshop.

The whole neighborhood awaited the comeuppance. It was the bitterest cold winter, even for Moscow, and everything just stopped. At night, the gangs would shelter in the rancid warmth of the Baikal, eat raw onions, and stare out of the plate-glass windows at the virgin snow, which should have been running with blood. Borka Starkhov and the Things stood stationed at the corner, dressed in matching silver inflatable jackets filled with foam rubber. Some looked like tractor tires, others like human condoms. To stave off the freeze, they sang *Here Comes the Night*, stamping their imitation Doc Martens to the beat, and their Wilkinson Swords flashed like sharks' teeth. "So what happened?" I demanded.

"Numbers never came," Sasha said.

"Then how did it end?"

"Snow melted."

When the last of the soup had been rendered, we went back on the street. Freezing fog wrapped tight around us like a tourniquet, smothered us blood and bone. To the east and west, Chinatown and TriBeCa were still awake, but Broadway was quite deserted, and every hidden doorway seemed to hold a Gum Lan, Born to Kill. So we went walking softly, softly, like two little maids from school.

A couple of blocks downtown, where we turned left, the buildings shrank, and we skirted Chinatown proper. Between a Lotto vendor's and a petshop, we ducked into a redstone, began to climb steep stairs in the dark.

Sam Wing lived at the top.

The man who came to the door was ageless, a small spry figure in baggy pants and a white waiter's jacket, an embroidered cap. His cheeks looked swollen, as though he'd recently had mumps, and two of his front teeth were missing. Even so, he exuded jauntiness, a birdlike alacrity.

The small sign beside his doorbell, printed in both Cantonese and English characters, read ORIENTAL HEALING MASTER: ACU-PUNCTURE—SHIATSU—MEDITATION + DISCIPLINES TO TASTE. But his true calling lay in massages.

He had not been long in the business. When Sasha had first met him, just a few months back, Wing had been a night waiter at the Plum Blossom. In those days, he had sported long moustaches, a lifetime in the growing, and they'd lent him a distinction quite apart from his younger colleagues. He didn't just fetch and carry, he served food forth, like a bhikku dispensing blessings. "I trust you will enjoy," he'd say, "and benefit."

When he did not serve, he slept. Five nights a week, while Sasha drank his duck soup, Wing sat nodding by the door, in a five-barred wooden chair, with a Chinese newspaper spread wide on his lap. According to the other waiters, he was studying the next day's Runners and Riders. If so, the contemplation seemed to bring him both pleasure and peace. But one night Sasha drove up to find the five-barred chair smashed to kindling, scattered all over the Canal Street sidewalk, and Wing himself in the back alley behind Lafayette, propped up against a dumpster, where two teenage hoods were alternately butting him and kicking him.

When Sasha ran up, the hoods took off down Lafayette. Wing's moustache hung in bloodied scraps, one ear was almost severed, and the whole left side of his body pulped. But he wouldn't let Sasha fetch the law, would neither name nor blame his attackers. "It was their right," he mumbled through broken teeth. "I issue no complaints."

So Sasha had brought him home, here to this redstone railroad flat, where he lived in two rooms with his married daughter, Jenny, and her husband, Yung Ng, their daughters Elizabeth and Harriet. Given time, he had healed up nicely, now seemed quite recovered. Still, he did not return to the Plum Blossom. Instead, the ORIENTAL HEALING MASTER sign went up. Wing did not advertise elsewhere, and he never seemed to have any clients. But in this, too, he issued no complaints. "It's better so. More restful," he said.

The first room of his apartment was a cave piled high with gadgetry. Two televisions ran at once, one tuned to an old movie, the other to MTV. There was a VCR, a Toshiba Boombeat cassette player, a Sony CD-video player. There were also Jenny, Elizabeth, Harriet. None of them looked up when we entered.

Behind a beaded curtain was a small plain cubicle, furnished only with a masseur's table and a spittoon. While Sasha waited outside on a plastic-covered sofa, watching *How to Murder Your Wife* with his left eye, *Like a Virgin* with his right, I stretched out beneath a raffia wall hanging touting JOY, LUCK, LONGEVITY and surrendered myself to a rubdown.

Wing was not possessed of the magic hand. His touch was leathery and scabbed, his rhythm jagged, and his joints clawed with arthritis. Under his fingers, my flesh was constantly jarred, snagged, twisted, as if caught in a barbed-wire net. "Ancient discipline. Lifetime study and mastery," said Wing, ripping fiber from sinew like barnacles off a seawall. "I myself am in awe."

His speech was unaccented, his delivery austere: "I am of Toishan," he said.

It was a rural area near Canton. There he had been a schoolteacher, like his father and grandfather, but he had early felt set apart, a stranger. "In me was never a shape to fit. Where the sunlight pointed, my shadow would not follow," said Wing. "Into the unknown only, my footsteps drew me on."

After the People's Revolution, he had fled to Hong Kong. "I searched. I *quested*," he said. He swam from the Chinese mainland with his family's library on his back, wrapped in strips of rubber tire. The books were old, some very rare. They were also very heavy, and Wing almost drowned. As he thrashed in the waters, he saw the figure three, writ in flame against the peak. At this, his strength revived, and he came safely to shore. The books were also saved. So Wing carried them to the nearest antiquarian, sold them off in a job lot. Then he took the money to the racetrack and backed every three horse on the card. They did not win.

He found refuge in a Buddhist monastery. There he taught Toishan, a classical dialect much prized in Hong Kong, where most novitiates were besmirched by street Cantonese; and he met an elderly Scotsman, name of Samuel Dree. Before converting to Zen, Dree had been educated at Fettes College, had tutored at Loretto. Now, in exchange for a smidgin of Fuchow, a smattering of Mandarin, the dominie drilled Wing in Lowlands Scots.

Soon Wing was vouchsafed another vision. In a silver ring, he glimpsed a card, the eight of diamonds. Instead of the usual markings, it bore the characters of his own name. So he borrowed from Samuel Dree, went over the wall, and hit the fan-tan parlors. He did not win.

That was the end of the monastery, the end of Samuel Dree. Other things followed, but he did not speak of these. He was not lucky, that was all. No Triad would take him and protect him. So any man might hunt him and kill him for free. It was very trying. For a moment, Wing almost doubted his fortune. Then he acquired a forged green card. The price was servitude. But it had brought him to America, *Gam San*—the Mountain of Gold.

This was in 1952, when Chinatown was still a secret enclave, twisted and teeming as a medieval ghetto. Its narrow streets had once been battlesites. Tong rivalries, the wars between the Hip Sing and the On Leong, had spawned mass gunfights. But that was a lost age. Tom Lee and Mock Duck, the great warlords, were long since dead, and the tongs defanged. Now Chinatown was ruled by allied guilds, its own style of Tammany Hall. The only war was the struggle for tourist trade.

Wing worked in a Pell Street laundry for four dollars a week, sixteen hours a day, 364 days a year, with only Chinese New Year's for vacation. Out of each four dollars, half went in payments against his green card. With interest factored in, and given good health, he would be out of debt in thirty-eight years.

In Toishan and Hong Kong, his name had been Hui Tang, but here he called himself Sam; it made him feel more at home. He slept in a garbage can, an oversized dumpster out back of the Phoenix Gardens, enwombed in chow mein and discarded porkballs. On payday, he gambled.

So did everybody else. In Chinatown, the sweatshops and duck-soup kitchens seemed filled with just one story—men who had sold themselves and could not buy themselves back. Their one faint hope was a windfall at fan-tan. So they scraped and starved, they went stampeding to the tables. At the end of the night, of course, they would be penniless again: "Still they had play," Wing said. "It was proof they were living men."

But he himself was cannier. Even at four dollars, he remained a visionary. Instead of fan-tan, he placed his faith in numbers. And in the seventeenth month, it paid off. In a dream, he saw a jeweled pig with a ring in its nose and, in that ring, was the number 427. He played it the next day. When it didn't come up, he lost his temper. As far back as he could recall, he had never lost control before, and it shamed him to recall it now. But he had stormed out of the numbers house, a Mott Street souvenir shop, and hurled a brick through its window. Then sanity returned, and Wing started running. A lamppost tripped him up, sent him sprawling in the street. He tried to rise but couldn't. From a cobalt sky, the plush, fatted moons of a lawman's buttocks descended on his head. Wing was pinned, paralyzed, to the cobblestones.

He was, as Samuel Dree would have said, afeared. And with just cause. In short order, he had been frog-marched off to court between two Irish beefheads, and when he could not come up with his fine, he served seven days in the Tombs.

It was a time of remorse, but also of rethinking, profound contemplation. When Wing was released, he made his way directly back to the numbers house. Humbly, he apologized. More humbly yet, he begged another chance. When the operator, a kindly man, at length acquiesced, Wing played the first three figures of his criminal-record number. They won him five thousand dollars.

As he talked, he had not ceased to torment my flesh. The fiercer his own deprivations, the more cruelly I was punished. But here the pounding was replaced by a slow, calm stirring, the lapping of cool waters. "From this reversal, I learned," said Wing. "We are surrounded by signs and omens. Ignore them all." His breath, a scent like vanilla extract, brushed damply against my ear, curled down the back of my neck. "To make dream come true," he said, "first omit to dream."

Henceforth all his bets were scattershots. "Do not seek and ye shall find," he said. Unlike most Chinese, he did not think of Americans as white devils or black devils. "I did not find them smart enough for devils of any stripe," he said. Instead of shunning them, shrinking from their touch, it was his pleasure to use them. He haunted their betting parlors, their racetracks. On Suburban Handicap day, he gladly shared their Getaway train to Belmont, and placed himself at the rails. Standing next to him was a pink stranger who smelled of sweetsop and onions. Her name was Edna Rosemary MacCracken.

"A good-sized person," she came from County Clare, weighed three hundred pounds. She was a qualified nurse. Loose

Lips paid $22.80 in the eighth, and they were married the following day.

The union was prolific. In twelve years, it produced three children, twenty-eight changes of address, and enough losing tickets to wallpaper the clubhouse at Churchill Downs. On each anniversary of their meeting, they would revisit Belmont, resume their first positions along the rail. "Gladsome days, by and large," Wing said, slowly stirring.

In 1966, there was a passing discord. In the fifth, his own selection was Cash 'n Carry, while Edna Rosemary espoused Persnickety. An argument ensued. "As husband, I was adamant," Wing said. But Edna Rosemary, as wife, prevailed. In a rare snit, she whacked down $2, Persnickety, win and show. "The horse paid $48.50. The winning margin was five lengths," said Wing, and the stirring became a chopping, fitful, out of sync. "Woman Edna let out one cry, and she was dust."

It may have been a timely demise. They had been living on Canal, right on Chinatown's borderline. They had been happy there. But for how much longer? The previous year, the Exclusion Act had been repealed. Suddenly hordes of immigrants came swarming, ten thousand new bodies each season. Most of them hailed from Hong Kong, that faithless isle. They brought ugly clothes, ugly dialects, ugly manners. Worse, they brought ugly ambitions. They had no respect for the old order, for permanence and balance. Tradition was not their concern. All they wanted was *Gam San*, the Mountain of Gold.

Once again the rhythm changed. Instead of chopping, I felt a series of small sharp jerks, like a suitcase being bumped down a steep flight of stairs. "Attend me now. Be guided," said Wing. "Perceive the picture."

For decades, Chinatown had had one supreme leader, Benny Ong, Uncle Seven. It was his genius, above all, that had given the Hip Sing victory over the On Leong. As a foot soldier, back in the thirties, he had fought in the great street wars, done time for a gang murder; as tong president, he had controlled the neighborhood's great industries—tourism, narcotics, gambling, protection; and now, as an old man, he craved peace. Side by side with opium and chopsticks, he provided free meals for the elderly, day-care centers for the young. The Flying Dragons, Hip Sing's enforcement arm, gathered rust: "They fly away," said Uncle Seven.

Not for long. By the late seventies, his lifetime's work lay in ruins. Not only were the On Leong resurrected, and the Tung On and the Fu Ching, but the Hong Kong Triads had moved in. Their warriors had names like Tiger Boy Wang, Alligator Chan, and, most feared of all, John Eng—Onion Head, Machinegun Johnny. Their battlefield was China White, pure heroin from the Golden Triangle, and their Godfather Eddie Chan, the Sixth Dragon.

"War, I know and esteem," Uncle Seven had said, a genial old gent. "Anarchy, I think, is not good business policy." But he was not granted the choice. In 1976, he was sentenced to eight years for bribery and retired to Lewisburg, Pennsylvania, where he grew squash and winter cabbage on the prison farm. The Hip Sing foundered; Eddie Chan took over. In no time flat, he'd annexed the On Leong. Fast Eddie, the cops called him then. He wore hand-tailored silk suits, rode in a chauffeured Rolls-Royce, took lunch with Mayor Koch. Borne up on clouds of China White, he owned his own bank. Down in the streets, meanwhile, his Ghost Shadows were shooting everything that moved. Their motto was *We Die Harder*.

Wing was outraged. Walking peacefully about his business, he found himself jostled, abused. Skinny kids with rickets and their teeth still in braces waved knives in his eyes. "This was not good," he said. A twist, a slight slap. "This was bad," he said.

Since Edna Rosemary's passing, he had lived cast out. Because he'd mixed his blood with the white devils, his fellow Chinese did not trust him. Even his children, whose birth had been his life's great joy, had come to doubt him. Pressured and mocked at school, they had forgotten their English, reverted to Hong Kong type. His first son had gone to work for Eddie Chan's United Orient Bank; his daughter had married a green-card immigrant. As for his younger son, Robert, he'd joined the Ghost Shadows.

Robert was then seventeen. Two weeks before his next birthday, he'd helped ambush a Flying Dragon clubhouse in Queens and been shot dead by one of his own comrades. "They took the body back to Pell Street and buried him the same night," Wing said. "His father was not informed but found out on the fourth day, through street talk, a washwoman's idle gossip. On application, a request for the dead boy's clothes and personal possessions was not honored. Instead, three thousand dollars cash was delivered in a wooden box, as payment for his lost life."

Wing's hands lay still on my kidneys. His fingers flexed but did not strike. Then they went away altogether. "All finish," Wing said. "The end."

When I'd put my clothes back on, he led me back through the curtain, out into the room full of electronics. Elizabeth and Harriet lay asleep on a corner pallet, but Jenny was still ironing their schoolclothes. Raidas, a Hong Kong disco group, blared from a cassette. The time was 2:45.

Underneath a wall hanging selling GOOD LIFE, BIG FORTUNE was a small inlaid cabinet, all crimson dragons and gilded scrollwork.

Wing squatted. His swollen cheeks, purple and green, were mottled like spoiled luncheon meat, and his white waiter's jacket was sweat-stained under the arms: "I have picture," he said. "Why won't you see?"

From inside the cabinet he drew a school yearbook, Seward Park High School. Robert's mugshot, surrounded by beaming white devils, showed a rabbit-faced youth with an outsize Adam's apple and a pompadour, a stare of frozen defiance. Only the fatness of the eyes suggested Edna Rosemary. "His name was Robert Eamonn," said Wing. "He called himself Bobby 2 Bad."

Across the room, his daughter Jenny went rigid, squawked like an outraged nightbird. Her brother's life and death were family business, she hissed, not fit to be exhumed before white-devil strangers. In protest, she switched up both TVs full-blast. John Wayne and Aretha Franklin merged with Raidas in a death chorus of stuck pigs, and we slunk back behind the beaded curtain, into a twilit haze of embrocation and staled sweat.

"My daughter has bad stomach," said Wing. She worked six days a week, seven in the morning till seven at night, hemming in a Bayard Street sweatshop, and she brought home $140. "Not enough for rent and children's food. Not enough even for horses." As for Yung Ng, her husband, he was a waiter on Mulbridge Street. While his green-card debt was unpaid, every cent he earned was pledged. So tonight would find him in some basement, at prayer and fan-tan: "In the world, all things change. Chinatown is not the world," Wing said.

With his missing front teeth and tiny stick body, his head cocked in permanent query, he looked a pensionable child. But his age was sixty-seven, and his joints hurt. Above the massage table, next to JOY, LUCK, LONGEVITY, was a Chinese calendar scrawled with handwritten figures. They kept track of Robert's age, day by day, had he lived.

Side by side, we sat on the rubbing board, feet dangling like urchins. "I issue no complaints," said Wing.

A few months after the shooting, he had received a last vision. In a whirlwind of the number six, he saw a shrine. At its altar sat a dragon with blood-slavered jaws. Then a purple cloud passed overhead, the shrine turned black, and the dragon burst into flames, was consumed.

"We are surrounded by signs and omens," Wing had said. "Ignore them all." Just this once, however, he had vetoed his own commandment. Rising up in the night, he threw on his clothes, went running through the streets to the United

Orient Bank, to watch it burn, watch the Sixth Dragon burn up with it.

As always, he had misread the signals. By the time Wing arrived, the bank was already blocked off by FBI men, its directors under arrest. But there were no flames, and Eddie Chan himself was long gone. Prewarned, he had escaped to Singapore.

The raging bonfire of Sam Wing's dream proved to be only lanterns and flambeaux to honor Benny Ong. In the Sixth Dragon's absence, Uncle Seven resumed his lost kingship. Eighty years old now, slow but stately, he could be seen every noon, crossing Pell Street to the Hip Sing Credit Union, to consult with tong officials. In a pinstriped business suit, complete with carnation and diamond stickpin, he then strolled the few yards to Sun Tong Gung, where he took Dim Sum with his wife and counsellors. Afterwards, he napped, he played cards.

And Eddie Chan? He ran from Singapore to Taiwan, then on to Manila, to Paris, to the Dominican Republic. It was rumored that he was plotting his return. Meanwhile, the United Orient survived, a four-floor pagoda on Mott at Canal. So did the On Leong, the Ghost Shadows, and the Flying Dragons, the Tung On, the Fu Ching, the Triads. So did the BTKs.

Inside his cubicle, Wing rubbed his clawed hands with Ben-Gay. "This does no good. Nothing does," he said. "It merely offers diversion, the soup of idle souls."

He did not cease to gamble. He never had. With the three thousand dollars left by the Ghost Shadows, he had carried himself through Aqueduct, Belmont, and most of Saratoga. After that, he'd gone back to nickel and diming. In flush seasons, he hit Atlantic City; in thin, he played skat. When he lost too much, there was trouble. "My family do not honor their progenitor," he said, without rancor. Truth was, they could not afford to. In direst extremity, Jenny might sometimes cough up a dollar or two. Otherwise, Wing's debts were paid the old-fashioned way, in fists and head-butts and steel-capped boots. "It is quickest," he said.

As for visions, he had none. "That is a young man's game. I am old," he said. "My wind is shot." The quest was done. "It is better so," said Wing.

It was 3:20. In the room through the curtain, Raidas had fallen silent and even Jenny slept. Sasha sat slumped on the clear-plastic sofa, reading *Only a Gilded Cage: The Lives and Loves of the Soap Stars.* The twin TVs blinked on.

Outside on the dark stairs, I fumbled for Wing's hand, got his sleeve instead. "You have the name correctly spelled? Robert Eamonn," he said. "Called himself Bobby 2 Bad."

In the streets below, the fog seemed colder, more impenetrable than ever. Groping by curbstones and blank walls, we edged our way back to Broadway and set our faces uptown, towards EmCee Marie and sleep.

Somewhere in the second block, a large body occurred. It was moving upstream in heavy hiker's boots, an overcoat like a tent. As it came abreast of us, the body seemed to waver, then it plunged on again and was swallowed up in gloom. But it did not go far. A few steps on, the sound of its footsteps faltered, then ceased.

When I retraced my steps, I found a face like a Halloween mask carved out of an oversized pumpkin. Its owner smiled fearfully. "Good sir," he said. "I search."

German? Silesian? Slovene? The accent escaped me. So did the words that followed, spilled out in a job-lot tumble. "What for looking? Searching what?" I asked, inane. The man raised his heavy shoulders in a shrug, then let them slump again. "I search I whatnot know," he said.

Interval

REALLY, IT WAS Barnum's fault. Before him, Broadway had been just a Main Street, the city's heart of business and affairs. Its history did not stem from any mystic quality of place, but simply from its centrality. *Der Hagh Wagh Way*, the High Wagon Way, it bound Manhattan together, a thick, strong spine. So great men gathered, great things happened there. But there was no abstract involved. Nobody came to Broadway on a dream.

Then Phineas T. Barnum appeared. Born in 1810, he was a country boy from Bethel, Connecticut, where his father was in turn a farmer, a grocer, a tailor, and a tavernkeeper. Phineas was an Old Testament name meaning "brazen mouth," but his childhood was placid, unstrained. Only Ivy Island enlivened it.

It was a practical joke. All through Barnum's infancy, his family kept telling him of this wondrous island that he owned, deeded to him by his grandfather. According to *Struggles and Triumphs*, it was painted as "the promised land . . . a land flowing with milk and honey . . . caverns of emeralds, diamonds and other precious stones, as well as mines of silver and gold."

When he was ten, his father took him to take possession of this Shangri-la. After a long trudge through muddy swamps and brambles, plagued by hornets' nests, he stood at last in his domain. And it turned out a mirage: "I saw nothing but a few stunted ivies and straggling trees. The truth flashed upon me. My valuable 'Ivy Island' was an almost inaccessible, worthless bit of barren land. . . ."

The incident colored everything that followed. For the rest of his life, he would invent his own Ivy Islands. That way they might fool others, but never again could they cheat him.

At sixteen, he moved to Brooklyn, became a clerk. He was quick, ambitious, big with energy and self-belief. On Sunday afternoons, he strolled on Broadway. It was an elegant promenade lined with poplar trees. But there was nothing much to do. There were a couple of theaters, a few grand hotels and restaurants. Above Canal, in the city's outskirts, there was also Vauxhall Gardens and Niblo's Garden, an open-air saloon and music hall. For the rest, pleasure got short shrift.

This was no accident. Among New York's arbiters, the prevailing belief was mass entertainment was dangerous, ungodly. "Laws were blue, and life was gray," wrote Irving Wallace in *The Fabulous Showman.* "Theaters and exhibitions were regarded by most as outposts of the devil. Sport was confined to intoxication, assault and battery, and discreet fornication."

Even these rough joys were denied to Broadway man. If he wished to roister, he must go wallow in the pig troughs of the Bowery, the grogshops of the Five Points. On the boulevard, he must be sober, heavy with gloom.

"Of curiosity and wonder and sensation there was little." To Barnum, even in embryo, this couldn't be right. "This is a trading world and men, women and children, who cannot live on gravity alone, need something to satisfy their gayer, lighter moods," he believed, "and he who ministers to this want is in a business established by the Author of our nature."

Almost ten years went by before he could start ministering in earnest. He ran a general store back in Bethel, he was a traveling showman, he dabbled in local politics. He edited a newspaper, the *Herald of Freedom*, and did sixty days in Danbury Jail for libel. He managed Signor Vivalla, who balanced bayoneted rifles on his nose. He was almost lynched by mistake, for the Reverend Avery, a Methodist minister and accused murderer. And then he found Joice Heth.

It was his first great scam; *humbug*, the word was then. Joice Heth was introduced as George Washington's nurse, now 161 years old but still full of running: "She weighs but Forty-Six Pounds, and yet is very cheerful and interesting. She retains her faculties in an unparalleled degree, converses freely, ●ings numerous hymns, relates many interesting anecdotes of *the boy* Washington, and often laughs heartily at her own remarks, or those of the spectators."

Her impact was prodigious. New Yorkers of all classes, "lovers of the curious and the marvellous," thronged to see and question her. Then Barnum took her show on the road. For eight months she toured and then, exhausted, she died. Autopsy revealed her to be a well-preserved eighty. But the point had been made. In 1841, just turned thirty, Barnum opened his first American Museum.

According to Irving Wallace, he was then "a Connecticut Yankee six foot two inches in height, a bundle of massive energy, with curly, receding hair about wide ingenuous blue eyes, a bulbous nose, a full, amused mouth, a cleft chin, and a high-pitched voice." Later on, his waistline would spread as his hairline ebbed, and his well-stuffed waistcoat, his beetling brows and knobby skull gave him more and more a Pickwickian look. But his energy level never dropped below volcanic. He was by no means a paragon. He could be money-grubbing and devious, exploitative, sanctimonious, cheap. Still sheer vitality, *animal spirits*, gusted all his sins before him, blown away by the gales of his own laughter. Self-styled the Prince of Humbugs, he was an overgrown child who recognized the child in all men, and it was this, more than anything, that made him Broadway's true inventor.

"His crusade," Wallace wrote, "was to make life a sinless carnival, to make mirth and play acceptable as a necessary portion of daily living."

Pleasure without guilt—it was no mean legacy. Before him, curiosity museums had been furtive, dust-ridden mausoleums. Usually they featured a few skeletons, a couple of death masks, perhaps a lecture with lantern slides. Barnum, by contrast, offered "educated dogs, industrious fleas, automatons, jugglers, ventriloquists, living statuary, tableaux, gypsies, albinos, fat boys, giants, dwarfs, rope dancers, live 'Yankees,' pantomime, instrumental music, singing and dancing in great variety. . . ."

It was only a preamble. From fleas and educated dogs, the showman moved on to General Tom Thumb, *the attraction of the ages*. Then there came the Mermaid from Feejee; Grizzly Adams; Jumbo the Elephant; the Great White Whale. Rival hucksters rose up in challenge, and Broadway filled with amazements. Not just museums and showplaces, but vaudevilles, concert saloons, and variety houses, giant department stores, theaters high and low. At every block, it seemed, there was *the latest, the greatest*. And somewhere along the line, the street became an idea.

The idea boiled down to a single word, the most potent in the language. And that word, of course, was *action*.

What Barnum had done was burst the dam; unpent all the energies, good and bad, that the blue laws and gray life had denied. The ultimate Ivy Island, Broadway became a synonym for release. You came to it on a risk. You packed up all your wit and nerve and endurance, your energy and your luck, and you brought them to the tables. Then you did not quit till you broke the bank or you were flat busted.

The medium varied. It might be finance or politics, show business, law or crime, prizefighting, magic, art, or sex. But all the men and women who played Broadway were driven, at root, by the same motor: the love and lust of adventure.

In another age or context, the same romance would have

spawned explorers, mercenaries, gold rushers. But this was the time of the city; New York was *the* city and Broadway its apotheosis. By 1900, its action stretched clear from the Battery to Forty-second Street. Downtown, the major games were money and power; from Fourteenth Street upwards, money and sex. In both, the stakes were all or nothing.

The turf had been staked out in roughly ten-block increments. As Broadway rode north, the smart money clung tight to its tail. At each successive crossroads—City Hall, Union, Madison, Herald, and, finally, Times squares—it would set up its lures, a fresh cavalcade of theaters and cafés, gambling dens, flash saloons, bordellos, then sit back, smug, and await the sound of those shuffling feet.

Rialtos, columnists called them. By day, they were mere shopping spas: "Jewels, silks, satins, laces, ribbons, household goods, silverware, toys, paintings, in short rare, costly and beautiful objects of every description greet the gazer," wrote James McCabe. Then came darkness, and the night-lights, and all of this glitter was set to work. "The vehicles in the street consist almost entirely of carriages and omnibuses, each with its lamps of different colors. They go dancing down the long vista like so many fireflies. Here and there a brilliant reflector at the door of some theater sends its dazzling white rays streaming along the street for several blocks. Strains of music or bursts of applause float out on the night air from places of amusement, not all of which are reputable. Gaudily painted transparencies allure the unwary to the vile concert saloons in the cellars below the street. Here and there, sometimes alone and sometimes in couples, you see women, mainly young, and all flashily dressed, walking rapidly, with a peculiar gait, and glancing quickly but searchingly at every man they pass. Some of them are mere children."

The lights, of course, were cardinal. First there were gaslights, then the silver electricity for which Broadway was rechristened the Great White Way, and finally neon. Now it was the Glittering Gulch, the Fabulous Floodway, the Stem, the Heavenly Hell. "There's a sucker born every minute," as Barnum may or may not have said, and they poured in from every lost corner of the planet. They were troupers; they were thrushes and hoofers, chorines, sugar daddies and stage-door Johnnies, gangsters and their molls, magicians, sword swallowers and flame throwers, bucket-shop floaters, speculators and prognosticators, touts, shysters and mouthpieces, honest rainmakers, faith healers, shamans, pols and fixers, lushes and hopheads, yeggs, dips, murderers and murderees, tunesmiths and rhymesmiths, half-hand bigshots, scribes and sob sisters, champs and palookas, sirens, swells, boobs, hayseeds, torpedoes and tomatoes, dames, quails, moustaches, gigolos, just guys and dolls. A few of them made it and most of them didn't and all of them wound up dead at the present time. It did not matter. They had had a piece of the action.

Numberless were the hymns of praise. *Give My Regards to Broadway* and *Lullaby of Broadway, Forty-five Minutes from Broadway, Broadway Baby, The Man Who Owns Broadway.* One of the most forgettable was *Broadway, the Heart of the World.*

Later generations would have their own theme songs, their own language and liturgy. But the basic nature of the adventure did not change. On Broadway you spun the wheel. At least you believed you did. In reality, of course, the wheel spun you.

Two

11 /
be spring," said Lush Life.

All winter she'd lived in the dark. At the Hotel Moose, her window was kept blacked out, a shellacked drop-curtain nailed tight, so that no hint of daylight could sneak in. Inside, her room was lit by Japanese lanterns like glow-worms. Then came March. One morning the blind snapped, bright sunshine rushed in. It caught her naked.

Lush Life's room, a cell much like my own, was lined with clothes and old magazines. Somewhere in the middle, she'd made herself a pallet on the floor, a thing of coats and scarves and torn curtains, foam rubber and wadded sacking, wrapped in the Stars and Stripes. There she lunched by night-lights, slept by Night Train. In between, she lip-synched to *Madame Butterfly*.

It was her season's religion. A new production was in rehearsal; Lush Life had seen the costumes previewed in a Sunday supplement. Now her room was awash in thrift-store Japanesque and Maria Callas albums, through which she moved with tiny mincing steps, miming to her pet arias. When Cio-Cio-San expired, so did she. But she did not stay dead for long. "It doesn't pay," she said.

Not at the Hotel Moose, it didn't. Here dying was *service*

compris. A lean and languid Jamaican, name of Motion, had the job of sweeping up the corridors, checking the rooms. When he found a body that his broom could not rouse, he called the cops or the ambulance: "Depends on de cause of departure," he said. "Demise, or is it decease."

Demise meant natural causes, decease did not. In this bitter winter, the whole city had seemed a killing field racked by plagues. Shelters overflowed, welfare hotels were reduced to funded crackhouses. Even doorways were disputed: "You want freeze to death, somebody beat you to it," Motion said. "You want slit your own throat, some mother son stole the razor."

He was not a man who hastened. Hence his name. "Other men move, I just motion," he said. Eleven years back, he and his partner, Reds, had left their wives and families, traveled here from Negril: "One cardboard suitcase, two pair pants," Motion said. That had been another bitter winter. They had slept in paper bags, crawl spaces, elevator shafts. But they neither demised or deceased. Instead, they'd met a fellow countryman, Captain Deliver he was called, who fed them two laws to stay alive. *Smile when you do*, he'd said. *Smile when you don't*.

Over the years, the smiles had acquired a rictal fixity. Passing them on the stairs, with a bodybag toted between them, Lush Life would squeak, curl back against the walls. But they did not get paid to carry corpses. "Only dust," Motion said.

A garden grew. It started down the hallway, in the wall by the fire escape. Nightly breakage of bottles and skulls had pitted the plaster like a firing range. All winter, pipes burst and were not fixed, water pipes and heating pipes, which caused the walls to weep. Crawling damp fed on the crevices, widened them into gullies. One day a patch of lichen appeared. Then suckers, then tendrils. Morning Glory swarmed the windowpanes. Through the rotted linoleum, which had once been patterned with ducks, a neat crop of toadstools sprang up.

A defunct party in Room 15 had left behind a paperback Nature guide. Motion consulted its index, picking whatever names pleased him, and christened the growths accordingly. "Crazyweed, ragweed, jimsonweed," he crooned, singsong as a lullaby. "Purslane. Spotted purge."

"Speedwell. Mallow," said Reds.

"Lady's Thumb. Cat's Ear. Beggar's Tick."

"Quack Grass."

"Poke."

Together, they kept the garden safe from the Brothers Kassimatis. In other days, Mike and Petros would have taken its incursions as personal affronts. But this winter had numbed them, too. The Moose had received its death sentence. In weeks or months, a couple of years at best, it would be razed to make way for one more high rise, a block of co-ops, a multi-story carpark. So they only rattled their nightsticks at the toadstools, spat. "Floral arrangements," said Petros, all disgust. He stared morosely at his wrists, the tangled backs of his hands, as if expecting deadly nightshade to sprout from their black undergrowth. "It's a jungle in here," he said.

The scent of blossom gave Lush Life allergies. She consulted the one book she possessed, *1001 Diseases*, and it appeared that she had all of them. "Jungle rot," she said. "Chancre. Grippe."

"Monkshood. Motherwort," said Motion.

"Pesthole. Fambesia. Thrush."

"Love Lies Bleeding."

"Yaws."

She lay doubled over on her pallet, shivering, in obi and slashed kimono, bound feet. Denise Denise had given her a stereo, an antique boombox that rendered male voices as foghorns, all females as squalling gulls. By night-light, her room became a harbor wrapped in mists. Sirens wailed, bellbuoys clanged. Somewhere high above, Cio-Cio-San wheeled and fluttered, mewling: "Brokenwing. Stigma," said Lush Life.

"Wolfbane," said Motion.

"Flux."

All along one wall hung summer dresses, waiting. Then the

blind broke, bright light flooded in. Naked, Lush Life ran to cover, arms shielding her bosom, her sex. "I'm not decent," she cried. But she could not keep from smiling. Her eyes closed, her arms fell to her sides. The sunlight ate her up every inch. "Oh, well," she said. "Oh, well."

We went out walking on Broadway.

This day it was enchanted. One dazzle of sunlight, and all the girls in spring dresses had come out at once. So had the sweet-talkers and slow-walkers, the street musicians, the palmists. "Let me read you a beautiful future," said Miss Sybil, a yellow girl with orange hair. "Five bucks is all."

"I got three," Lush Life said. "What future is that?"

"Short," said Miss Sybil, "but sweet."

At every corner, pushcarts peddled hot dogs, cold drinks. Sucking on a Popsicle, her lips a perfect O, Lush Life was a young Tuesday Weld, a teendream in bobby sox, flipskirt, flick-ups. When she held my hand, I felt like Eddie Cochran playing hooky: "Who's Eddie Cochran?" Lush Life asked.

We rode downtown. In the taxi, the radio deejay played L. L. Cool J, Jazzy Jeff, the Real Roxanne. All winter, it seemed, I had been mired in the past, that dark and soggy land that Sasha called UsedToBe. Now Lush Life stuck on pink eyelashes like spiderlegs, the bike messengers wore lime-green spandex. On the corner of Broadway and Thirty-fourth, a blonde model in a frilly white dress posed over the subway vent, legs flexed wide like Marilyn Monroe, head thrown back and tossing. The deejay played *You Be Illin'*; Lush Life sang *Un Bel Dì*.

Down the block from Union Square, she led me into Julian's Billiards. As Geraldo Cruz, she had shot a mean stick. These days her game was rusted, and her shakes did not help. Still she could sweep whole tables clean, Straight Pool, Eight-Ball or Nine, quicker than I could chalk a cue.

Julian's was an upper room, held sacred. According to the man who punched the clock, it was the oldest working poolhall in America, went back beyond the First World War. Here *The*

Hustler had been shot, and Willie Mosconi had crushed Minnesota Fats. "You could look it up," said the man. But why bother? The long ranks of tables, the slow-whirring fans and unspotted greens, told all: "You shoot pool in Julian's, you chalk with the ghosts of giants."

Even at noon, most tables were occupied. Gaggles of teenage Koreans, both boys and girls, interspersed with older, graver sticks. Over by the high windows, which were muddy brown with grime, two sailors played. One was tall, the other squat. Save for the clack of balls and squeak of chalk, the odd smothered curse, they made no sound. But when the tall one sank the black, he whirled his face at the light, flashed one white smile, and Lush Life was lost.

"Pinkerton," she whispered. But he looked more like Jerry Lee Lewis—a rawboned and towheaded youth with freckles, big hands, bigger feet. Though a certain manic glint spoke of crossroads, of family Bibles and whiskey rivers, he shook hands shyly, blushing. "Tommy Blalock," he said.

"Vida Lujuriante," said Lush Life.

"A pretty name," said Tommy, "for one pretty lady."

He came from New Iberia, Louisiana, World's Capital of Capsicum, the hot pepper that made Mace and Tabasco sauce; and his voice held a Cajun lilt, an accordion's lurch and ramble. With Hap Cowley from Plaquemines Parish, he'd been ranging the streets for two days and a night, and now they were broke, sore, disgusted, for nobody would talk, not a soul give them time: "Excepting they get paid," Tommy Blalock said.

It was his first time in New York. All the way up in the train from Norfolk, Virginia, he'd kept humming *On Broadway* by the Drifters: "Like a sick headache, won't let you be," he said. *"They say the neon lights are bright. They say there's always magic in the air."*

Hap Cowley preferred the next verse. *"They say the girls,"* he began, *"are something else."*

"But how you gonna make some time?"

"When you ain't got . . ."

"But one thin dime?"

"Good question," said Lush Life.

"One thin dime, and a diamond watch."

"Good answer," said Lush Life. "Good answer."

Blurred sunlight, dancing with motes, slanted on her blonde wig, her pink lashes. Beneath her thin dress, her shoulder blades rose sharp and brittle, toy wings. "It's bright in here," she said. "In a bar, it's dark." She was shivering again. "In a movie, it's even darker," she said.

"Pitch black," said Tommy Blalock.

"But warm. It's warm," said Lush Life.

Back on Union Square, the Farmer's Market was setting up. The promenade was riotous with color, scent, growth. Stalls spilled over with asparagus and arugula, radicchio, spring greens. A poster advertised *Bitch Dyke Fag Hag Whore*, a new performance piece by Penny Arcade. By the entrance to the IRT, a sidewalk artist was sketching black orchids. "Daddy, buy me," said Lush Life, crooning low. "Buy me some new shoes."

They went their ways, I went mine. On Eighteenth, I fell across the Old Town Tavern, a place of battered tin ceilings, deep mahogany booths. On the bar, a fat tabby cat sat toasting, its image trapped in cut-glass mirrors.

A drunken man, the color of a chocolate milkshake, went weaving out of sunlight into shadow, then back again into sun. At my booth he stopped, swayed low in my face. His breath was bitter almonds, the stuff of cyanide, but his mouth was much obliged. "Spring be sprung," said the drunken man.

Sunstoned myself, I dozed; when I woke, it was dark.

Back at the Moose, Motion was weeding the floorboards with a kitchen fork. "A little bit compost is all it takes, we could make grow our own vegetables," he said. "Plantain, pawpaw."

"Cassava, callaloo, calabaza," said Reds.

"Ganja. Canned ackee."

"Rum."

I sat reading in my room, lost in *The Fabulous Showman*. I had reached the passage where Barnum's museum burns down: "From Maiden Lane to Chambers Street, Broadway was lined with forty thousand people watching a blaze worthy of Nero's art. . . . Great billows of smoke invaded the upper stories, and many freaks were overcome. Fortunately, innumerable fire engines clanged up before the building just in time."

From a room across the street, a reporter called Nathan D. Urner had witnessed the rescue of Anna Swan, the seven-foot-eleven-inch giantess from Nova Scotia, who was found at the top of the third-story staircase. "There was not a door through which her bulky frame could obtain a passage. It was likewise feared that the stairs would break down, even if she should reach them. Her best friend, the living skeleton, stood by her as long as he dared, but then deserted her, while as the heat grew in intensity, the perspiration rolled from her face in little brooks and rivulets, which pattered musically upon the floor. At length, as a last resort, the employees of the place procured a lofty derrick which fortunately happened to be standing near, and erected it alongside the Museum. A portion of the wall was then broken off on each side of the window, and the strong tackle was got in readiness, the tall woman was made fast to one end and swung over the heads of the people in the street, with eighteen men grasping the other extremity of the line, and lowered down from the third story, amid enthusiastic applause."

An orangutan, meanwhile, had made his way to the nearby New York *Herald* and invaded the editor's office. "The poor creature, but recently released from captivity, and doubtless thinking that he might fill some vacancy in the editorial corps of the paper in question, had descended by the waterpipe and instinctively taken refuge in the inner sanctum of the establishment."

Panic-stricken, the book editor, the music critic, and sundry cub reporters rushed the beast and tried to subdue it. Flinging them off, the orangutan leaped over Bennett's desk, made a wild dash for the window. As the crowd watched horrified from below, it teetered on a narrow ledge, eighty feet above Park Row. Flames seemed to shoot from its eyes. An agonized cry curled its lips. "Don't ask," said Lush Life. "Just don't ask."

Bending low above the marigolds, she kissed my cheek, my chin. She was crying and wearing new shoes, high-heel scarlet slingbacks, a couple of sizes too big, which made her look like a child masquerading. "It must be love," she said.

"How come?"

"It hurts," she said, "so good."

Her feet also hurt. Like her mother, she was a martyr to fallen arches. Of all her parts, her dogs alone defied her, remained inescapably male. Flatfoot floogies, calloused and carbuncled, they belonged to a trainee cop.

Normally she kept them bound, out of sight. But tonight she kicked them high. "Tommy knows. He already saw," she said, "I have no secrets from him."

She had not meant to come so clean, not when they'd entered the shoestore. They'd gone to the Paradise Bootery, famous for its six-inch stiletto heels. She shopped there all the time; all the girls on Times Square did. But she was bashful, even so. Young Tuesday Welds wore size six, but Lush Life took nines. So she told Tommy not to look. But he did, of course. And he touched her. Right there in the shop, in front of the salesgirl and everyone, he reached out his hand, took her whole naked foot and cupped it in his palm. His hand was hairless, raw pink, the color of fresh bubblegum, with thick blue veins, and her foot was swallowed whole. All that stuck out was her big toe, fat and twisted, with a scabbed blister on its joint. And Tommy bent his head, he kissed the scab. So you see. He kissed her foot. He bought her red shoes. The biggest red shoes in the house, they were ten wides, much much too big, but he said they fitted perfectly. "It's just your feet," he said, "they're so small."

Afterwards, they had not gone to the movies. Instead of hiding in the dark warm, they'd spent the afternoon at Broadway and Fiftieth, pressed up against a hole in a wooden fence, spectators at a high-rise building site. Lush Life's feet hurt. The red shoes opened up her blisters, made her limp. Tommy was concerned. *He was a perfect gentleman.* He lifted her up in his arms, to get a better view. He bought her ice cream, a magazine. *He promised me the world and all its glories.* But he could not drag himself away from the cranes and hods, the gloppiter-gloppiter machines, the dirt. "The sea is his meal ticket, but construction is his first love," Lush Life said. "When he gets out the service, he hopes to construct himself."

His uncle was a bricklayer before him, but his grandfather preached, and his father ran a bar. Outside of New Iberia, on Avery Island, Tommy himself had picked hot peppers. Then he got in a little trouble, had to go see the world. *He knew sorrow, he knew shame. But he's put it all behind him.* In five more weeks, his voyaging would be done, and he'd be free to go home, settle down. Meantime, he was dating but not going steady. *He's still looking for Miss Right.*

Out in the hallway, the nightbloods were gathering. Motion had invested in some Bacardi. The bottle clinked against the wall, the radio played torch songs. Kicking off the red shoes, Lush Life began to massage her big feet. "Vida Lujuriante," she said. "So bind me."

Dried tears smeared her cheeks. Along with the powder and paint, weeping seemed to have stripped off fresh layers of skin, so that she looked more naked than ever. "Make it tight," she said. "Tight, tight." Her teeth chattered, jarred on her bottle of Night Train. "He's just a boy," she said.

She felt reborn. The world was started over. This very night, on her way home from Tommy Blalock, she'd turned into our block and found the street full of nattering corpses, dead men who would not lie down.

It was a movie set; a fire was being shot. On the site of a razed hotel, a plywood theater had been built, scripted to burst into flame. But there was a problem with the extras. They were

disgruntled with their wages, or they mistrusted the safety pre-
cautions. Whatever, they would not work. The producers threatened, the director cajoled, but the extras were adamant. Unless
they got satisfaction, they would march off the set, leave the
whole scene hanging. So you see. Fire sirens were wailing, spectators catcalling, the whole street lit up and waiting. But the
extras only stood around, drinking coffee.

Finally, the producers had laid down an ultimatum. Either
work, they said, or get lost. "So what d'you think the dead men
do?" Lush Life asked.

"Don't know."

"They walk," she said. "They walk."

said the sign.

I had entered another realm. Lower Broadway had been ruled by old men, and young men born old. But now I had crossed Canal, and the climate was reversed. To the north, it was the young who reigned, and those who weren't young pretended.

On the corner of Grand was a red-headed stripling selling Consciousness. A Giacometti figure, splindle-shanked in sandals, shorts, and red woollen socks, he offered Insight at discount, *A Whole Other You*: "Deals you cannot, you dare not turn down."

For fifty cents, I bought a neat blue package stamped BE AWARE. But the warning came too late. When I opened the packet up, it turned out to contain a booklet entitled *Cockroaches*, put out by AmYork, Laboratories of Pest Control.

Its author was Mohammad U. Shadab, PhD. He had actively worked with bugs and spiders for the last fourteen years, said the blurb. He had always been concerned with roaches and their problems.

At a Cuban luncheon counter, I drank *cafe con leche*, read on. "Roaches are not only disgusting but dangerous for health," Shadab wrote. "They drink water, milk and beer. They also eat dead insects, their own cast-off skins, dead roaches, fresh and dried blood, excrement, sputum, finger- and toenails, and they lick the saliva of sleeping or comatose people. *They are active at night so that their dirty habits are not seen or known.*"

"Vampires. I fuckin' despise 'em," spoke a voice, reading over my shoulder. "They suck my blood, I suck theirs."

The voice belonged to a Hell's Angel, a small, furry creature in leather and chains. "Only one thing worse, that's a splash," he said.

"Splash?"

"Painter. Fuckin' artist," the Angel said.

The grievance was new, still raw. Five years before, this had been an art-free zone. Now the stuff was everywhere: *Not only disgusting but dangerous for health*, the Angel quoted. He picked his nose, contemplated the spoils. "Disfuckingusting," he said.

Leading me outdoors, he sniffed the air suspiciously, pointed like a chained setter. But I could detect no odor of creation. On the contrary, Broadway smelled bracing as Cape Cod.

It happened every March. All winter New York reeked, a toxic wasteland. Then suddenly, as if ozone-bombed, it would come up cleansed, brand new. For a week then, maybe two, the air held a zip and fizz, a glamour that made Angels sing: "Splish fuckin' splash," sang mine.

Broadway was superb here. In its entire length, twenty-one miles through Manhattan and the Bronx, no stretch was finer than these few blocks, Canal Street to Houston.

In the 1840s and 1850s, the first fine flush of Barnumism, this had been the heart of Night-town. Hell's Hundred Acres, as SoHo was known then, was a hidden swamp of brothels and low taverns. But Broadway was an open tumult. Along this strip lay theaters and gaslit cafes, concert saloons such as Niblo's, amusement parks such as the Vauxhall Gardens, and the grandest of grand hotels—the St. Nicholas, the Carlton House, the Metropolitan.

On the balcony of the Carlton House, Charles Dickens sat making his *American Notes*, glassy-eyed at the evening promenade, the carriages and their coachmen, the ladies in silks, the gentlemen preening their whiskers and, above all, the pigs: "Ugly brutes they are, having for the most part, scanty brown backs, like the lids of old horsehair trunks, spotted with unwholesome blotches. At this hour, just as evening is closing in, you will see them roaming towards bed by scores, eating their way to the last. Occasionally, some youth among them who has over-eaten himself, or has been much worried by dogs, trots shrinkingly homeward, like a prodigal son; but this is a rare case—perfect self-possession and self-reliance, and immovable composure being their foremost attributes."

Picking their way through the scavenging swine, the Broadway crowds swarmed into Wood's Minstrel Hall, and the Olympic, home of West's Amazing Circus, and the Chinese Rooms. These last became Barnum's second American Museum when the first burned down; and that too ended up in ashes.

No trace of such revels now remained. What *had* survived were the commercial buildings raised after the Civil War, and many among them were beauties. Prefabricated cast iron, they'd been designed purely as workplaces, as factories and showrooms, department stores, and so were lumbered with none of the false pomps of Lower Broadway. Their architects had kept function first, ornament for lagniappe. So the Haughwout, the Little Singer, and others were perfect in proportion, glorious in detail, but their grace was carried without fuss, no straining for effect.

The Haughwout's fate was typical. Built in 1857, it had been among the most fashionable of carriage-trade emporia, its design modeled after Sansovino's Library in St. Mark's, Venice, with a chocolate-columned façade, a fine clock, and the first Otis elevator in New York. Now it manufactured bras and wholesale knickers, and the clock had a vacant face, no hands.

Splash began at Spring.

It had come oozing up out of SoHo, which lay simmering to the west, so glutted with galleries that it couldn't contain them all. Earlier the overspill had seeped south into TriBeCa, east to Alphabet City. Now Broadway caught the lees.

SoHo itself was Boomtown, rabid with gold-rush fever. Twenty-five years back, only trucks had lived here. Its narrow black canyons, gaunt with warehouses, were full of welding shops. Then the first few artists had snuck down from Greenwich Village, lured by the emptiness and the unobstructed light, by floor-through lofts at $10,000.

It was the moment of the minimalists. Their raw materials—steel plates and blocks of Styrofoam, industrial felt, daubed bundles of rags—lay ready to hand in these streets, tumbling out of every basement and manhole cover. So a cabal formed. Paula Cooper opened one gallery, Max Hutchinson another. Then came the critics.

Among the first was Robert Hughes.

A long-haired and black-leathered Australian, newly imported from London by *Time*, he was a young man with a motorbike and fitted right in. Above the SoHo Heat-Treating & Pacivating Company, he found a floor-through loft of his own. Already the price had upped to $25,000. He bought it anyway.

His neighborhood, solidly Italian, was as minimalist as its art. Apart from a single Puerto Rican bodega, the only shops were two pork butchers, a greengrocer, a trattoria, and one lone bar, Fanelli's, in which the art colony huddled, molelike, most earnestly disputing. On wintry nights, Hughes could step out through the snow for an evening's revelry and find his footprints untouched on returning.

Money was no issue. In that age, painters were not moguls. Wealth was reserved for museum artists, the Jasper Johns and the Willem de Koonings. In SoHo, success was paying your rent.

All of this changed in a hurry. A rash of articles began to appear in the Style sections of the glossy magazines. Leo Castelli and Andre Emmerich, uptown dealers, opened downtown branches. Soon West Broadway was lined solid with bistros and chic saloons, art-supply stores, gourmet foodfares: "Came the dawn," said Hughes, "came the boutique."

Overnight, it seemed, SoHo was crammed, not only with painters and sculptors, but potters, art historians, framers and canvas-stretchers, professional girlfriends, professional boy-friends and, above all, assistants, a locust-plague of assistants. On one West Broadway wall, a lone graffito, crying in the wilderness, wailed SOHO SUCKS, BRING BACK THE TRUCKS. Double-quick, it was painted over, replaced by a daubed proclamation from René, a Labial Formalist, announcing I AM THE BEST ARTIST.

From a neighborhood, SoHo was transformed into a theme park. "ArtWorld," Robert Hughes called it.

And now the show had opened on Broadway.

In the manufacturies, whole floors had been annexed. Above and below, regiments of Hispanic women still churned out bikinis, pantyhose, garter belts. But sandwiched in be-tween, like miniature shopping malls, sat clusters of bright white galleries, each peddling a different brand name: Neo-Geo or Retro-Abstractionism, Hyper-Realism, Postmodern Recidivism, Conceptual Art and/or Anti-Art.

The Broadway Restaurant was not impressed. A dim and cavernous bunker, heavy on the Lysol, it was not impressed by much. Deep in its recesses, men played cards and sipped sticky drinks, disputed the *Racing Form*. When strangers approached, the players froze, stiff as cardboard cutouts. "Art? Don't tip worth shit," said a man in a porkpie hat. Fluttering his hand in shadow play, he made silhouettes on the wall, a squawking bird, a flapping of black wings. "Cheap, cheap," he said.

At the counter stood a young Englishman, cash in hand. He

glanced left, then right, then shrugged, then twitched. Then he ducked his head, he opened his mouth half an inch. "Pack Winstons," he hissed.

"And what else?" the cashier asked.

"Depends," said the Englishman.

A slightly built youth, curly-haired in a feather-tweed jacket, he had the face of a very old child. Pocketing the Winstons, he edged away from the counter, glanced left again, glanced right again. "All depends," he said, and made good his escape.

His name was Paul Kasmin; he ran a gallery upstairs. At this moment, it was a small empty box at the end of a blank corridor, containing nothing but a few kissee beads from Mozambique, short black banderillas like barbed-wire kebabs. But more was expected. If present plans worked out, there would soon be drawings, photographs, even paintings. "Art," said Paul. "And then." He wiggled his eyebrows, wrinkled his nose. "Or maybe not," he said.

Hidden behind a white partition, a girl scribbled notes, answered phones. "Are you in?" she asked.

"Up to a point," said Paul.

His father dealt art in England, had done so for three decades. In the sixties, he had helped package the generation of young and disparate English painters—David Hockney, Patrick Proctor, R. B. Kitaj, Allen Jones—that journalists lumped together as Pop, job-lot stars of Swinging London.

Paul himself, aged six, had had his portrait drawn by Hockney; had grown up immersed in Splash of all persuasions. In his twenties, he had studied art history at the Courtauld Institute, hustled prints in the Kensington Market, collected Brancusi photographs and, when England burned out, made his way to New York. He had drunk a bit and traveled a lot; he had met many people with money. Now he was turned thirty, and it was time to get serious.

To that end, he had rented this white space. With assistant, secretary, three-hour lunches at Da Silvano, and flights back and forth to art fairs around the globe, it cost him some $18,000 monthly, and he really must think how to fill it. He had drawers full of fine photographs, he had contacts and connections, his name was Kasmin, and he wished devoutly to be rich. Was that enough? "Yes," he said, "and no."

Everything was fine in theory; but in practice, he had a sharp and urgent problem. This same evening he was due to try selling a Donald Baechler oil to a young French couple. Laurent and Gaby Pelletier, their names were, and they made a perfect team. "He is a man with lots of money, she is a woman with lots of legs," Paul explained. But selling was not his strong point. "I know art. Or I think I do," he said. He made a small choking sound. "But my song and dance, it's not. I mean it isn't." He gulped. "It never has been."

Normally, he left the merchandising to his assistant, Marina, a dark girl with bottomless black eyes. Buyers needed to be nuzzled, led sweetly by the hand, and Marina could have sold life insurance on the *Titanic*. But she was out with the flu. That left everything up to Paul, and his gift of gab.

It was an all-important role. In recent years, a new breed of collectors had sprung up. They were primarily investors, not art lovers, and they paid in brand-new money. They'd made a killing in Hollywood or real estate, videos, computers, junk bonds and, as professional salesmen, they expected good sell in return. Just hand them a painting, however splendid, and they felt cheated: "Premature ejaculation. *Coitus interruptus*," said Paul. "One of those, anyway." His eyes flickered over the blank white walls of the gallery, the blank brick walls outside his window. "For every painting, there's a—. You just have to find the—." Rumpling his already rumpled hair, he dragged at an unlit Winston. "The key," he said. "The magic words."

Glumly, he thumbed through past catalogs of Donald Baechler's work. Baechler was very much a coming young artist, still in his early thirties, and Paul believed in him strongly. But words? "Oh, crumbs," he said.

In Baechler's paintings, deliberately *naif*, there were figures of fat naked mothers and dinosaurs and little girls, the backs of heads, black-haired or bald, and faces howling and jeering, weeping, praying, just staring. Set against them, gaudy as picturebook cutouts, were soccer balls and Christmas trees, onions, okras, potatoes. "Great stuff," said Paul.

"Why don't you just say that?" I asked.

"Single syllables," he said. "Are you mad?"

His face was never still. He had pinkish eyes, small pink ears, a small tight mouth and, at every question, the little eyes would go darting every which way, desperate for boltholes. So he looked like a rabbit at bay, but a streetwise rabbit, an Artful Dodger indeed.

Seeking inspiration, he read out of the catalog of Baechler's last exhibit. "His recent drawings provide the viewer with an experience of simultaneous attraction and vexation. Subtly attenuated surfaces layered by an indispensable fluctuation of line on the one hand, and the disorienting, claustrophobic image of a plenum; a sea of faces internally constrained and yet held from expanse by the paper's edge on the other, is reflective of this concomitance. What is offered by the density of these images is both the allure of commiseration and the negation of a subjective gaze (in an impedance of communicative intention), through the specific placement of profiles at once bearing a plethora of expressions and rarely addressing the viewer directly."

There was an extended silence.

In this white space, the phone failed to ring, the blank walls outstared the starer. "Oh, crumbs," said Paul again, and he plunged out into SoHo, went searching for magic words.

Inside Fanelli's, there were boxing pictures on the wall, a bar scarred deep by expressionists. But Mike Fanelli himself was long gone. He had always been a ghostly presence, his figure so cadaverous and flesh so parchment-thin that he'd looked like one of those dried Japanese blowfish with a guttering candle inside. On frozen nights, when the pipes failed, an ancient Coleman stove would be hauled out. Its flames, refracted, shadow danced on ceiling and walls. Then the long bar seemed a cavern, a Hogarthian thieves' kitchen. In the men's room, above the marbled Edwardian urinals, some unknown hand had scrawled ARTIST OUTLAWS ALTOGETHER. Until the drink wore off, it had almost seemed true.

Now credit cards were accepted, and the salads were dressed with Balsamic vinegar. Wedged tight against the bar, hemmed in by day-trippers, two German dealers stood drinking Harvey Wallbangers, poring over their art-map. They'd just flown in from Stuttgart; they were here for forty-eight hours. Middle-aged STABs, they had covered six shows this morning, were expected at eight more this afternoon. But that was not enough: "We must see faster," said Dealer A.

"One more beer, we go," said Dealer B.

"No more beer, we go now," rapped Dealer A. "After Twombly, then we drink. After Twombly, *mein Gott*, we drink till the crows come home."

Snatching the space they vacated, we called for ardent spirits. We were surrounded by the images of Mickey Walker and Young Griffo, Packey McFarland and Paul Berlenbach, the Astoria assassin; but no painters. "The thing about art. It is or it isn't," said Paul. His hands described a pair of plump and bulging half-moons, reminiscent of Edam cheeses or Jayne Mansfield's breasts. "But ArtSpeak?" he said. The moons crumpled, dissolved. "Who knows?"

Tony Shafrazi knew.

He was the acknowledged SoHo rap-master, an emblematic figure whose rise had paralleled ArtWorld's own and whose fall, if it came, would prove its darkest fears.

Iranian, born of Armenian parents, Shafrazi had grown up in England. Coming to New York in 1965, he tried to be an artist himself, without success. "I was strapped in a waiting position, isolated, in a Kafkaesque state," he said later. And so, in 1974, when Picasso's *Guernica* was on view at the Museum of Modern Art, he'd smuggled in a can of red paint and defaced it with the sprayed slogan *Kill Lies All*.

In its moment, it seemed a promising debut. Conservatives raged, blackballed him for life, but that was because they failed to understand. "I did it," Shafrazi said, "because I wanted to take on a greater responsibility."

Wrist-slapped for a misdemeanor, he published a book of photographs and notations, started buying American art for the Teheran Museum. By the early eighties, East Village artists such as Keith Haring and Kenny Scharf had started making Graffiti Art, and Shafrazi brought them to SoHo. Their opening on Mercer Street was riotous with noisemakers and balloons, a hundred squealing male models.

Since then, Shafrazi had been unstoppable. Andy Warhol had showed with him, Charles Saatchi sold through him. Now of an age he declined to divulge, he had recently leased a new gallery on Prince, the size of a small museum, which was said to cost him $40,000 a month. But this new palazzo was not open yet. For the moment, Shafrazi still worked out of Mercer, in a clean, well-lighted airplane hangar.

Seated plump behind his office desk like a bank manager, he proved a fashion plate. Forget mad bombers, red paintcans in hand—late-model Shafrazis came with distinguished gray hair and year-round tan, an Italian suit, a custom-made striped shirt. "I don't use the word *dealer*. I am a gallerist," he said, looking everywhere but at us. "It involves more creative involvement and depth of responsibility."

Responsibility was *his* magic word. His overheads and commitments, and the many personality wars in which he was embroiled, might have daunted a less unselfish man. But Shafrazi did not flinch. "It is always the task of those with vision and integrity to forge ahead," he said. "Art is my religion. With such a passion, it is my duty to address it at every level, the financial as well as the poetic and creative. That is my cross to bear, you might say."

"To make money, you mean?"

"If necessary," said Shafrazi, "even that."

Black Monday's shadow lay heavy overall. What if a major depression were brewing? It was a horrid thought. All those forty-thousand-dollar rentals and hundred-thousand-dollar pricetags up in smoke. And the miniskirted assistants with them, the power lunches at Da Silvano, the weekend raids on Paris, Barcelona, Los Angeles. Yet Shafrazi betrayed no dismay. "I take the positive view. Pioneers always do," he said. "With integrity, a proper sense of *responsibility*, even periods of upheaval may result in contextual reinforcement."

"Meaning profit?"

"I call it creative enhancement."

In the gallery outside hung a Donald Baechler, a large oil and acrylic featuring a black-coated man with a black stovepipe hat and a brightly colored beachball. It made me think of clockwork toys and decals, Indian pickle cans, *The Mystery of Edwin Drood*. But this was not my call. "What do you see?" Shafrazi demanded.

"No, please," said Paul cannily. "What do *you* see?"

"The first caveman making the first mark, saying 'I am Man, I exist, This is my testament.' "

AROUND THE BLOCK, inside a converted diner called Jerry's, Sasha Zim sat drinking iced milk with Alexei Alexandrovich and drawing a scarlet beard on a New York *Post* picture of Madonna. "Is *my* testament," Sasha said. But his public was not impressed. "Art is dead," said Alexei.

He was a bird man; some species of crested grebe. Twin white tufts and a silver plume flared from his bald pate, and his face was split by a purpled blue beak. "Dead. Kaput. Bought the farm," he said. His right arm, polio-crippled, hugged his chest like a broken wing. "Come speed the friendly bullet," he said.

He wasn't from here. His home was in the Lower East Side, in a basement studio underneath Ludlow Street, and he only ventured out in need: "When my gut feeling is my gut needs filling," he said. In those hard times, he'd peddle his canvases on the sidewalks of Cooper Square, along with stacks of used paperbacks and *National Geographics*. If that failed, he played the balalaika and sang Russian songs in the subway.

It was singing that I'd first met him. That was three years ago, long before I'd begun to Broadway. Alexei was midway through *Moscow Nights*, serenading the A train at Thirty-fourth Street. His high-pitched voice beat helplessly against the din. I gave him a dollar and requested *Stenka Razin*. "It's not enough," he said.

"It's what I have," I replied.

"Then here. Take this," said Alexei. And, reaching inside the beer mug that served as his tin cup, he handed me a crisp new five.

Afterwards, in the basement at Ludlow Street, we got drunk on buttermilk laced with potato vodka. There was no glass in the windows, only blankets. Inside, there was a German shepherd called Leon, and the walls were lined three-deep with paintings, unframed expressionist oils.

There were only two subjects: still lifes and crucifixions. "I try other stuff sometimes. Nudes, landscapes, what you like," said Alexei. But the nudes always ended up eating raw produce; every landscape sprouted a cross. "Aubergines, zucchini, nails," he said. "It's what I see. Only I can paint what I see." And what he saw was ruin. The moment his brush approached it, all matter took sick. Fruit rotted, meat turned green; the savior's flesh turned to ooze. "Putrefaction," said Alexei. The thought seemed to give him a backhanded pleasure. "The Abattoir School," he said.

As we drank, sundry Russians had wandered in, ambled out. They acted as if they lived here, but Alexei said they were just resting. One, a Mongoloid, started riffling through the paintings. When he came to a study of Christ's martyred feet, he burst out laughing. Somebody cursed him, and the Mongol flushed crimson, ran away. But Alexei himself took no offense. On the contrary, he seemed reassured. "You can't fool the jester," he'd said.

This basement doubled as a safehouse; a home for Soverican waifs. Alexei Alexandrovich had been living there for thirty-two years. In that span, he claimed, he had also sold thirty-two paintings. Meantime, he had sheltered a thousand dispossessed: "The army of the lost," he said now, sipping his iced milk in SoHo. "And their drums."

His own journey had started in Odessa, in 1935, the third child of six. His father had been a tailor and a flautist. When the Germans came, the family took the clothes they stood in and the father's flute, and they stowed away on a fishing boat. Halfway across the Black Sea, a storm came up and the boat capsized. Alexei's mother was drowned; two brothers and a sister perished of exposure. The survivors clung to the debris until they were washed ashore in Turkey, where they were picked up by coastguards and interned. They stayed in the camp for seventeen months. A second sister died of malnutrition. When the camp burned up, the family were shunted off to another, and another. Somewhere in transit the last brother disappeared. That left Alexei, and his father, and the flute.

By 1944, they were in Algeria, in a camp outside Biskra. Alexei came down with polio. No doctors were available, and the medicines he needed had all been stolen. So he lay down to die. In the absence of a rabbi, a Catholic priest baptized him and gave him the last sacraments. His father played Papageno's trills from *Die Zauberflöte*. Next morning, when the guards came around, Alexei was alive and his father lay dead.

He had stayed Catholic ever since.

After the war, he had lived in Oran and Meknes, Tangiers, Algeciras and Málaga, Barcelona, Toulon, Marseilles. When he reached Paris, he was seventeen, left-handed, and he made his living by sleeping with men.

One of the men, a New Yorker, was an archbishop by trade. When the divine returned to America, he took Alexei Alexandrovich with him, bought him a green card, and set him up as a butler at the Swiss Embassy. There Alexei met and married a chambermaid. Her name was Kirsten, she was an earth mother, all buttocks and breasts, and she loved him half to death. There was so much of her, he never knew where to begin. So he never did.

When Kirsten was not chambermaiding, she doubled as a life model at the Cooper Union. Alexei used to sneak into classes and watch from the back row, a man in a dirty raincoat. He dreamed to draw her, just once, his own wife. But he didn't dare. Instead, he went out by himself on Good Friday and got blind drunk. When he came back home, Kirsten was sprawled face down and naked across their bed, fast asleep. Alexei took out his sketch pad. He drew what he saw. Then he fell asleep himself, his mouth buried deep in his wife's round belly.

In the morning, when he looked at what he had drawn, he found a rear view of Christ crucified, nestled in a julienne of aubergines, zucchini, nails.

It was the end of a marriage. "I went mad, my wife went bowling," he said. "She found her home in the Broadway Lanes, and me they placed in Creedmore. The booby hatch. Fourteen months of white walls and enemas, no nails allowed. And the vegetables all were canned."

When they let him out, Alexei Alexandrovich moved downtown, became a janitor at St. Stanislaus Parochial, found the basement on Ludlow Street. In between, he taught himself painting in oils.

It was the late fifties, the early sixties; nobody on these streets was scared yet. Every night that it did not rain, Alexei would sit out on the doorstoop, sketching. Late one August night, a slate fell off the roof above him and tomahawked his scalp. In return, he took ninety stitches and a lifetime's compensation.

The monthly checks had kept him afloat ever since. If you looked long and close, you could just detect the faint white line on his pate where the slate had hit. Even now, he suffered violent headaches, nausea, the occasional fit of self-loathing. But mostly he was at ease. In the long months of his convalescence, shut up in his cellar, he had reached a type of resolution. "My skull was bound up in bondage, my mind running wild. So what? I start to ask the questions."

"What questions?"

"Same questions like any man else: Who am I? How am I get here? So why?"

"And the answers?"

"There was none. Only except," said Alexei, "once I was some Russian."

It wasn't much to go on: "But a start. A commencement," he said. As soon as he could climb off his sickbed, he traveled to Brighton Beach in Brooklyn, out by Coney Island. Under the D-train el was a neighborhood called Little Odessa. Everything out there—the foodstore signs and the newspapers, the restaurants, the graffiti, the crime—was in Russian. Alexei bought a balalaika in a junkshop, started strumming it on the street. He strummed it down the block and overhead, up the B-train stairwell, on the platform, all the way back to Manhattan. When he got off the subway at Times Square, seven homeless Russians were ranged out behind him.

He had carried them home like trophies. They'd filled his basement with noise, flesh, healthy stink; he had cooked them cabbage soup and *pierogi*. When one squad was replete, another replaced it. And another: "One good thing about Russians. They never run out," said Alexei.

They were his sanity. His own Russian was minimal, a few basic phrases. Still, the sound of his lost language kept him rooted, secured him from flying away.

It was a needed restraint. Many nights in the dark, he'd feel himself sprout wings and rise up, fluttering. But, of course, he could not fly with a maimed arm; all he could do was hurt himself. That was why he put no glass in his windows, in case he dashed himself against the panes. But it rarely came to that. Before he even got aloft, the dog would growl, or some drunken voice start singing of Lake Baikal, and Alexei would subside.

Come morning, there was always more soup to be made, a fresh batch of *pierogi*: "So day by day, I remain discrete," he said. "In tact."

As for his paintings, he couldn't make up his mind. He had never taken lessons, he knew that his technique was crude, and many times he felt absurd. Other times he was swept away. He'd stumble on some canvas he had forgotten, or glimpse another in a strange light, and their force would knock him sideways. It was as if some other hand had painted for him, used him for public transport. Then the crudity didn't matter, and being absurd was an honor: "Only is the living thing. New life created, that was not alive before."

On this day in SoHo, his morale was at a peak. The week before, for the first time in years, a professional dealer had shown real interest, had even seemed willing to buy.

The story went back a month. One of Alexei's Russians, a retired watch repairer, had died and left him some antique gilt frames. Alexei had used them to set off his latest paintings. And somehow they'd changed his luck. The next time that he struck his pitch in Cooper Square, a smooth man in fawn leather pants and Gucci loafers came strolling by, took one look, and was entranced: "Like he seen some vision. Or other," said Alexei.

The smooth man's name was Harold, he ran a gallery on Cape Cod, and he offered to buy the lot, five paintings and five frames, for five hundred dollars. He would have closed the deal on the spot, only he did not have the right money on him. Still, he swore he'd return that day next week, cash in hand.

That day was today. Inside Jerry's, the framed paintings sat propped between Alexei's feet, neatly done up in Christmas wrapping. Within the hour, he was to meet his man Harold here and be made over, reborn as a gallery artist.

Sasha was not sanguine. "Three to five isn't kosher. Even stevens is doing bunk," he said.

"Of course," said Alexei. "Art is dead." But he would not permit me to wait and see for myself. When the time appointed drew close, he drove me out in the street. Arguments and pleas got me nowhere. "Ill-omen bird, begone," said Alexei. So I went. It was time for lunch.

LUNCH, IN SOHO, was the critical meal. Da Silvano, the trattoria of choice, was crammed with dealers. Leo Castelli ate here. So did Shafrazi, and Larry Gagosian. And here Paul Kasmin brought me to break bread with Donald Baechler.

"What's he like?" I asked.

"Oh, you know," said Paul, and handed over a critique by the art journalist Robert Pincus-Witten, snappily titled "Increments of Inaccessibility." "He [Baechler] is obsessive," it read. "Working in isolation and filled with angst he revealed that by moments he fears he may hurl himself through the plate glass wall of his working loft. In a depression marked by an inability to paint he passed long hours abed watching daytime TV; weeks of this diet ensued. In a fever-dream he imagines that he is hurling the television set through the glass and awakens in terror. The next morning he steels himself with a view to act out the impulse suggested by the dream and, in so doing, be 'cured' of the fantasy as well as liberated from the depression. But he reconsiders, thinking of all the waste, and instead gives the television set away—only to regret, even more, the unrealized beauty of the act. It's a god-myth, of course, life, death, resurrection, allied to Gide's *Acte Gratuit*. And now he's got no TV."

"No TV at all?" I asked.

"Only black," said Paul, "and white."

The man who came to lunch had a bland and circular face, milky white, and a voice both sweet and low. Any trace of TV-hurling was kept buried beneath a natty black suit, a spotless white shirt, furled at the cuffs. "I'm sorry I'm late," said Baechler. "There was a line at the bank."

He had large and liquid eyes, a forelock that kept flopping down across his forehead. This gave him the pampered, slightly babyfat look of a fifties' rock and roll star, a bobby-soxer's dreamboat. And a star he was. Courteous and smiling when it pleased him, pouty when bored, he had the star's self-absorption, aloofness from human struggle and mess.

In his presence, Paul turned hedgehog, pulled his head so deep inside his jacket collar that his face all but vanished. Only the small pink eyes were revealed. "Your painting," he said.

"Well?"

"Oh, nothing," said Paul. "Not a thing."

Da Silvano was full of travelogs. Everyone present, it seemed, had just flown back from Barcelona or Venice, from Rio de Janeiro, New Delhi, Dusseldorf. Baechler himself was lately returned from Holland and had printed up his sketchbook journal: "How it all started was, I thought I was on my way to India, but they talked me into going to Amsterdam first," the first page kicked off. "Two days in the Krasnapolsky with Paul Blanca, ordering room service and drinking the entire contents of the mini-bar, first the beer and the scotch and the vodka, then the sticky shit like Cointreau and Cheery Herring nobody normally touches. I thought about asking him for a blow job, but I saw him beating up his girlfriend once on Bond Street, so I figured he probably didn't like boys too much."

Reading this, I thought of Shafrazi saying, "I am Man, I exist, This is my testament." But Paul's mind was elsewhere.

Popping up out of his collar, he flicked one glance at Castelli, another at Gagosian. Then he plunged. "Your painting," he said again.

"What about it?"

"Describe it."

Baechler did not flinch. Breaking off in mid-sip, he put down his wineglass, laid his large white hands palms down on the tablecloth. His forelock fell across his eyes, but he did not brush it back. He sat quite still, he pondered. "It is," he said, "a picture."

There was no time for subclauses; the clients were due at five. So Baechler returned to his painting, and Paul sweated over grappa.

Lunch done, we walked back through the heart of ArtWorld. West Broadway was now given over utterly to galleries and their outcroppings—health-food stores, slimming spas, Italian fashion marts. But every so often, glancing up a side street, one could still catch a glimpse of forklifts and loading bays, broken cobblestones, great looming redbrick warehouses.

"Great stuff," said Paul. Away from Da Silvano and the yellowed eyes of the trade, he was full of fervor, a born fan. Every beautiful image stirred him. Confronted by a first-rate Rauschenberg, or even a second-rate Man Ray, his whole body swung back on its axis, a Shetland pony wheeling on its hind hooves. His pink flesh turned pinker; his eyes screwed up so tight they almost vanished. "Yes, oh yes," he cried. He could look at paintings all his days and not be bored for one beat. "If only it wasn't. I mean, if you didn't have to," he said. His front hooves came back to earth. "I mean, words," said Paul. "Bloody words."

We moved up Spring, hemmed in by a thousand canvases. It was a street that held a sacred place in New York mythology. A few blocks to the east, one morning in the 1820s, workmen arriving for the day's labor had come upon a large group of men and women equipped as if for a long voyage, with wagons and building tools, food supplies, sled dogs. When asked what the fuss was about, the group said that they'd come to saw off Manhattan Island. It was getting too heavy at the Battery end. Too many buildings had made it dangerous. The only solution was to slice it through at Kingsbridge, then swing the whole island around, using sea sweeps, till north was made south.

The workmen thought this over. Then one spotted a flaw. "What about Long Island?" he asked. "Won't it get in the way?"

"Hard to say," a voyager replied. Some experts claimed that the trick could be turned without moving Long Island at all; that the bay and harbor were large enough for the island of New York to swivel round in. Others believed that Long Island must first be detached and floated to sea, held at anchor until Manhattan's somersault was completed, and only then returned to its former site.

I told Paul this tale while we peered through a gallery window, transfixed by a blinking TV screen, which endlessly repeated YES IS NO, NO IS YES. Behind us, a large man in an Afghan blanket kept jostling and thrusting, straining for a better view. But when we moved on, the man came trailing behind us. "So how did it come out?" he demanded. "Did they saw it off or not?"

"Up to a point," said Paul.

At Jerry's, I left him again, went back to Sasha and Alexei. They sat in the same booth, fixed in the same postures, as though they'd never moved. But the Christmas wrapping had vanished from between Alexei's feet, and his iced milk had changed to wine. "I am a happy man," he said.

He did not seem it. His white tufts of the morning now looked murky gray; his blue beak sagged on his breast. Clenched tight in his twisted hand, however, was five hundred dollars in crisp new bills.

His man Harold had shown up spot on time, glorious in jodhpurs and a yellow silk cravat. He stood drinks, slapped backs, and paid up with no murmur. Then he took his leave.

It had all happened in such a rush; Alexei did not want it to end. To draw out the moment, he offered help in carrying out the paintings. But Harold had said no need, he was parked right down the block. "Your work is done. God bless you," Harold said. "Paint well." And he was gone.

Without him, the restaurant had seemed dimmed, somehow flat. Instead of exultation, Alexei had felt oddly deprived. So long he had ached for this. Now Harold had left him dangling, his thirst only halfway slaked. Though he did his best to jubilate, his stomach felt bound in coils. He must have air or be sick. So he'd run out in the street, set sail for an art-supply store.

The spring air had felt good. At the corner of Prince and Broadway, he stopped in a shaft of sunlight, let it wash out the throbbing and ache. When Sasha caught him up, he stood sniffing with face upraised, beatific, breathing deep. "What is?" Sasha asked.

"Fresh paint," said Alexei.

Together they walked towards the smell. But they did not reach it. Ten yards down the block, they passed a large oilcan filled with trash. Inside were Alexei's five paintings, cleanly ripped from their antique frames.

UPSTAIRS AT THE Kasmin, promptly at five, the Pelletiers arrived to view the Donald Baechler.

Both were tanned to a crisp. Laurent was a short, plump, and fussy sort, big with self-importance, who looked like the mayor of Clochemerle. Apparently, he had made many millions in Club Med–style resorts, then turned in his first wife for Gaby, who was an ex-model, and looked it. Blonde and statuesque, almost dressed in a white crochet miniskirt, she was newly flown in from Aspen, where she'd broasted herself the color of a Frank Perdue oven-stuffer. As she stood getting kissed, she kept flexing her nude thighs, flashing her bright teeth. Girlishly giggling, she twirled and pirouetted, showing off her pantyline.

The Pelletiers, it was understood, were not to be shown the painting itself. For the moment, they must be content to glimpse a Polaroid. Afterwards, they'd have twenty-four hours to make up their minds. And they were lucky, as Marina had reminded Paul in a pregame note, to be granted even that: "Donald Baechler is a MAJOR artist," the note read, "and this is a MAJOR work."

The major work in question, titled *Forest*, showed a blank face in profile, a green Christmas tree. "Not one of his best," Paul confessed, though not to Laurent and Gaby, "but big, you know. It really is quite big."

The price was only fifty thousand dollars. But something was not quite right; the Pelletiers failed to exult. "I don't find it quite howyousay," Gaby said. "It is the tree, I think. Too green."

"Trees *are* green," Laurent pointed out.

"You would say that," said Gaby.

Bending over the Polaroid, she kept her face rapt, most solemn, in artistic contemplation. Below the countertop, however, her buttocks and bare thighs did not cease to flex, clench, flex, clench, unwearying in their fight against cellulite. "I like it. I do," she sighed. "But then."

"But then?"

"But then."

Forgotten, Paul slumped lower and lower in his chair, his pink head almost buried between his shoulder blades. He stared out through his window at the blank walls across the airshaft. He gazed at the David Hockney drawing of himself, aged six, that hung beside his desk. He lit a cigarette, stubbed it out. And at that moment, out of some forgotten deposit box of memory, he himself could not later say what, a lost phrase came back to him, bore him away. "Ironic obliquity," he said.

Gaby's buttocks froze in mid-flex, wobbled like *blancmanges* before a storm. "Ironic?" she queried.

"Obliquity."

The words hung in the air, a lightbulb. Green trees, however one cut them, were only trees. But obliquely ironic green trees? "Of course," Gaby said.

For form's sake, not to undercut the rituals of the dance, she asked to borrow the Polaroid overnight, hold it up against her living-room wall. But her twirls and pirouettes were ecstatic, and her pantyline bulged tauter, more muscular than ever. "Obliquity," she said.

"Ironic," said Laurent.

Hand in hand together, they walked away down the long blank corridor. At the elevator, they kissed, they hugged. Gaby held the Polaroid to the light. Her face, upturned, glowed with ardor and Max Factor.

"But of course," she said.

said Sasha Zim.

It was his *abraxas*, the name he invoked against chaos. When he felt himself free-falling, it held him down, sat on his head till he sobered. "Dirty old street. But dirty good like sweat, my own armpit smell," he said. "Sweet like homemade sin."

The past was much on his mind this spring. He had just turned twenty-five, and still his drums had no home of their own. For the first time, he felt the lack.

At the Pearl River, he had bought himself a coffeepot, a furry blue bathmat, a ceramic lamp in the shape of a clothed girl whose kimono melted when the light went on, assorted Christmas decorations—tinsel, fairylights, iridescent plastic balls—and a stuffed toy dragon with red eyes and a footlong purple-red tongue. "Is time to own some stuff. Be possessed," he said.

He took his new life with him everywhere, parked beside him on the front seat of his Checker. Sunny days, he'd roll down the window and wedge the dragon's head in the gap, its tongue hanging down and flopping, half-hard, like an enormous spent cock.

Instead of just a vehicle, the taxi was turned into a mobile romper room. Possessions apart, every square inch of surface was plastered with pictures of athletes, musicians, Playmates and Penthouse Pets, cowboys. Cowboys most of all, for Sasha's long-term ambition, beyond Broadway, beyond even his drums, was to end as a Marlboro Man.

Of late the vision was dimmed. His welcome had worn out with EmCee Marie, and he now split his nights between a Mormon waitress from Utah, a lady bodybuilder from Bangor, Maine, and the floor at the Hotel Moose. More often than not, he slept in the Brooklyn garage where his taxi berthed.

He was not concerned for himself, he said. But the drums, that was something else. He'd had them five years, almost six; in that time they must have known a hundred beds. It was not right, not respectful. If he didn't straighten up, fly right, they would end up stolen or ruined, worn out. Or maybe they'd just up and leave: "Find some man who's playing them right, *dosvyedanya* is all she wrote."

He thought about his father.

It was a bad sign. Any time he thought about Lev Mikhailovich, he risked contracting failure, and he had not come here to fail: "Who's going Helen Handbasket?" he demanded. "Not Zim, that's who."

But he thought about his father.

On Houston, right round the corner from Splash, was a jazz club called the Knitting Factory, where Sasha had sometimes sat in. It was a throwback, a rathskeller out of the Beat years, full of beards and sandals and baggy sweaters. Lev would have killed to spend one night there.

He'd been a fifties *stilyag*, a hepcat, in love with bebop. In those years, jazz in Russia meant conspiracy—basements, passwords; rags shoved into windowcracks and doorjambs, so that no sound might escape; x-ray plates. For men like Lev, it wasn't just music, it was a whole system of belief, an outlaw creed for which they would risk family, jobs, their freedom, their very lives.

The x-ray plates were paramount. Willis Conover's Voice

of America radio show, beamed nightly from Tangiers, was taped religiously by shortwave hams, then transferred onto plates by hospital-lab technicians, one of whom was Lev Mikhailovich. Sasha's earliest remembrance was of crouching under his parents' bed, staring down into a whirlpool blur of ribs and intestines and bronchial tubes, while *A Night in Tunisia* played.

The sound itself was mostly a distant burbling, more static and fuzz than music. What stayed with Sasha were the x-rayed innards, and his father's bare feet hanging down off the edge of the bed. They were scabbed and black-toed; they smelled of dirty secrets. When Charlie Parker soloed, high-flying Bird, the black toes would twitch and jerk uncontrollably, spasming: "Like dangling men," Sasha said.

His father was large, loud, disheveled, catastrophic; "man of faith and great thirst." His friends called him *Rhyzhi Muzhik*, Big Red, but he was not truly red, not a slab of raw meat like Ellen Fogarty's Dad, more flaming orange. When he got to drinking, which was most every night, the freckles that covered his whole face would swell up like tiny raisins, fat enough to burst, and heat would come off him in waves, he'd burn up, a human brazier.

He was a one-man demolition derby, could not cross a room without wrecking it, couldn't touch any life without leaving it for dead. He had no malice, and needed none. Simple bull-headed blundering turned the trick every time. For months each year, he'd save up for Sasha's birthday. And each year the presents would emerge from their wrappings in pieces, crushed, mangled beyond all repair. "Each man must have his own talent. My father, his talent was falling down," Sasha said. So Lev got kicked out of the Party, kicked out of the hospital lab, kicked out of every apartment his wife ever found. Turning taxi driver, he drove three cabs into three walls in three months. He even failed in sanitation: "Only man ever in history of sewers, they give him cash in hand to leave, go flush himself away." That left the black market.

Across a tarpit from Novokuz, the Zims—mother, father, Sasha, and his younger brother, Pavel—found a room on the fifth floor, tucked right beneath the eaves, with a sweatshop below and only pigeons above. The closets were crammed with dead chickens and canned cherries, nylons, radios, and Lucky Strike cigarettes, always Lucky Strikes. When Sasha, then eight, asked what all this stuff was in aid of, Lev would stroke one orange nostril with a broken-knuckled forefinger and misquote the motto of the Young Pioneers, their pledge of allegiance to the Soviet. *"Gotovy na Trud i na Zastchitzu Zhop?* Ready for Labor and the Defense of Your Ass?" he would recite, burning up, grotesquely leering. *"Vsegda gotovy*, Always ready," he'd reply.

"Was typical Russian humor. No laughing matter," Sasha said. For certain, his mother was not entertained. Varya Petrovna, a curdled woman, pinched and hungering, she worked in the telegraph office, she was a Party member in good standing, and she hated Lev Mikhailovich with a hatred almost religious.

The saxophone was the last straw.

Lev bought it off a sailor, carried it home in a coalsack. It was a sulphurous summer night, and it must have been a Saturday, because there were lights on late across the street and you could hear music behind the blinds, Vladimir Vysotsky, Volodenka, with his hoarse rasp like a rusty hinge and word-drunk ballads—"Wild Horses," "A Village Wedding." Songs raw as a running sore, they made Lev cry in his cups.

All music did. "This big lug, drunk oaf crazyman," he wept for Volodenka and he wept for Bud Powell, for Billie Holiday and the Red Army Choir. But he wept hardest for dead tenormen—Lester Young and Chu Berry, Honeybear Cedric, Wardell Gray. And it was a tenor that he brought home, an old tarnished Selmer, all bound up with tape and rubber bands.

Sasha was dozing by the window. It was cooler there, the reek of boiled cabbage less vile. Propped upright like a tailor's dummy, he went drifting on the music behind the drawn blinds, the smell of heat and melted tar, the party girls squealing, the hellfire night sky. Then the door crashed open behind his back, and there was his father, brandishing a coalsack.

Picked out in silhouette by the hallway light, he was solid blackness with a rim of gingery orange. He stood lowering, swaying. He took the Selmer out of the coalsack. Only the bell was visible, a golden cobra's head upreared. And Lev blew. Just once, an obscene *blaaarrp*. No tone, no song, only noise. It burst in the room like a bottle of homemade cherry brandy exploding. Sasha's mother sat up stark in bed, a gray sheet clutched over her breasts. But she did not scream, she didn't speak, she just walked to the door and slapped Lev's face, a single blow, with all the force she possessed. Then she turned him around, kicked him back down the stairs. The Selmer and the coalsack followed. So did his clothes, his chamber pot, three dead chickens, and a suitcase full of Lucky Strikes: "No Lev, no more," Sasha said.

Now downstairs at the Knitting Factory, the tables were asymmetrical, all angles and sharp points, and the tenorman was an earnest white boy in horn-rimmed glasses. His music was ferociously avant-garde, all honks and howls and strangled squeals. But its props—the tiny stage at the end of the darkened cellar, the rapt solemnity of the audience, the anorexic girls in their mauve lipstick and black tights, the wisp-bearded hipsters in shades and BIRD LIVES T-shirts—were sempiternal. "Black music, white meat," said Sasha. " *'Relaxin' at Camarillo.'* "

Camarillo was the California asylum to which Charlie Parker had once been committed; it was also the Novokuznetskayan bunker, underneath a rubber-boot factory, to which Lev Mikhailovich had retired with his Selmer, his chamber pot, his three dead chickens.

Monday to Friday, it served as a storeroom and Lev as its

janitor. On weekends, the *stilyagi* moved in. Middle-aged now, red-eyed men with bad breath and broken teeth, they made Sasha think of *The Wild Bunch*, displaced desperadoes worn out by battles yet unable to abide peace. By this time jazz could be heard quite openly, the latest American records picked up at any sly corner. But the *stilyagi* clung to the dark. Underground at Camarillo, they still smoked their joints jail-style, cupped in the palms of their hands; spoke out of the sides of their mouth: "Was like *war is dead, long live war.*"

To Sasha, this was his father in aspic: an ancient Vox box-stereo, circa 1953, on an orange crate between two candles; some half-dozen decayed hepcats crouched down before it, like voodoo cultists before some forbidden godhead; choking black smoke; distant music, almost lost in crackles and pops; and Lev Mikhailovich, crying.

Sasha was ten, eleven. Sometimes on Sundays, Lev used to take him on day-trips, out into the country or to Serebryany Bor, the Silver Wood, and the Selmer came along for the ride. After their picnic lunch, if Lev had had enough to drink, he'd try to find some secluded spot, a pool or riverbank, and then he would mime playing, just to see how he looked reflected in running water, a real-live jazzman, a Novokuz Coleman Hawkins.

So one afternoon, it must have been October, the first snows were just beginning, and they got lost deep in the woods. Through a copse of silver birches, they came on a rotting wooden jetty reaching out into a small stagnant lake. So Lev walked the creaking planks to the far end, the Selmer dangling from his throat. Outdoors, he always wore the same long coat, not black precisely, more a midnight purple, the same color as the bloom on black grapes.

"Picture," Sasha said. "Trees are silver, water is pea-soup green, sky is cement gray. Brownwood boards are brown like shit, snowflakes are white as snow. And Lev Mikhailovich is big orange, pissdrunk with great gold horn. And purple coat is flapping open, sucking on legs like black-grape shroud." He closed his eyes, held still. "Forgeddaboudit," he said.

At the last plank, Lev lurched to a halt, stuck the mouthpiece between his lips. Inflating his cheeks like water wings, he bugged out his eyes, and silently he blew. He rocked way back, for balance, and then he rocked forward, overhanging the lake. To see. And the Selmer slipped through his fingers. Very gently, no fuss, it slipped into the lake.

So mucous the water was, there was hardly a splash; the cobra's head simply vanished, sucked under without trace. "One poof, all was gone," Sasha said. For maybe ten seconds, Lev stared at the ripples, stupefied. Then he turned around, like a man sleepwalking, and walked in a strict, straight line back down the jetty to land. He did not even weep.

Two weeks later, the KGB picked him up. To keep out of jail, he volunteered for an Arctic Circle work camp, out beyond the Finland Station. He was gone three years.

Varya Petrovna had already divorced him, remarried. Her new husband was a retired dentist, a smiling man in a shiny blue suit and schoolgirl white socks, who wore sterilized rubber gloves at the dinner table. He lived far away in the suburbs, out beyond Lyublinsky, where the apartment blocks looked just like projects, mile on mile of prefab-gray. In the dead center of his living room stood a voodoo godhead of his own, a vintage toothpuller's chair complete with solid-steel drills, red-leather trim, a floral gargling bowl.

Sasha was fourteen. He ran back to the city, to Novokuz; turned Fruit Eating Bear; and he took up lodging in the cafeteria at the Paveletsky railway station, which had been Lev Mikhailovich's office, was the office of every penny-ante hood in Moscow.

It was a twenty-four-hour Exchange and Mart, an A–Z of petty crime. It had no tone, no class whatsoever. A big-time racketeer like Yan Rokotov, Russia's *capo di capos*, would not sully his fur coat here. But for workaday hustlers and black marketeers, *fartsovschiki*, it was Club Paradise. Pimps and dope dealers worked the bar, whores and pickpockets the tables. Twice a day, the KGB men came by to collect their cut, but that did not slow the action.

The flow of suckers seemed inexhaustible. Young soldiers in transit, mostly, blind on sweet champagne. Swilling, they gorged on whitefish and cold potatoes, paint-stripper vinegar, until they passed out. Then the rogue taxi drivers, *pidzhachniki*, would sweep them off the floor, bring them round with vodka, and drive them away for one last fleecing.

Sasha staked out a spot beside a hissing radiator, snug in the murkiest, greasiest corner. There he sipped on sticky orange drinks and smoked Herzegovina Flors, which tasted of tarred rope dipped in sheep's piss. Sometimes he ran *zhelazka* games, based on the numbers printed on rubles, and sometimes he sold a little reefer. With the profits, he went to Hollywood movies.

These, in the late 1970s, were not yet shown openly, but they were not hard to find. To keep up a semblance of official disapproval and avoid paying royalties, the Party simply changed the titles. Thus, *The Roaring Twenties* became *The Fate of a Soldier in America*, and *Mr. Deeds Goes to Town* was *The Dollar Rules*. But Sasha's own favorite was *Sweet Smell of Success*, which he sat through fourteen times. Its Russian title was *Dead Souls of Broadway*.

"Every man is having one savior," Sasha said. And Tony Curtis was his. As Falco, the low-life Times Square press agent, he had seemed glamour incarnate: "Cool like Yule."

The mystique owed all to place and time. Just recently, Sasha had seen the film again, for the first time since Novokuz, and had been shocked to find it changed, completely garbled. Once you knew English, Falco stood revealed as a rat fink, "a cookie full of arsenic"—treacherous, venal, all things vile. But back in Moscow, there had been none of that. No words, no plot, no moral—just the Times Square night, and a thin man running.

This was Sasha's first vision of Broadway: a self-contained cosmology, a system of brightly lit oases set in a sea of unremitting black, and this lone thin man, Falco, "the boy with the ice-cream face," racing and sweating through its neon galaxies, whirling out of jazz clubs into white-plush restaurants, out of restaurants into horseshoe bars and Automats, newspaper offices and TV studios, plate-glass penthouses, elevators like golden cages, hands flailing, mouth flapping, a starving man, consumed.

Why the thin man ran, Sasha did not know, could not guess. But he recognized the hunger. It was his own.

And then there was the suit. In one of the earliest scenes, Falco dresses himself in his bedroom mirror, a stately and rhythmic ritual, every move just so. And the threads he put on were the pure stuff of dreams. Single-breasted but double-vented, what Fruit Eating Bears and Pretty Things called a bugger-baffler, the jacket was lean as mean, tight as night, with a sheen so subtle that it did not seem to glint, merely to suffuse. Set off by high-waisted matador pants, a Skinny Jim tie, and a dazzle of white shirt, it made Sasha hard just to gaze on it.

On Arbat, there was a hunchbacked tailor called Yul, the only Moscow tailor who could duplicate American style. Three months' hustling bought Sasha a sharkskin two-piece, avocado green with a faint reddish underthread, like a subliminal glow: "Crease so sharp you could be stropping razor. Chest and shoulders so narrow, was like coffin, you could not breathe. What I mean, was perfect perfection."

Embalmed like so, he sat very still and very straight for eighteen months, stuffed in his corner at the Paveletsky cafeteria. Sometimes he messed with schoolbooks, more often he just sat and watched. The airlessness and steam-heat kept him drugged, half-asleep. Then somebody slapped his face. When he jerked awake, it was Lev Mikhailovich.

Lev Mikhailovich, but not Big Red. That man was long gone, lost someplace out beyond the Finland Station. The person who now stood shaking, free-floating inside a suit of denim coveralls, was reduced to half-size and no longer orange, more faded ocher. He had cancer in his guts, cancer up his ass, so much cancer in his throat that he couldn't speak, could only communicate by penciled notes.

He used a kindergarten magic slate, each sentence painstakingly printed in block capitals, then snuffed out. But the questions did not compute, asked either too little or much too much: ARE YOU FINE? WHAT IS IT NOW? WHO CAN SAY?

Sasha could only blink and mumble nothings. His trouser crease was not falling quite right. It bothered him, stopped him from relaxing. Lev ordered champagne, and they drank together, sweet, sticky stuff like a glucose drink. Some drunken soldier kept yelling obscenities, claiming he'd been robbed. HOW DO YOU KNOW? Lev scribbled. Then he drew a cartoon self-portrait on the paper tablecloth. When you looked at it twice, it transmuted into an anus, a purse-lipped, prissy-smiling sphincter. "*Gotovy na Zastchitzu Zhop?* Ready for Defense of Ass?" it simpered.

Sasha's crease was still not right. He bent to correct it, and Lev went out to get some cigarettes. In his absence, Sasha bought a joint from a Pretty Thing, something that two could share. But his father did not come back. So he smoked by himself.

At the Knitting Factory, the tenorman had ceased and desisted. A stray pianist wandered up onto the stage, began to frame soft chords.

Sasha sat in.

The drum kit, in keeping with current fashion, was a leviathan. "Why I'm not playing tenor sax, drums are better swimmers," Sasha had said, recalling the drowned Selmer. So now he set sail on the back of a monstrous octopoid, all cymbals and gongs and cowbells, vibraphonic tubes, Tibetan chimes. And he played the twelve-bar blues.

The music was not much. But the stance—eyes rolled back

and sightless, head tossing in quasi-narcotic trance, cigarette at droop on slack lower lip—was a dead ringer for the young Sal Mineo, vintage *The Gene Krupa Story*.

Catching sight of his crazed reflection, distorted in a cymbal, Sasha laughed just like a boy. And when the number ended, and he was back safe in the dark, he went on laughing still. "Crease you could be stropping razor. Was perfect perfection," he said. The tenorman started bleating again, and Sasha called for 7UP. "*Vsegda gotovy*," he said. "Always ready."

Street News was called "How to Make Pigeon Stew," by Cleveland Blakemore. It read: "It was too late to go to the soup kitchen on 80th Street. The evening meal was shut out by 4:30 and it was 5:00 now. If you didn't get a food ticket you were beat when they started handing out the chow. I was starving to death. My stomach felt dull and lumpy, and my head was light from low blood sugar.

"It had been raining all week long, and it was wiping out my small supply of cash. I liked to tell people that I was "the only homeless man in New York who was never broke"—but now I was. I had sold all the umbrellas I kept for my rainy day back-up, and I wasn't collecting aluminum cans while it was pouring.

"I tried to sell paperbacks in front of Tower Records earlier that morning, but a flash flood had ruined all the books before I could even throw a sheet of plastic over them. I lost about three hundred like-new books I found in a dumpster near Central Park. I tried to lay out a couple of copies of *Architectural Digest*, but they got ruined by more surprise precipitation and I got really depressed. I never cry, but I felt like I could when I pushed my cart back under the bridge on 59th Street and collapsed on my foldaway bed.

"I tried to turn on the TV, but something was wrong with our makeshift electricity again. It looked like the rain had seeped onto the cables overhead and shorted out my juice. I read for a while and felt bad. I couldn't seem to make myself get up and do anything.

"Then all of a sudden I was awake and rested and hungry as hell—and it was starting to get dark outside.

"A few minutes later my roommate Steve straggled into the makeshift hut I had built. I knew he had a drug problem, and we weren't talking much anymore; just a hello whenever we happened to pass. I knew he never stole from me, so I liked having him in the hut whenever I was gone, to keep an eye on the books and stuff. He was a good guy deep down, but he was screwed up on drugs.

"The thrum of the cars overhead as they sped across the bridge was like weird occult music. It lulled me to sleep at night, like hearing the roar of your mother's blood around you in the womb. And through the rumbling, I could hear the soft cooing of the pigeons roosting in the dark girders trying to stay out of the rain.

"Steve brought everything that we had left in the way of groceries and set them down on our "dining table." A pack of 50-cent chocolate chip cookies. Four-for-a-dollar Ramen Instant Noodles. A can of sweet corn. A bag of day-old bagels from the Bagel Factory on 79th Street. A half bottle of Wesson cooking oil and a box of Corn Flakes.

"He lit a fire in our oil-barrel stove, put our 'wok' on top of it, and went to get some water from the open fire hydrant across the street to boil up the noodles with.

"I sat down on a cinderblock and watched as he tried to put together an Instant Noodle Corn Soup.

"I knew what my father would say if he were here.

" 'Ordinary men are weak. Don't be weak. Do whatever proves necessary. Be strong. Don't be wretched or overcivilized.

Harden yourself inside and just do it. At one time, it was the stoic who survived over all others.'

" 'How about a little bird meat in that?' I said as I rose to my feet and strolled over to a pile of rubbish and bricks.

"Steve watched me as I selected a dirty orange chip from a brick and hefted it in my hand. He grinned. 'You're bullshitting me,' he said, continuing to stir the noodles.

"The sun was almost gone. I could still hear the soft coos overhead. They seemed to be coming from one particularly dark corner of the bridge in a complex intersection of girders.

"I drew back and winged the chip as hard as I could. It sailed into the darkness, vanished, then clattered to the ground seconds later. 'You don't want to do that,' Steve said, sounding uneasy.

"I pretended I didn't hear him. My second throw stirred the birds up overhead. Several of them fluttered off in fright, like gray spirits in the fading light. My third throw was wild, and I never heard it come down.

"The fourth rock was a disc which had been honed to a jagged edge on all four corners. I found it under an old sweater. It felt heavy and lethal.

"It was closer to a handaxe, probably looking a lot like the ones they found in Olduvai Gorge in Africa, where chipped flint weapons bear testament to the favorite tools of our ancestry.

"I tried to imagine what it would be like to be a hominid on the African savanna, after a day of hunting with no food and desperate for even one kill. What kind of stone would that carnivorous, primitive mind select from the rubbish pile? Probably a stone just like the one I had in my hand.

"I knew even before it hit, it was a perfect throw.

"The pigeon was still alive, shaking and twitching its broken wing when it hit the ground. I used to hunt doves with my father when I was eight, so I knew exactly how this worked. I gave the head a quick twist. The neck cracked, and the head came off like a cork out of a bottle. The wings still moved in a reflex action. My hands felt warm and wet.

"I squeezed the lower parts of the bird, and the entire body slipped out from beneath the feathers like a silk purse. A small lump of meat the size of a large apple. I opened the breast with my thumbs and cleaned out the entrails.

" 'Boil it good,' I said to Steve as I dropped it into the hot pan and poured in the rest of the contents of the Wesson bottle. 'No telling what sort of disease these birds might have. Leave it in there at least an hour.'

"I walked away and washed my hands under the open hydrant. Steve was still gaping when I got back. I sat down beside him and watched the fire. 'Get over it, homeboy. Everything on earth lives by consuming something else. It's no big deal.' Steve didn't say anything.

"And then we ate the pigeon, the noodles, the corn. And finally the cookies.

"I went to bed on a full stomach."

Cleveland Blakemore in person was a golden boy. He came from Richmond, Virginia; was full of Confederate dash. Standing outside Tower Records in NoHo, unmarked and gleaming, he looked the perfection of the doomed Southern hero, a reborn Jeb Stuart or John Pelham. But he was not homeless now, he was well rested and plump. Cookbooks and shiny picturebooks were flying off his cart at a rate of two hundred, three hundred dollars a day. Still he wanted more. "It's the time we live in," he said. "If you don't get more, you don't get any."

He had lived in the shantytown beneath the Fifty-ninth Street Bridge for a full year. In that time, he had steeped himself in Nietzsche, Darwin, and Robert Ardrey's *The Territorial Imperative*, and they had left him with a theory. "The lion roars. In any jungle he is king," Cleveland Blakemore said. His voice was brisk and dismissive, a bark. "The lion rules," he said.

The homeless could not accept this; that was why they were homeless. They watched TV and saw consumer heaven, *The*

Wonderworld of Plutography, and knew they couldn't measure up. So they fell by the wayside. They took refuge in booze or dope, and they ended up underneath the bridge. "Not because there isn't enough to eat," he said. "Because they're not equipped to grab their share. They're not fitted."

When first he landed in New York, he'd not been fitted himself. Promises were made to him and broken, golden lures extended, then snatched away. For a time, he had lost hope. "Just gave up," he said. "I was sickened. It was like, if I couldn't play on *Dynasty* or *Falcon Crest*, I would not play at all." But the night of the pigeon had saved him. In the whirl of the sharpened stone, the fall of the broken bird, he had discovered his proper self, the true order of Man: *"Everything on earth lives by consuming something else. Get over it, homeboy."*

It was that simple. "Ordinary men are weak," his father had said. But he, Cleveland Blakemore, was not an ordinary man. Selling books off a handcart was only a beginning. When he had built up a stake, he would move on, escalate. Where to, he did not yet know. Or maybe he did, but was not saying. Either way, his homeless days were done.

He spoke with self-pride but no malice. Caught by the morning sunlight, he glowed with recklessness and ardor, the image of Aryan glamour. He cast a disowning hand at Broadway, not at the shoppers who thronged the sidewalks but at the loafers, the lost, the whole doomed city beyond. "These people," he said, smiling with white teeth. "They don't think that they can make it." His eyes glittered but did not connect. "And you know what?" he said. "They can't make it."

Stranded midstream across the boulevard, as if waiting his cue, a man in a dirty pink blanket stood teetering on one leg and feebly flapping his arms, like an oil-slicked flamingo. "Fuck that shit. Fuck that shit," he kept saying. Then he lay down flat, face down, defying the traffic to run him over. "You can't do that," a lawman said.

"I'm doing it," said the man.

"Well, you can't," said the cop.

"Fuck that shit," said the man.

On either bank, the shoppers passed by with locked eyes, staring straight ahead. Tower Records on a Saturday was the hottest spot on all Broadway, a daylong cabaret. *These people* were not invited.

Still they came. A short stretch upstream, more men in blankets sat hunkered against the brick walls of Hebrew Union College. Cleveland Blakemore called them Banquo's Ghosts.

The district had traveled full circle. In 1800, Astor Place was Manhattan's last outpost, a narrow country lane, north of which lay farmland. Then Broadway arrived, and it became the Bohemian Woods, lined with dance halls and bordellos, the last word in gambling hells: "The sole purpose of the area is riot," the New York *Herald* wrote.

The Astor Place Riot of 1849 was definitive. It was whipped up by the Know Nothings, a political party/secret society sworn to purge America of immigrants, especially the English and the Irish. The announcement that William Macready, the British tragedian, was going to play *Macbeth* at the Astor Place Opera House signaled war, and fifteen thousand assorted hooligans came swarming up out of the Five Points and the Bowery. "So fair and foul a day I have not seen," Macready began, and then the mob stormed the building. Rocks were hurled, pavements ripped up. The police fought back with clubs. Ned Buntline, one of the Know Nothings' leaders, brandished a sword and yelled, "Shall the sons whose fathers drove the baseborn miscreants from these shores give up Liberty?" At this, the militiamen raised their muskets and volleyed into the air. A rioter ripped open his shirt, exposing red flannel underwear, and dared them to take aim. "Fire into this! Take the life of a freeborn American for a bloody British actor! Do it!" he cried, and the militiamen did. They fired point-blank into the crush, New Yorkers gunning down New Yorkers.

Twenty-two were killed, 150 wounded. Inside the theater,

meanwhile, Macready ploughed on undeterred. "The cry is still *They come*," he declaimed. "Our castle's strength will laugh a siege to scorn." A chandelier came crashing down into the center aisle, and the Opera House went dark. Outside, the street was wedged solid with the fallen. "Here let them lie," said Macbeth, "till famine and the ague eat them up."

Afterwards, the neighborhood hushed. Broadway moved on uptown, the brothels and blind tigers went with it, and what remained was a backwater, a fringe of Greenwich Village. Walt Whitman and Fitz-James O'Brien frequented Pfaff's, a rathskeller at Bleecker Street, where the beer was watery, the conversation windy, but they played a mean game of skittles. Then that too was gone.

For a hundred years nothing stirred. It was a place of wholesale dry goods, of millinery, ready-made suits and button factories, always more button factories. New York University abutted it, and a couple of student bars clung on. Otherwise, it was Broadway's dourest stretch, a sunless Death Valley between the West and East villages.

Now it was a playground again; realtors had renamed it NoHo. Instead of Bohemian Woods, its theme was born-again Carnaby Street. Unique Clothing crowded haunch to paunch with the Dome Boutique, the Antique Boutique, and Pepito DeJoiz, the Home of the Chino Latino, and the sidewalks were lined with vendors, with jewelry stalls and used books, $5 wads of frankincense, Ghanaian necklaces of wood and bone, Islamic tracts, puff earrings shaped like giant shrimp.

Hipshot from Tower Records there was a weekend flea market, a parking lot filled with Keith Haring T-shirts and turquoise love-pendants. On the redbrick wall out back, some hand unknown had scrawled the neighborhood's new deal. POEMS AND CONDOMS FOR SALE, it read, ONE SIZE FITS ALL.

It was a sign that Sasha would have enjoyed, but Sasha was not around. Three nights after the Knitting Factory, he had been mugged and left for demised.

He had been sleeping in his cab, off Broadway on Lispenard. It was a practice that his dispatchers had warned him against many times but, for Sasha, all warnings were incitements. "So on I sleep. And how I am dispatched," he said.

The details were fuzzy. All he could remember was a noise of shattering glass, a blast of freezing night air. Then some hand unseen had knocked him sprawling. His wallet and all of his treasures—the Christmas decorations, the stuffed dragon with the footlong tongue, even the girl with the melting kimono—were removed. Footsteps moved off down the sidewalk. Two sets, he thought. Then one set had returned, nice and slow.

"Not to ask," he said. Propped up in his hospital bed, his skull festooned in white tape, he looked less like a victim than a snow-decked Christmas tree. Total strangers burst out laughing when they passed. This did not improve his mood. "Is not to whistle Dixie," he said. But he himself could not forget. He had taken sixty stitches; his skull screamed every time he moved it. Worse, his belief had been betrayed. "Right off Broadway. Twenty yards, maybe less," he said. His red mouth, framed by white, turned down like Al Jolson filmed in negative. "How could she?" he said.

With NoHo coming up next, what was more. "My best bit. My own village," he said. Shutting his eyes, he strained to float back down to the street, cruise its sidewalks this bright Saturday. "All world is stirring there," he said. "Is total pot of melt."

The mix was dizzying: homeboys from Bed-Stuy and Fordham Road, ACT-UPs from Christopher Street, NYC activists and upstate preppies, street artists from Alphabet City and con artists from Jersey City, Bush Leaguers from the Upper East Side and sons of STABs from the Upper West, Psychedelia Nows in acid-dyed culottes, radical lesbians in combat boots, disco divas and postpunk transsexuals, undercover cops done up as Rastas, bikers done up as Pentecostal priests, Pakistani B-Boys with shaven skulls and Cambodians with rat-tails, Albanians all in matching denim, white-robed Muslims, and one lone Zoroastrian, name of Myron, pushing pamphlets outside Top Tomato.

There were civilians, too; Shopper Joes, bastions of the new bourgeoisie, flashing Billy Joel CDs and Nelson Mandela T-shirts. But they were merely background, a blur. What registered, vivid as a schoolyard mural, was the cavalcade: Big Youth.

Its clubhouse was the sidewalk outside McDonald's. For generations, kids on the loose had idled in Washington Square Park, three blocks to the west. But the coming of crack had put that off-limits: "Too many dealers, too many cops," said Rashan Ray Perry, "Too hard to tell the difference." So they'd shifted their gift to Big Mac's.

Rashan Ray Perry himself was nineteen years old. At six feet three and 143 pounds, he looked like a *Soul Train* scarecrow, the advance man for a famine. On the street, his name was Stretch.

Days he worked at a TriBeCa loading bay, hefting sacks of dog food and artificial fertilizer. That made him an exception, for most of the McDonald's Jacks were either in college or school. A few were Korean, the rest Hispanic and black, and they hung here each weekday afternoon, all day Saturdays.

Fashion plates, this month they favored elephant-baggy pants and Brooklyn Dodger baseball shirts, newsboy leather caps, subway-token earrings. Gold chains—*cables*—were Out; gold toothcaps—*fronts*—were In. So were glass-bead bracelets, shark's teeth necklaces. But the greatest glory was their coiffures: "This is," said Rashan, "the year of serious hair."

Fades, braids, and designer dreads: Rearing up above the traffic, like trophies stuck on a battlement, were thirty-seven heads, each carved in a different shape. There were Mohawks and Checkerboards and classical Shags. There was Warlord hair, brush-cut like a privet hedge in front, a Chinese pigtail in back; and Samson hair, a footlong waterfall on the right side, shaved bald on the left; and Trenchtown Dreads and Uptown Dreads; and Plague Dreads, a field of blighted cornrows dyed yellowdog and ocher; and Tremont Fades, Brownsville Fades, and Koran Fades inscribed with Islamic characters. Baddest of all, there were Messageheads, cranial billboards blazoned with the owners' names and/or beliefs. I AM THE JAM, said Rashan Ray Perry's.

He also wore sky-blue bib coveralls, a spotted green ascot, a whitebone skull earring. But his speech was muted, his manner discreet. "Conservative style," he said. "Don't play me no slamming doors."

This sidewalk served him as meetinghouse, newsdesk, street disco. Three, four times a week, he'd slope up Broadway after work. Benny and MoRitz, his homeboys, bussed tables at a nearby saloon, and he used its men's room to change coveralls, get right. "Lock the door, turn off the light, just sit in the dark, in the stall, breathing deep," said Rashan. "I don't move till I see myself glow."

The bathroom was sprayed with pine essence. At squat in the blackness, Rashan liked to think himself lost in a deep dark forest with no way out. It was a game his mother had taught him. When he was seven, they'd used to hide together from Mr. D, his father at that time. They'd be cooped up in a closet under the stairs, twelve hours, twenty-four at a stretch. That closet had smelled of pine essence, too. And his mother whispered stories, she'd tell him, *Be still, keep hush, they wolves out there. They wild animals, they killers, be still, keep hush.* So he'd freeze, not make a sound, just crouch and hug in the pine-scented dark, till Mr. D sobered up or got tired of hunting.

When D went away, he'd leave the hall light still burning. It hung right outside the closet door, but at first it was invisible. Then it started gleaming, just dimly, through the cracks. Rashan didn't know what it was. *The North Star,* his mother told him. So they followed it.

He laughed at that now, something so womanly and weak. *Slop,* he called it. But the habit was ingrained. One whiff of pine essence, and it was as if something outside his knowing mind took him over, made him repeat the same child's game. Beyond the bathroom door, the saloon was filled with wolves and gorillas, birds of prey. So Rashan was still, kept hush. *See they eyes glowing red, feel they breath all stinking and hot, whiskey-mean*, his mother had said, and he did see, he could still feel. A crack of light showed under the door. It widened and grew brighter, till the blackness broke apart. When he could see his hands, Rashan rose up. When he saw his own face, he walked out.

He was ready then. He wore the dark's imprint like armor, the same way that Sasha Zim wore duck soup, strong to ward off evil. In the cluster outside McDonald's, he stood a little apart, aloof. The coveralls and the spotted cravat gave him a harlequin look, a smack of the street performer, and he kept a performer's distance. "Nobody know this man. I mean, this is the man nobody know," said Benny. He was a Stiff-Stuff Fade, built like a middle linebacker. "The Invisible Man. The Alien," he said.

"Stretcho," said MoRitz. "The man that ain't."

Their voices were taunting. But that didn't mean they lied. They were Rashan's partners. They cruised the clubs with him; they ate with him and danced with him; they even mopped up his women after he got through. Still somehow he escaped them. "When he's gone, he gone," Benny said. "When he's not, he still gone."

Rashan himself didn't know what they meant, did not much care. Under questioning, he simply shrugged and fell back on his mother's pet motto, picked up out of Shakespeare: *"To be is not to be,"* he said. *"Only moreso."*

It was the first thing she'd taught him, the one thing he never forgot. As an infant, he'd been a freak, all head and neck, no body. His blood father took one look and joined the merchant marines. Even his mother moved house. Her born name was Edwina Elizabeth, and her family lived in a Mount Vernon brownstone; they owned their own pharmacy. She herself had trained to teach school. But when she gave birth out of season, she took two rooms in Morrisania, the South Bronx, and she called herself Lizbeth.

Rashan was Arabic for "warrior." Lizbeth had wanted to name him Jadda, the root-word for Mujaddid, "the one who makes anew." But Mujaddids were not long on survival, not in the South Bronx. Rashan seemed a safer bet.

Even then, he hadn't survived by much. At age three, he could not walk, could not say one word. All his movements were uncontrolled, limbs flopping every whichway. His Adam's apple filled his throat, a buried hand grenade, and no hair grew on his skull. Then some infection caused his eyelids to droop at half-mast. He looked, Mr. D would say, like a goddamn turkey buzzard.

In Morrisania, his home was the last tenement still occupied in a block of gutted shells. The walls were so rotted that you could look clear through. There were holes like open wounds, straight out into the weather. Rats sat in them, polishing their whiskers: "Ate up my food and all my clothes, stole my toys. Traps didn't bother them none, but they love to watch TV. The weather, news and sports, the Saturday morning cartoons," Rashan said. "First I fear them, but then I got used. They bit my momma, all my sisters, but they never mess with me. Word got out, I guess—*Don't fuck with the freak.*"

Eight years he sat in that place. At the start, social workers came by. They tried all sorts of tricks to make him respond, but Rashan kept silent, never made a sound. So then they tried to send him to remedial school, but his mother would not agree. She said he was fine, just dandy. To prove it, she carried him to day school. The kids there parceled him in feathers, tarpaper, dogshit, and sent him back home, COD. After that, he stayed sitting in his room.

Fathers came, fathers went. For remembrance, they left him sisters. Violetta, Latisha, Mylene, Lenore—four girls in five years, and all of them walking, all of them talking nonstop. From a whole room, Rashan was reduced to a corner.

He was not unhappy there. As best as he could recall, he'd lived quite content. The others all clustered round the tube, learning English, like Sasha, from *One Life to Live*, but he stayed by himself; he still did not make one sound.

At age five, he suddenly started growing. Having taken so long to begin, he could not stop. His arms and legs shot up like tangleweeds, it seemed overnight. They grew so fast and straggling, his trunk could not support them. His mother propped him up with cushions, tried to wedge him between two chairs, but he kept overbalancing. He'd topple on his face, and then he couldn't move.

"Felt good. Felt just grandiose," he said. When nobody was looking, he'd lay his cheekbone flat against the linoleum, enjoy the dirt and the grit on his skin, soak up every last spot of grease. Hog-wallowing, he'd breathe in the soapy water and lemon wax his mother used to clean, the cloudy sweetness of escaped gas. Faraway, he could hear the TV burble, his sisters flip, flop, and fly. "Then guess what? I got satisfied," he said. And one day he shouted out loud.

According to his mother, the sound he made was not human. Lizbeth, at that given moment in time, was on the toilet down the hall. Suddenly she heard a stuck pig crossed with an exploding gas-main. Her first thought was, somebody shot the TV. But when she came rushing in, her flimsies all awry and her wighair in her hand, she found only her mute son, face down in a mess of cookie crumbs, serenading the roaches.

How to describe it? It was as if, all his life, he had sucked up every sound and tremor, every bang, siren, whisper, whistle, slither, screech, and stored them away, made them his. He wasn't even conscious of hearing them; seemed to take them in automatically, through his skin, his nerve-ends. Sometimes he saw them as objects, solid as a fist; other times they were tastes, smells, aches, or they tickled, way deep in the back of his throat. They goosed him, rode him, made him shiver. Or else they made him fat. First his head would swell, then his belly. The day he shouted out loud, he guessed now, he'd simply been so stuffed and bulging, big with sound, that he couldn't hold it in one minute more: "I didn't speak. I burst," Rashan said.

The din brought back the social workers. A Miss Tweedle— the name was not easily forgotten—desired to have him committed, shut up. So did Mr. D. Even his mother was tempted.

In her darkness and confusion, she sought guidance from Rashan himself. When Mr. D left for the bar, she crouched down in front of the roaring boy, tried to cut through the sheets of sound. Though they seemed like random ranting, she thought they might be a secret code. So she started to mark down cadences, the shifting beats. She prayed to jump in his skin, ride shotgun behind his eyes. *"Bil'lisaani. Bilqualbi,"* she said. "With my tongue. With my heart." When Rashan barked, she barked back. When he screamed, so did she. *"Aamantu.* I have faith," she said.

Teetotum-style, he rocked himself on his base, back and forth, back and forth, his cries growing louder, more frantic, till he wet himself. His piss made a golden lake on the linoleum, and this sight seemed to calm him. Then his mother rose up smiling; she dusted off her hands, case closed. "It's just his song," she decided.

She bought him a Horner electric keyboard on sale; he attacked it like a box of chocolate eclairs. He would not sit to make music but crouched. The keyboard was laid flat, its cheek against the lino, and Rashan hovered above, teetered with flapping arms, turkey buzzard on a highwire.

For nine years, he had breathed in sounds. Now he poured them back out. "Slamming doors," he said. "Sirens in the street, rat whispers in the dark. Squeaking shoes, toilets flushing, TV jingles, rain, frying fat." He played in the hallway, not to bother Mr. D. He replayed all existence, percussioning in rhythm, with his fingers stiff as drumsticks. "Mostly, I just played weather. Played clouds, thunderbursts, sunshowers, hailstorms. And lulls, I played a lot of lulls. Then I played dinner, then I played ice cream and Jell-O, cherry soda, meatloaf. Then I played kisses. Then I played sleep."

After Mr. D, hungover, threw the Horner against the bathroom wall, Lizbeth kept it locked away. By day she worked odd jobs, sweeping up, checking out. Rashan sat home by himself, propped on his cushion, and did not cease to howl till she got back, released his music.

Outside their tenement, Morrisania was in flames. The city had abandoned it, left it to burn. Rather than make repairs, landlords burned their buildings for the insurance payouts. Most every night, through the holes in the walls, Lizbeth watched the fires across the wastelands. Her own landlord wanted her gone, she wanted it herself, but there was no place to go. At first the landlord sweetmouthed her, then he threatened. The lower floors were stocked with angel-dust junkies, the damned. Mr. D moved out and was not replaced, Miss Tweedle stopped calling, raw garbage was heaped in the stairwells, and the Seven Immortals used the cellar for gang rapes. Still Lizbeth clung on. In the end, the landlord tossed a match.

Rashan remembered waking up choking, his sisters screaming. Afterwards, in a hospital hallway, aged nine years and seven months, he spoke one word. His mother heard it as *bilaahi*, In Allah. His sisters heard *baloney*.

Homeless now, the family was shunted from department to association, shelter to welfare hotel. Sometimes they were kept together, more often cut apart. Only Rashan and his mother always counted as one. The Horner keyboard made two.

Rashan played fire, played burning. He played heat and cold, angry priests, plastic plates, burlap blankets. When the Horner gave out, he howled instead. To hush him, the Sisters of Mercy let him use a stand-up piano. It stood out back of a soup kitchen, overlooking the back alley. He played garbage cans; he played stench; he played scavengers. What he liked best, he played birds.

At last, after four years' drifting, he and all his family washed up at the Hotel Carter on Forty-second Street, the Deuce, half a block from Times Square.

It was the middle eighties. President Reagan had decreed, and Mayor Koch confirmed, that having nowhere to live was not a misfortune but, like dissent in Stalinist Russia, a disease. "Primarily, homelessness is a mental health problem," the Federal Task Force believed.

In the Hotel Carter, there were maybe sixty families, 250 kids, no more than a dozen grown men. The Perrys had Room 417; it measured fourteen feet by nine.

Rashan slept in the closet, under piles of his sisters' coats. He could talk now, and walk at the same time. Still neither seemed natural. His body, too long atrophied, shot up at hazard, groped like a creeper towards the light. He grew eighteen inches in three years. Arms and legs filled the closet, festooned the clothes racks. So weak he was from sprouting, he kept tripping over himself, entangled in his own parts. But at least he did not look like a buzzard: "More like an ostrich with the bends," his sister Violetta said.

The Carter was a subsidized snakepit. In a previous incarnation, as the Dixie, it had offered sanctuary to writers and ecdysiasts, all manner of magicians. Delmore Schwartz had lived here; and Belle Liberty, star of *99 Tricks with a Banana*; and even Colonel Stingo, the idol of A. J. Liebling. Now the denizens had renamed it RTC, the Rahway Training Center after the New Jersey State Penitentiary. The hallways were full of moonrock, of crack pipes and used condoms. The bloods called Rashan a geek and beat him up daily, twice on Sundays. *"To be is not to be. Only moreso,"* Lizbeth said.

She had reverted to the Reverend Calvin Butts and his Abyssinian Baptist Church, West 138th Street. In Rashan's closet, right next to his picture of Magic Johnson, she tacked up another poem, hand-printed. "Pain that cannot forget," it read, "Falls drop by drop upon the heart / Until in our despair comes wisdom / Through the awful grace of God."

But the pain failed to register. "I never was wired for hurt," he said. Somewhere beyond his memory, he had been equipped with an unbreachable shell. Time and turmoil had only thickened it. So now he could walk through battlefields, with deadfalls and landmines at every step, and never blink. Night after night, the Deuce was full of gunsong and sirens. Inside the Carter, right down the hall, a pregnant woman was cut into strips with a blunt penknife. "Is that a fact?" Rashan said. "I was not aware."

Only afterwards, when the noises died away, he played them back, pitch-perfect. His sisters were all in school; his mother hung out with friends. Left alone in Room 417, Rashan played just one person: "Rashan Ray Perry," he said. "I and I."

At sixteen, he had stopped growing on the outside, was ready to start on internals. He was dyslexic, but his mother had taught him school talk, his sisters had taught him streets. After dark, when the TV went on, he took to voyaging.

Mostly he traveled Times Square, five blocks up, five back. Raffy, a Dominican from Room 407, mapped out the turf, which hustles went where, whose sex fitted what. But he was not shaped to run with crowds. What he most enjoyed was to squat on the steps of George M. Cohan's statue, cast away on the Forty-sixth Street traffic island. From there, safely distanced, he studied riot in peace.

He had a great gift for this. "How to be alone in hordes," he called it. In his eye, it was the whole art and secret of streetlife. To sit apart at the heart of Broadway, to see and not be seen: "Conservative style," he said. "When the sickness hits, you not home."

Upstairs in the Carter, his sister Mylene was best friends

with a girl named Xanthia. She came from El Salvador, and she was fourteen; she had green eyes any fool could get drowned in.

Her brother Isidro was Rashan's prime tormentor. He had a withered arm—the bloods called him Crip. In the whole hotel, only Rashan was worse enfeebled. So Isidro took to hiding in stairwells, pouncing in the dark. Late at night, when Rashan strolled by dreaming, a twisted hand came snaking out of shadow and grabbed him by his throat, sprayed his eyes with Mace.

Rashan thought it was acid. Clawing at his ruined face, he went bouncing off the walls, plunging blindly down the hallways, scattering the little girls playing Double Dutch and their mothers gossiping, the crackheads and the dicemen and the baby carriages, till he hit an open doorway and fell through it, smack into Xanthia's lap.

She sat curled up in an armchair painting her toenails tangerine. It was a steam-heat night in August; she was wearing short shorts and a halter top. Rashan's head seemed shooting flame. Plunged between her thighs, it felt like a firebrand dipped into running water. "I heard the sizzle. I smelled the scorch," he said. But he did not make noise, he couldn't; the burning gutted his cries. "I was still. I kept hush," he said.

Xanthia bathed his eyes, first with a wetted rag, then with her fingertips. As the scalding ebbed, his sight crept back. Still his eyes felt swollen, peeled raw. So he hid deeper in her cooling flesh. She was not wearing shorts anymore. She was not wearing anything. So then she sighed, lifted up his freak's head. Her green cat's eyes looked down into his, and she giggled, kind of shy. "Pretty boy," she said.

Remembering now, Rashan giggled too. "Tangerine toenails," he said. But it had not seemed foolish then. When he was swimming upstream through Xanthia, half-blind and burning up, it had not seemed foolish whatever. "Felt just grandiose," said Rashan, "To bury the geek and get gone."

In his room, he played Reeboks and Nikes, he played Jerri Curls. Come fall, when his mother was moved on again, he didn't move with her but stepped out by himself. He had a young lady in Loisaida, her name was Lashuan. Then a young lady in East New York, her name was Tonya Laverne. After her, the stuff he played, no Horner could contain.

He needed a scratchboard, a minimum synth, a drum machine. There was a young lady on East 118th, her name was Esther and her brother was Hilario, he worked in a music store. For fifty dollars cash and 20 percent forever, Hilario provided a sound studio, a tincan storage shed behind the Kanawha Political Club. There Rashan could play out all creation: "The history of the universe," he said, "in the uncut version."

The music that he made was not rap, not hip-hop or house. It used elements of all three, but its key was Rashan's own beat, a lurching rhythm that pumped like a bloodpulse, then dangled, a skipped heartbeat.

"I sing the body electric," Walt Whitman wrote. Rashan sang it too, but this body was out of sync, riddled with arrhythmia. Every time it seemed in stride, it broke apart, its flow snapped short and twisted: "Like Johnny Staccato got a bum ticker," Rashan thought. So he called it Stack Attack.

He wrote lyrics, made tapes. When he played them to deejays, they complained of chest pains. But setbacks did not faze him. He understood that cardiac arrest was not automatically dancer friendly. To break big, it would need to become a habit, second nature: "Like breathing," he said, "or not." Meantime, he hefted dog food in TriBeCa, had a room in Alphabet City.

On Broadway, outside McDonald's, he was a rusted color, bronze and ocher mixed, like oak leaves late in fall. Above the Rube Goldberg body, his head rose like an Amharic carving, long-necked, austere, with high scimitar cheekbones and high forehead, a high hawk's nose.

The year before, he had met Benny and MoRitz at the Paradise Garage, the Home of House. Up till then, dance clubs had repelled him. Growing up, he had seen *Saturday Night Fever* and thought it cretinous. All those Guineas drawn up in ranks, time-stepping, like androids on parade: "The sucker wrote that shit, we talking serious asshole," he said. And there was something else. "Tell the truth," he said, "I was scared. Like I didn't trust my own body. Like maybe I thought, deep down, I was still the turkey buzzard, the no-dick ostrich with the runs. So if I start to dance, *expose myself*, I might be blowing my cover. Then everybody see through me, the thing I really am," Rashan said. "A fuckin' freak."

Just one thing only could make him rethink. There was a young lady from Red Hook, her name was Paulette DePaul, the girl had a dancing Jones. If you did not take her clubbing, you did not take her at all. So Rashan went to the Garage. Under protest, but he went. And was swept away.

"My pants were turned upside down," he said. In this place, freakishness was no deformity, no disgrace. On the contrary, it was the beau ideal: "Like you gotta be fucked up, I mean fucked up *good*, before you can get right."

Instead of dancing automatons, the floor was jammed with creatures that earth forgot. Some plunged and leaped like dolphins, some burrowed, some flew high, some seemed to swim underwater. Inside a chalked circle, Benny and MoRitz mirror-danced, bodies rigid and twitching. Rashan, without thinking, stepped into the circle with them and started to twitch along.

Volume plus beat equaled joy of pain, the fiercer the more ecstatic. If the walls did not sweat and your eyeballs fry, if you could taste your own mouth next morning, it was not true house. "Takes a sickness to ride the high," Benny said. "Soak up the punishment, then bounce it back."

"*Fight the Power*," said MoRitz.

"Right," said Benny. "And love it, too."

They went clubbing from midnight till dawn, Thursday through the weekend. On this sidewalk outside Big Mac's, they'd meet to collude and conspire, rehashing the night before, charting routes for the one ahead. Mostly they followed their favorite deejays, Clark Kent and Kid Capri. Tonight, the word was, the Kid was due at Powerhouse: "Bird's the word," said Rashan.

His left eyelid still drooped, a half-shut blind, and his speech was hesitant, as if the words had been learned by rote, a foreign language too systematically mastered to sound quite his own. But dancing, MoRitz said, he was just beautiful. On the floor, where there were no rules, no limitations, he was whatever he made himself—a corkscrew or a stormblown sail, a pissing dog, a samurai: "A mighty man," Benny said.

"A warrior," said Rashan.

On this sidewalk gathered the house elite, a loose-knit inner circle that called itself the Corps. Most of its conscripts were refugees from street gangs and the projects, who had refused to be typecast. Instead of festering in the neighborhoods and getting dead, they'd dared to bust out, play Broadway: "Ax for more," said MoRitz.

He was a Barbadian from Washington Heights, born to shrug, with a MO KNOWS Messagehead. If you were down with the Corps, he said, you had it made. So Rashan had it made. "But that don't make it easy. It's not," MoRitz said.

"Snot meant to be," Benny said.

"No pain, no brain," Rashan said.

Across the street, against the wall of the Hebrew Union College, the homeless men still sat in line and stared. The man in the pink blanket was crouched at the far left. He kept rocking on his heels, shouting *Fuck that shit, Fuck that shit.* Then he came lurching across Broadway. Up close, there was blood on his lips, in his mouth, and he stopped right in front of Rashan, stood swaying and mouthing, his forefinger stabbing the air. "Who he?" Benny asked.

"Just one of my fathers," said Rashan. Deadpan, he turned away, began to pose in Big Mac's plate-glass window. "Only kidding," he said. But the man in pink was not amused. Reddish froth clung to his chaps, blood red was in his eyes. Shooting out his right hand, he grabbed Rashan by his spotted cravat, pulled him close. "And who the fuck?" he cried, "are you?"

"*I Am The Jam,*" Rashan said.

Freeing himself, he moved off down Broadway. It was early yet, hours to go before Powerhouse got going, and he needed rest. Outside Tower Records, where Cleveland Blakemore was dismantling his book display, Rashan bought a Sesame Street picturebook. There was a young lady off Seward Park; her name was Candy; she was teaching him to read. "Rough sledding," he said. "But I endure."

He was so long of leg, he seemed to be walking on stilts. At Great Jones Street, young girls in bright dresses were sucking on Popsicles, young boys were watching them. A boombox blasted *My Generation*: "Who wrote that?" Rashan asked. "Elvis Presley? The Beatles?"

"Pete Townshend."

"That a fact? I knew it was some dead mother." Unsmiling, he started to move away, turned left into the night. "It always is," he said.

lounged in Union Square. Leaning on his broom, immaculate in new coveralls and designer sneakers, he looked like an Ivy Leaguer slumming, and that's what he proved. His name was Calvin Palmer, his alma mater, Cornell. A Wall Street broker with Merrill Lynch, he had lately been convicted on drug charges. The nimbleness of lawyers had kept him out of jail. In lieu, he was performing community service.

Leaning on a broom was the least of it. Most of his sentence, Calvin said, was spent babysitting trees. Plant-pirates were marauding the city parks, ripping off shrubs and saplings, every growing thing. Barbed wire and chains had failed to prevent them. So had grappling the roots with buried spikes. Now it was up to Calvin Palmer. "I have to stand sentry," he said. "Then when the thief shows up and starts molesting a tree, I blow on a little tin whistle."

"What happens then?"

"He takes the tree," Calvin said, "and he goes away."

It was draining work. Some nights he was so tired, so absolutely fed up with it all, he couldn't face dining out. The rest of his set, Bush Leaguers, were living it up at Mortimer's or some Young Republican fundraiser, while he suffered cold cuts in his bedroom and watched reruns of *Cheers*. And still he had a hundred hours to work off. His broom was clogged with sticky black glop, God knew how it had got there; he had a blood blister on one heel. "Free Calvin Palmer," he said.

"There's no such thing," said Lush Life.

Union Square was her new playing field. Tommy Blalock, his stint in the navy completed, had taken rooms in Brooklyn Heights and was working on Fourteenth Street, selling T-shirts off an army-surplus blanket.

His pitch sat tight to the entrance to the IRT, the very spot where he and Vida Lujuriante had first pledged to go shopping for shoes. Scaffolding and a low ceiling of wooden boards gave it a subterranean feeling, cool and musty like a cellar. In the recesses of its deep shade, Nigerians sold beads and Senegalese sold tape cassettes, a Korean sold Oyster Perpetuals. But T-shirt vendors were steadily cutting them back.

The shirts themselves were not Tommy's choice. If he'd had his druthers, he would have featured his own travel trophies, souvenirs of Louisiana and Virginia, Caracas, Singapore, a dozen other stopovers. His favorite came right from New Iberia, his own hometown—a McIlhenny's Tabasco shirt, with the red-pepper bottle burning up in hellfire and flame-licked letters proclaiming HOT STUFF.

"Tommy comes from an artistic bent. All his family do," Lush Life said. But street sellers must take what they were allotted: white Bart Simpsons and black Bart Simpsons, MOM AND DAD WENT TO THE BIG APPLE AND ALL I GOT WAS THIS LOUSY T-SHIRT, a hundred variations on I ♡ NEW YORK. "Demeaning," Tommy thought it. "Tossing the cowchip."

"We have each other," Lush Life said.

He only grunted. He was a creature of strong attachments, fierce pride. His mother, who had raised him, had taught him never to take second best. That was why he had joined the navy. *Be All That You Can Be*, the army urged. But Tommy would not settle for so little. "All you can be, and then some," was his own belief. "One hundred and ten percent."

His speech was heavy on footballese, the jargon of pigskin war. Every play of his life seemed fourth and inches, goal to go: "This is the big one. There are no tomorrows. For Tommy Blalock," he said, "this is the one for all the marbles."

"Hut, hut," said Lush Life. But she was no longer Lush Life, not really, or even Vida Lujuriante. Outside the Hotel Moose, she was just Tommy Blalock's girl. "His intended," she said.

Or so she trusted. For the moment, no rings had changed hands, no vows were exchanged. It was Tommy Blalock's belief that a man did not plight his troth till he could pay his way. "No property of Tommy Blalock's is going to end up on no damn welfare line. That isn't the way Tommy Blalock was raised," he said.

"His mother is a dental assistant," Lush Life supplied.

"My mother," said Tommy, "is a saint."

One long summer's toil, he reckoned, and he would achieve a basic stake, down payment on a little house someplace near his mother's house, maybe even enough to get a start in construction. "Ten grand and we have first down. Move the chains, stop the clock," he said. Till then, he practiced strict economy. He even hesitated at sex. "Roughing the passer," he called it. "You get caught one time, it's a major penalty. You get caught again, it might be a game ejection."

Lush Life did not argue. In her secret heart, she was relieved. "Don't ask," she said. For years, she had been meaning to go to a plastic surgeon. She had saved up, even set a date. Then she'd run into International Chrysis, the Brazilian transsexual, in the ladies' room at Mars. Her measurements, proudly proven, were 38, 24, 36, and 9. Lush Life was awestruck, enraptured. First thing next morning, however, she had canceled her doctor's appointment. *"C'est magnifique, mais c'est pas la guerre,"* she said. Besides, she was scared of needles.

For herself, she had no regrets. But what about Tommy? What if he was disappointed? "Those Southern momma's boys, you know how they love big chests," she said. "They're udderly crazed." In her room, she lit candles and stripped, breathed out like a highboard diver. But her mirror was too cheap to lie. "He won't like me. He won't approve," she said. Glinting in the candlelight, Night Train ran down her sleek flanks like oil, an unguent. Her nipples were rosy and hard, no fatter than an infant's. "Ladybeard, I'm not right," said Lush Life. She flung herself down on her pallet; she hid her ribs in Madame Butterfly's silks. "I never will be," she said.

The black mood did not sustain. The morning after, beneath the scaffold at Union Square, she dazzled in and out of sunlight like a snapdragon, singing stridently off-key. From Cio-Cio-San and Nagasaki, she'd made a right turn into Nelly Forbush and Bali Hai, *In Love with a Wonderful Guy*: "I'm as corny as Kansas in August," she blared, a vision in white shorts and boater, a navel-knotted, sky-blue shirt. "High as a flag on the Fourth of July."

Her feet in open-toed gilded sandals were torpedoes, yet she floated through the Farmer's Market like Mary Martin on a tightrope. "No more a smart little tart with no heart," she sang. On the corner of Sixteenth Street, outside the Metropolis Cafe, she stuffed her face with Tootsie Rolls. The blockage muffled her voice, but could not still it. "Kansas in August," she crooned. "I'm as normal as blueberry pie."

Union Square, like NoHo, was not so much changing as reverting. It had started brilliantly, gone through a long passage of dimness, and was just beginning to flourish again. Coming to it from below was like surfacing from Atlantis.

By now the physical business of walking Broadway had settled into one pattern, endlessly repeated. For days and miles on end, you quarried underwater, passed along a bottomless tunnel. But periodically—Trinity Church, City Hall Park, Canal Street—the darkness broke, and you floundered into light. Most often, these breaks came without warning. At Union Square, however, the rest was signaled four blocks in advance, where the road broke stride, hitched a sudden dogleg.

According to legend, this was Hendrick Brevoort's doing. He was a Dutch tavernkeeper of the early nineteenth century and, as Broadway kept pushing north, its proposed route had run through his apple orchard. In that orchard, he had a favorite tree, which the planners wished to cut down. And Brevoort had flatly refused. Architects, master builders, City Hall delegations had come to him pleading; the innkeeper would not be budged. In the end, Broadway was rerouted, went lurching off to its left.

That, at least, was the story. If true, Brevoort's apple tree had changed the whole of Manhattan's topography. Without it, Broadway would have run into Fourth Avenue, the two combined would have made Park Avenue, and the Rialto would have been an East Side show. Instead, it went west, invaded the creeks and untouched farmlands of Bloomingdale: "To flaunt itself," Dr. Davitt said, "and make a mock."

His own flaunting was discreet. A willowy youth of fifty, he wore lime-green chinos with a tight white sweater, rose-tinted glasses, just a hint of eyeshadow. In his shoulder bag, he carried a deck of printed cards, deep purple ink on a plain cream ground. DR. DAVID DAVITT, the cards announced, WORD-SURGEON.

This was not his only commercial. Neatly fanned into separate pouches, like the segments of a purpled mandarin, there were also testimonials for DR. DAVITT, COSMOLOGIST; DOCTOR DAVID, YOUR PAIN IS MY PLEASURE; and DAVE'S CARPENTRY, CLOSET CASES OUR SPECIALITY. But the word-surgeon was his favorite. "Master Writing with the Master Writer. Produce Deathless Prose," said the card, and then, in gold copperplate letters, "How Can You Lose with the Muse I Use?"

They were, he admitted, just teases. Back in the sixties, before the pulp-magazine market collapsed, he had been Brett Houston, short-order scribe. *So Young, So Lovely, So Dead,*

Pardon My Corpse, and *The Morgue the Merrier* were just three of his. He had even knocked off a novella, unpublished, called *You'll Be Sorry*. But his own writings had failed to satisfy him. Deepest down, he'd always felt that he was a teacher: "Born to preach, not practice," he said. So Dr. Davitt was born: "My mother's maiden name, my first love's profession."

He placed classifieds in *True Detective* and *Jet*, wrote up a two-page prospectus. "Is this feeling familiar?" it began. "Did you ever finish reading a literary classic and think to yourself *I could have written that?* Did you ever feel, if only you had the necessary know-how, that you too contained the seeds of a timeless masterwork? If so, READ ON, for help is at hand. Dr. David Davitt, world-famed word-surgeon, is here to show you how you, too, can unlock the door to genius. . . ."

He had printed up five thousand Free Introductory Booklets. But the ads had failed to generate a serious response. "Which is my life's history," the Doctor said now. "I meant it for real. I always mean it for real. But somehow, I don't know why, I make it come out sounding phony. It's like a tic, some kind of nervous reflex. So everyone thinks it's a put-on, a great big yuk. And all the time—this is so sick—it is my heart out there."

The failure to communicate had hit him hard. "Give me half an hour each day, just thirty little minutes, in the privacy of your own home," the Master Writer's prospectus promised, "and you, too, can soar with the eagles, weave word-dreams for pleasure and profit." But he received only two replies. "One from a retired banker in Wisconsin, a spiritualist, who was trying to reach Pierre Louys," Dr. Davitt said. "And the other was from my half-brother in Panama City, he wanted three thousand dollars."

Looking back, though he'd tried to shrug it off, the experience had been his life's watershed. Afterwards, he ceased to write for profit, drew back on himself. For the last eighteen years, he had been working intermittently on a history-cum-

daybook of Union Square, *News on the Rialto*. He did not expect
to complete it in his own lifetime.

He was a little trim man, freshly laundered, but his cheeks
had a mottled cast, blue where they should have turned pink,
like a failed litmus test. He'd lived in this same neighborhood,
off and on, from the age of eleven months.

When his mother left his father, a Long Island City phar-
macist, she went to work in S. Klein's, the bargain clothing store
on Union Square East, where the Zeckendorf Towers now stood,
and she roomed on East Eleventh. Now eighty-three and wheel-
chaired, she was still in the same apartment. So was her son,
the Doctor.

"Call me Davitt. I want you to," he said. But his mother
called him Hyman. Among his first memories was his infant
self, aged three years and seven months, standing screeching on
Fourteenth Street, right outside Lüchow's, screaming *I'm not
Hyman. I'm not, I'm not.* For years afterwards, he couldn't walk
that block, or he'd be swarmed instantly by packs of street
urchins, guttersnipes, squawling *I'm not Hyman, I'm not.*

What was the neighborhood like back then? "Dispossessed," he said. Somewhere it had lost its charter. In *News on
the Rialto*, the Doctor wrote: "Union Square was to be the last
word. All Broadway led up to this place. This was the place
where the city was going to end. Where everything would end.
It would be the flower forever. Only everything would not stop
growing. It moved on beyond."

It left behind a dumping ground. Looking back into childhood, what Dr. Davitt remembered most clearly was mess, a
perpetual morning-after feel. "It was like there'd been the party
to end all parties, only nobody had bothered to clear up," he
said. "So all the dirty glasses and the leftover food, the party
favors, the funny hats, they'd just sat there and gone bad." He
sniffed the stale air, wrinkled up his nose in distaste. "It was a
hole," he said, "where a place used to be."

The days of Union Square's greatest glory had followed the Civil War. For thirty years then, it had been *the* Rialto; the hub. Solidly from Eighth Street to Twenty-third, Broadway was lined with smart hotels and smarter stores, the strip called Ladies Mile. Tiffany's was here; so were Colonel John Daniell, Arnold Constable, and Lord & Taylor. But Union Square's greatest stardom was as the heart of the theater district.

It was the city's first. There had always been playhouses on Broadway, but they'd sprung up haphazardly, just like the street itself: Edwin Booth's Winter Garden at Bond Street and Niblo's Garden at Prince, Wallack's at Broome, the Astor Place and the Broadway Theater itself, where Adah Isaacs Menken used to climax her performance in *Mazeppa* by charging up the central aisle strapped, seemingly naked, aboard an Arab stallion. Then there were the concert halls, like the New Oriental and Harry Hill's on Houston, "where murder is almost unknown"; the minstrel shows, like the Christy's Mechanical Hall at Grand; and the first of the skin palaces, Wood's Museum, where the Lydia Thompson Burlesque Co. displayed four strapping blondes laced into black corsets and sporting pink-flesh silk stockings. "If this is not the end, what is?" James Gordon Bennett's *Herald* shrilled.

Union Square was the salty answer.

Within its bounds, all forms of entertainment, high and low, were tumbled in one bed: "Vice wears a fair mask at every corner," wrote Junius Henry Browne, "and Art smiles in a thousand bewitching forms. Hotels and playhouses and bazaars, and music halls, and bagnios, and gambling hells are radiantly mixed together; and any of them will give you what you seek, and more sometimes."

At one extreme was the Academy of Music, an opera house whose boxes were reserved for Mrs. Astor's four hundred; at the other Tony Pastor's, the first house of vaudeville, whose reigning muse was Maggie Cline, the Irish Queen, with her boxing ballad, "Throw Him Down, McCloskey."

Off Broadway, the back streets filled with basement bars and hockshops, theatrical boardinghouses; and the sidewalk outside Keith's Union Square Theater so overflowed with vaudevillians seeking work that it was known as the Slave Market. "Happy days," Davitt said, "filled with song, dance, and loathing."

He treasured one feud in particular. As recorded by George Jean Nathan, a certain Aug. Allaire of the Three Bounding Allaires wrote to a showbiz publication protesting that Flo D'Arcy of the D'Arcy Sisters had pirated his trademark one-armed back spring. In the next issue, Miss D'Arcy replied:

DEAR EDITOR,

I dislike to be unlady-like, as my conduct as a member of the famous team of D'Arcy Sisters who have played successfully in all parts of the world is well known to all my dear friends in vaudeville to be strictly ladylike, but I can't let the remarks of one, Aug. Allaire, of the Three Bounding Allaires, go by unnoticed. I want to say to Aug. Allaire that if he claims I stole the one-armed back spring from him he is a liar, as I copied the one-armed back spring from Oscar Delarmo, of Delarmo and Astor, with his kind permission. Mr. Oscar Delarmo has used the one-armed back spring for twenty years and twenty years ago Aug. Allaire of the Three Bounding Allaires, was probably still sweeping out some Baltimore Lunch place on the Bowery.

> Faithfully yours,
> Miss Flo D'Arcy, Of the D'Arcy Sisters
> —booked solid for one year.

After 1900, Broadway had pushed on and taken the Rialto with it. The luxury hotels and theaters were boarded up, torn down, and Fourteenth was reduced to a bargain basement, no-

torious for its bootleg furs and contraband silks; its nine-cent
record stores; its pretzel and chestnut vendors, its sheet-music
peddlers; and the ninety-eight synchronized timepieces in the
windows of Korn's Klock Korner.

Came the depression. The square filled with Wobblies and
soapbox orators. On March 6, 1930, some two thousand Communists demonstrated there and fifty thousand came to gawk.
Grover Whalen, Mayor Jimmy Walker's police commissioner,
refused permission for a march down Broadway to City Hall.
When the Communists started marching anyway, they were met
by mounted police. Then, wrote Edward Robb Ellis, "hundreds
of cops and detectives, swinging nightsticks and blackjacks and
bare fists, rushed into the marching columns." The marchers
fought back, and the law rushed harder. "A dozen plainclothes-
men and uniform cops beat and kicked two unarmed men until
they nearly fainted. Women screamed. Men shouted. Blood
began to trickle down faces. Soon a score of men sprawled on
the ground."

It was the worst riot that New York had seen this century.
No guns being used, only twenty major injuries were reported,
a hundred hospitalizations. But the bitterness cut deep: Union
Square did not recover.

By World War II, when the infant Davitt arrived, the Academy of Music was a rattrap movie house. For fifty cents, twenty-
five at matinees, it offered a double feature plus eight live vaudeville acts. On weekends, it threw in free popcorn and pretzels.

Everything here was secondhand, used up, despoiled. The
loudest sign on the block, gold and scarlet neon, read ALL
MERCHANDISE REDUCED 200%. It was advertising the hostesses
in a taxi ballroom.

DANCING, it also said, IS A SOCIAL NECESSITY.

In this place, Davitt had grown up solitary: "A little queer,"
he said. He was never any good in school, dropped out at fifteen,
but he was an obsessional reader. He'd pick up books at random,
devour them piecemeal. So his knowledge had come in a jack-

daw's ragbag. He could quote from Dante and Walter Winchell, the Book of Job, Dale Carnegie and Mickey Spillane. But he did not know who Lenin was, or Jackie Robinson.

Union Square was no place for little queers. When he was twenty, he got tired of the sight of his own blood. He'd had enough of healing just to get scarred again, and he moved to the West Village. He wrote for the pulps; he doubled as the Master Writer. But he found that he missed his roots. However he had hated and feared the place, Union Square had hooked him. "It was the hopelessness," he said. "The ugliness and meanness, the whole squalid mess." He shook his head wearily, fondly, a mother hen clucking at a wayward chick. "A runt," he said. "But *my* runt."

He recalled the day and hour when the pact was sealed: "May fourteenth, 1971, two o'clock in the afternoon. I had just finished a story. *Blood in the Blender*, it stank. I was living in the West Village, Bank Street, and hanging out at Julius. That was the time right after the Stonewall Riot; the whole gay pride thing was blowing up and it wasn't me." He spoke with measured cadence. In the same steady rhythm, he tapped a menthol cigarette six times on its packet, passed a match three times, sucked in twice. "I never was a joiner," he said. "I just wasn't made for groups, coalitions, whatever. Ever since I knew I liked boys, I hated the word *gay*, it seemed so false somehow. The old names were better; they were vile and dumb but they didn't lie. *Faggot, flit. Other*, I always liked that."

After four puffs, his cigarette was thrown away, a fresh smoke produced. Six taps, three passes, two sucks: "I was past thirty. A word-surgeon with no patients. And blood in the blender," he said. "I packed up my belongings in a brown paper bag. I came back to Union Square." He tossed aside the cigarette, reached for a third. "To be Other," he said.

By Grace Church, walking but not seeing, he'd bumped against an old and evil-smelling Greek who trundled a pushcart full of stuffs—shoelaces, cheap cottons, polyester pants. Jarred, the Greek stopped dead, measured Davitt with a fierce glare. He was a stranger, but not a bit shy. Oozing garlic, he grabbed the Doctor by the arm, commenced to rattle him like a cocktail shaker. Then he brought his dirty mouth up close, he hissed. "Queer. You dirty little queer," he said. And Davitt was back home.

"Saul on the road to S. Klein's," he said. Arriving at Union Square, he bought himself a cheap notebook, plumped down beneath the hooves of George Washington's horse. "And there I made my stand. Or sit," he said. "The second coming of Joe Gould."

Gould, Professor Seagull, had been a Greenwich Village landmark before World War II. He had spent his life in downtown cafeterias, diners, barrooms, and hobo jungles, tormented by "the three H's—homelessness, hunger, and hangovers"— and compiling *An Oral History of Our Time*.

According to Joseph Mitchell, who wrote Gould up in *The New Yorker*, he wrote in school-composition books and filled them with "a great hodgepodge and kitchen midden of hearsay." In one chapter alone, "The Good Men Are Dying Like Flies": "Gould begins a biography of a diner proprietor and horse-race gambler named Side-Bet Benny Altschuler, who stuck a rusty icepick in his hand and died of lockjaw; and skips after a few paragraphs to a story a seaman told him about seeing a group of tipsy lepers on a beach in Port-of-Spain, Trinidad; and goes from that to an anecdote about a meeting held in Boston in 1915 to protest against the showing of *The Birth of a Nation*, at which he kicked a policeman; and goes from that to a description of a trip he once made through the Central Islip insane asylum, in the course of which a woman pointed to him and screamed, 'There he is! Thief! Thief! There's the man that picked my geraniums and stole my mamma's mule and buggy'; and goes from that to an account an old stumble-bum gave of glimpsing and feeling the blue-black flames of hell one night while sitting in a doorway on Great Jones Street and of seeing two mermaids playing in the East River just north of Fulton Fish Market later the same night; and goes from that to an explanation made by a priest of old St. Patrick's Cathedral on Mott Street of why Italian women are addicted to the wearing of black; and then returns at last to Side-Bet Benny, the lockjawed diner proprietor."

This description was the closest that Davitt or anybody now living had ever got to glimpsing the original. *An Oral History* was never published. There was a fire someplace, all the composition books burned up, and then Gould died. Or maybe the order was different. Whatever, the story never hit the stands: "But he wrote it, didn't he?" said Davitt. "He sat, he saw, he wrote."

Sight unseen, Joe Gould's book had still changed Davitt's existence; inspired him to *News on the Rialto*. He understood that he lacked Professor Seagull's universality. His own canvas was restricted to Union Square. Still, he didn't see this as a limitation. Far from it. By chronicling this one spot in every detail, through the tales of its inhabitants, *ancient and infant, forever and just passing through*, he hoped to achieve a synopsis of all humankind: "The Cosmos in Cliff Notes," he said.

So far he had written some two million words. Completed notebooks, handwritten in a miniscule schoolgirl script, filled an entire sea chest. Still his task was just begun.

He had not lost faith. He still believed in his vision, more intensely than he'd ever done. But he was paralyzed by shyness. He could approach no stranger, couldn't manage the lightest small talk. Every day the newspaper vendor said "Have a nice day," and each day Davitt meant to respond. He never did.

I myself had only met him by running into his mother, Eugenia, while she was wheeling through her corner deli. She wanted Blue Mountain coffee; I possessed the last jar; we traded for her son. Even then it had taken four letters, maybe a dozen phone calls, before he would speak out loud.

Every day of these last eighteen years, he had followed the

same ritual. Rising at six, he wrote for exactly three hours. Then he took breakfast with his mother; then he rode his bike three blocks to Union Square. The bicycle was a vintage Rudge from Wolverhampton, England, high-barred and erect, a thorough-bred. Old friends of his mother's, cigar makers, let him stash it in their hallway. When he picked it up at night, the saddle smelled faintly of Cuban seeds, rolled Dominican leaf.

And then what? "I take notes. I amble," Davitt said. "I think the big thoughts."

Most of the time, he sat on park benches, working up his courage to approach some stranger and start intercourse. Courage never came. So he settled for the next best thing: "I watch. I imagine. I lie."

The Union Square we sat in this day was all of bits and pieces. On the east was the Farmer's Market, organic, pure; to the south were Tommy Blalock's T-shirts; to the west, juveniles and winos. Before us were statues of liberty (assorted)—Lafayette, Lincoln, and Gandhi—and the equestrian George Washington, eyes filthy and right arm beckoning, with a look of promiscuous entreaty, like some Bourbon Street tout crying "Live! Naked! Live! They're naked and they dance!"

"You have to understand," David said. But he did not say what. In conversation, his style was to sneak up on a subject, make a sudden dart, then dash back to shelter. "It's hard to say," he said.

"What is?"

"Everything."

His voice was breathless, very small. Bound rigid by the tightness of his sweater and lime-green pants, he sat flinching in the shadow of Washington's horse. A massively built charger with a rump like rolling thunder, it gazed down askance, one hoof raised and pawing. "Cream rises, scum sinks," Dr. Davitt said, and he led me inside Grace Church.

It was the very best of Gothic Revival—vertical, strait, austere, with no stick or stone of empty rhetoric. Henry Holiday's

Pre-Raphaelite windows washed the nave in a cool twilit glow, as soothing as a cold compress. "This is loveliness," Davitt said.

The fat girl at the altar said, "God is."

The other fat girl said, "Aren't we all?"

The spot was hallowed in Barnumania. Here, on February 10, 1863, General Tom Thumb was wed at last to his Lavinia Warren. Grace Church was then less than twenty years from consecration, but already it had surpassed Trinity in chic. "The First Temple of Christ Our Lord in Knickerbocker Society," a gossip columnist called it. Washington Square lay just to the south, Gramercy Park was sprouting to the north. Within a square mile, the whole of New York's richest and finest were gathered, and Tom Thumb's wedding had brought them all running.

This was Barnum's shining hour. So far he had made money, news, sensation. Now he made the Social Register. Two thousand guests were invited, and more than five thousand showed up. Among them were four state governors, thirteen army generals, untold rabbles of mayors and millionaires. President and Mrs. Lincoln sent a gift of Chinese firescreens, and seats were scalped at sixty dollars per pew. "I know not what better I could have done," Barnum wrote, "had the wedding of a Prince been in contemplation."

Fittingly, Grace Church loomed over the corner of Tenth, Broadway's elbow, where the streetcar bent the corner round. From its steps, you could face both ways at once, be in a straight line from Wall Street and also from Times Square. *"Nel mezzo del cammin di nostra vita,"* said Dr. Davitt. Across the street, a custom-made billiards store preened, its windows rich with mahoganies, gleaming oaks. "I just love dark woods," Davitt said.

In the years of his observation, many superficials had changed. The secondhand bookstores that had dotted Fourth Avenue were gone, and the antique warehouses that recycled salvage now charged three thousand dollars for fake art nouveau Ganymedes. Instead of ninety-eight timepieces, the site of

Korn's Klock Korner now offered twenty-three styles of goat cheese.

"*Yuppies*. Another despicable word," Davitt said. "What was wrong with *Bourgeois Curs?*" On Union Square itself, post-Nouvelle hash-houses and Eurotrash ginmills scarred the sidewalks once sacred to dime-a-dance. In the whole square, you could buy no sliced white bread, only honey-raisin-in-cinnamon rolls, cream-cheese-almond croissants. "What does it make you?" Dr. Davitt said. He lit a fresh cigarette. "Sick," he said.

The thought of an upscaled Fourteenth Street threatened him profoundly. All he asked was to grow old ungracefully, evolve into the style of curmudgeon that made children scream and run away just by smiling. You couldn't do that with a mouth full of kiwi fruit.

But he need not have worried. Beneath the New Age trappings, the square's essence remained as shiftless as ever. High fashion might swank on the piazza, but along Fourteenth Street, the shops looked tacked together with Elmer's Glue, the vendors changed with the seasons. "No tomorrows, let it all hang out, it's now or never," said Tommy Blalock.

"Have some Night Train," Lush Life said.

He didn't, she did. She had been nip-sipping all day, and now it began to show. Nelly Forbush's green eyes were fuzzed; the boater wilted at tilt. "Normal as August, I am as Kansas as blueberry pie," she sang. "Heart too tart for the Fourth of July."

Her nerve was primed, her mind made up. On this afternoon, when trading was done, she would lug Tommy Blalock to the Arlington Hotel, Broadway at Twenty-fifth, where they rented by the hour. In any room with a three or an eight, her birth numbers, she would take her best shot—no holds barred.

Behind the ranks of Bart Simpson T-shirts, on the hoardings by the IRT, theater posters advertised a Bertolt Brecht revival. IN HER MOUTH LINGERS THE TASTE OF ANOTHER MAN, the caption read. But Lush Life swore it was not true. "You are my first," she said.

"And only," said Tommy Blalock.

It was a statement, not a question. Scooping up his T-shirts and army-surplus blanket, his profit and his love all in one formless bundle, he bore them off through traffic. Truck horns blared, Brooklyn voices cursed, but he never broke step. "Tommy Blalock," he said, "could give a fuck."

And Dr. Davitt? "I could. But I don't," he said. In the shadow of George Washington's horse's rump, which blotted out the sun, he hugged his notebook to him like a shield. "A place to disappear in," he said.

Not for too much longer. His mother's health was failing; they were planning to move to Cape Cod. In six months, perhaps a year, he'd be gone, and *News on the Rialto* would be out of time. After eighteen years, he did not regret that it wasn't complete. But he did wish he'd dared to begin. "All of the people sitting. All the bodies, all the lives," he said. "I might have asked."

What he would miss most was the hopelessness, the sense of waste, and the echoes they struck in him. The square, he believed, was a seine for the foredoomed. "Streetsweepers of the soul," he called them. Across the piazza, Calvin Palmer still circled his broom, idly stirring a peck of pigeons. The sight stirred Davitt to pity, an existential rage. "Poor misbegotten bastard," he said. "What chance did he ever have?"

Fourteen half-smoked menthol cigarettes were spread in a neat fan around his feet. Rising now, he picked them up one by one, carried them to a wastebasket. "Time for tea," he said. But before he went, he made a brief recitation. In a voice like a squeaky hinge, he read again from the first page of his life's chronicle: "*Where everything would end,*" he breathed. "*It would be the flower forever. Only everything would not stop growing.*"

He lit a fresh cigarette; he sucked twice. "*Blood in the Blender* was better," he said.

When Dr. Davitt went home to his mother, I went back to

the Hotel Moose. Face down among the marigolds, I tried to read more *Struggles and Triumphs*, but could not concentrate. Even the tale of Madame Josephine Fortune Clofullia, "the most astounding wonder of the nineteenth century," comely, feminine, with a "full-grown beard and whiskers that the most fastidious dandy would be proud to wear," failed to grip. Soon I slept.

When Lush Life woke me, it was two in the morning, and Motion was watering his garden, singing *No Woman No Cry* up and down the corridor. Sugary rank wine ran down my face, in my mouth. I reached out blindly, but Lush Life was not to hand. "Well?" I asked.

"We are one," she said.

with Satan lately?" the quiet voice purred. "You know that he's
waiting your call."

The voice belonged to a man who called himself Smith;
Archie Smith. A warm and beaming presence in a gray business
suit and button-down Brooks Brothers shirt, he was standing
outside the locked silver gates of the Palais de Beauté, a black-
leather briefcase in hand. "Well, have you?" he insisted.

"Why me?"

"You seem darkness friendly," he said.

Chins juddering, fat paw outgrabbing, he looked like an
encyclopedia salesman. And that, to hear him tell it, was just
what he was. "The arcane knowledge of the ancients, the timeless volumes of forbidden lore. The black books," he said. "All
lie within your grasp. Just reach out and claim them, they are
yours."

"No money down?"

"Not a cent." When he smiled, his red cheeks swelled up,
his eyes almost vanished. His resemblance to Porky Pig was
quite remarkable. "The Black Arts are not about lucre. They're
about belief. About trust," Archie said. "About potential for
inner change and growth, and your willingness to explore them."

Opening up his briefcase, he displayed a wide range of

portfolios stuffed with reading matter. Spoiled for choice, I vacillated. "Which would you recommend?" I asked.

"For beginners?" He stroked invisible whiskers, seemed to pick out a pamphlet at random. "*Satan: The Real Deal*," he said. "Not flashy, but a good solid read, full of meat."

"Such as?"

"Just meat." He looked at me a little sideways, like a tailor measuring. "A feast for the hungry mind," he said.

The vagueness was not by choice; just a needed self-defense. When first he'd taken his message to the streets, he had been too open: "I led with my heart, not my head, and I got hurt," he said. He shook his chins at the remembrance. "Some people, you know, they're so prejudiced," he said. "They close their minds, tight like clams, and you just can't get them to open up again. If you try, they turn sarcastic. Even threatening."

"The police?"

"Worse. Far worse." The thought seemed to make him nervous. His cheeks subsided, his eyes reappeared, and this time they did not seem so jovial. "Perhaps I misread your signal. I thought you were a seeker," he said.

"I am."

"Yes. Well, yes." He snatched *Satan: The Real Deal* from my hand, then snapped his briefcase shut. Suddenly, he was twenty yards away. "Where could I find you again?" I shouted out.

For a moment he seemed to waver. His missionary self drew him back towards the potential convert. "Don't worry," he called. But his prudent self was the stronger. "We'll find you," Archie said.

It was a Friday twilight, the streetlamps were just going on. Wall Street was out for the weekend and, minute by minute, the streets were filling with unleashed marketeers, hot for the new night's spoils.

Broadway between Union and Madison squares was their latest amusement park. Five years before, this had been nowhere in particular, a hiatus. It did have a few portentous buildings left over from the days of Ladies Mile, but most of their street levels were given over to wholesale toymen peddling carnival items—false beards and grab bags, whoopee cushions and carnation squirts. Now all that was overthrown. The toymen had been routed, their sites taken over by slicker, more expensive games. There were pool parlors and singles' bars; Manhattan Raceway, a slotcar club; the Palais de Beauté, sacred to transvestites and arbitragers; and there was Cafe Society.

"The room that defines the nineties," its night manager called it. If he was right, we were in for a schizoid ride. On weeknights, it was a tango palace. When you walked by its wraparound windows, you looked in upon a Busby Berkeley set. Floor-to-ceiling columns framed the dancers, superb in formal dress, who dipped and froze, spun and surged cheek-to-cheek. Soft lighting bathed them in pinks; through the windows, the music sounded tinny, a long way distant. The whole charade, self-consciously nostalgic, conjured up music boxes and mechanical ice dancers twirling.

Then came Fridays. The live orchestra was banished, the lights turned electric rainbow. Three chained pedestals were placed inside the windows, and go-go girls placed upon the pedestals. When the music started blasting, it was *Ride on Time* and *The Power*, and two of the girls acted out a lesbian soft-porn routine. The blonde wore blue-denim cutoffs, thigh boots, and a see-through bra; the brunette, spandex and sequins. When the blonde lay down on her back, the brunette crouched low above her, grinding her crotch in her partner's face. Then the brunette lay down beside her; they touched but they did not look.

Macy's window had nothing on this. Inside Cafe Society, the drinkers seemed only amused. But outdoors, shut out by the plate-glass windows, Broadway stopped dead. Police in their patrol cars, taxi drivers in their cabs, a hundred Bourgeois Curs—all stared transfixed. "Disgusting," said one suit.

"Pigs," said another.

"Disgusting pigs," said a third, which seemed to settle things. And all of them stared some more.

When the first two girls, who were paid, had finished their routine, they were replaced by volunteers. Girls alone, girls and girls, girls and boys, they came bumping and strutting, mincing and twitching, black leathers and gold G-strings, bodystockings, scarlet ruffles, satin peek-a-boos. "Have you spoken to Satan lately?" I heard Archie Smith saying, lost somewhere in the crush.

"Sure, I called him up. He was engaged," a woman's voice replied. "The asshole always is."

She stood a little aside, lolling against a streetlamp and dragging on a small cigar. Tall and lean, somewhere in her thirties, she was a woman in black.

First impressions were grim. In studded, black biker's jacket and black dancer's tights, dyed black hair, bitten black fingernails, she looked like a Juliette Greco left too long in the oven. But she wore no shades, and her stare was direct, unstyled. "A drink wouldn't hurt," she said.

At the Old Town Tavern, she ordered a double orange juice, but she must have left her money in her other jacket and now she felt just awful, she truly did. The go-go girls had upset her. So had Satan's salesman. "I hope he rots in hell," she said.

"So does he."

"I suppose." But she was not appeased. She worked just round the corner, quality checking for a Japanese stuffed-panda importer, and these Real Dealers were getting her down. "If it was only one, I wouldn't mind. But they're everywhere," she grouched. "All of them dressed the same—business suits, shiny shoes. And all of them called Smith." She wolfed down her OJ, slapped her hand on the bar for another. "*Arcane knowledge of the ancients. Inner change and growth.* Or did you get the one about investment? *Satan's Stock Exchange?*" The rim of her glass was smeared black with lipstick. "The nerve of those guys," she said.

Her name was Sadie; she was a recovering addict. "Smack, coke, booze, ludes, love," she said. Six nights a week, she went to meetings, and on the seventh she watched people in bars get loaded. "Have to do it. Just have to." She swiveled on her barstool, looked me over, as if I'd just sat down. "You ever been to a meeting?" she asked.

"One."

"*Hello, Sadie.*" Her face split in a simper. "*Admit that you are powerless. Admit that a power greater than you can restore you to sanity. Humbly ask Him to remove your shortcomings.*" She shuddered theatrically, flathanded the bar one more time. "Rather Hell than Well," she said.

The voice was rough. So was the skin. But the mouth, even propped up by a cigar, would not stay hard. Laugh lines and pain lines spread from its corners in a force field, like an ordinance survey map, minutely scaled, marked out in iron filings.

Spotting them in the backbar mirror, she went rigid, she stared herself down, Travis Bickles in *Taxi Driver.* "You looking at me?" she said. Ash from her chico fell into her drink, she laughed. "What a maroon," she said.

The Old Town was a day bar; it shut down in the dark. Strolling back to Broadway, Sadie took my arm. Her black nails dug in like talons, gouging the weak flesh inside my elbow. The crowds were still milling outside Cafe Society. Now an olive-skin boy, stripped down to his jock, was being toyed with by a streaked blonde. Bending double to touch her toes, she pushed the crack of her ass up and out, straight into the watchers' faces. But they had seen too much already, they did not even ripple. "Not a sausage. Not one solitary sausage," Sadie said. Away from bright lights, black-leathered and rock and roll skinny, she was a woman who could almost have passed for a girl.

The evening throng overspilled the sidewalks. By Ralph Lauren out of Calvin Klein, they came stepping two by two, the doctors and the lawyers, the brokers and the bondsmen, each bearing their own set of trademarks.

Sadie, who knew all this stuff, rang them up like walking closet-racks. "Omega Speedmasters," she said. "Bossini Challengers. Hermés Silk Twills." In the window of Cafe Society, the blonde knelt before the olive-skin boy, her wet, orange mouth three inches from his crotch, and pantomimed sucking. One fat cop, half-asleep, stepped from his prowl car and started to cross the street. "Yves St. Laurent. Tommy Hilfiger. Yohji Yamamoto," Sadie chanted. The blonde waved to the cop, the cop chewed gum. "Noblia Moonphase Chronographs. Lancôme Exfoliating Gel Scrub." The cop spat out his gum, and the crowd drifted on. The olive-skin boy, eyes shut to show off his fine long lashes, popped a pimple on his butt. "Giorgio Brutini. Ronaldus Shamask," Sadie said. "Ozone Protective Layer."

A few yards down Broadway a Winnebago van pulled up outside Johnny Rockit, disgorging a joblot of transvestites. After midnight, they would be voguing at the Palais de Beauté, safe-sex titillation for the investment counsellors. They were the city's new goddesses.

Among them was Denise Denise, Lush Life's friend. "We came a long way from St. Louis," she said. Five years before, she and most of these other bodies had been hiding out in Harlem, at Andre's on 125th Street. It was New York's oldest gay bar, a safehouse in all troubled times. And those times were troubled indeed. Gay bashing was in open season, and transvestites, *dressers*, its prime targets. Denise Denise had been beaten up four times in one winter: "Not just trashed. Hospital stuff," she said. "Broken ribs, busted teeth. A boot in the throat." So she had holed up inside Andre's. "Just me, my pussy, and five hundred close personal friends." And there, she and her friends together, they had created vogue.

"Defiance, I guess. Or just self-defense," said Denise Denise. In repose, a deep purplish brown, she was tall and stately, austere as a fashion plate. But her voice was a squeal of brakes, tires burning rubber in the third turn at Indy. "Disco throat," she said. "A case of dance or die."

Andre's was not easy to describe; harder yet to explain. "Feets fail me," she said. All those wintry Harlem nights, the wind a witch up and down 125th Street, and the wolfpacks waiting to pounce. And inside Andre's, sanctuary. "Such beautiful boys and girls. Such lovely things," said Denise Denise. "You'd hit your spot, strike your pose, and everything would just go *zwooosh, vzooom*. You had so much time, all the space you'd ever need, it was almost like you were tripping. Of course, some nights you *were* tripping." She hit a Valentino pose, long and languid, a weeping willow. Then she switched to a veiled mystery, after Coco Chanel. "Dance or die," she said. "I danced."

Voguing had spread from Andre's to other clubs, from dressers to the whole Other world. In due course, its moment done, it went out of style. Soon after that, the news had reached Madonna, and she'd turned it into a video. Suddenly, Vogue was a national craze: "All-American as a blow job," said Denise Denise. And dressers were downtown divas.

Georgette and Lyzy, Perfidia, Vanessa the Undresser, Cherry Sunday—not since Harlow and Andy Warhol's Superstars, way back in the late sixties, had TVs been so hot. No fashion show or dance club was copacetic without them, no night crawl complete. "Divinities," said Denise Denise.

Playing Broadway, she struck random poses. Surrounded by Armanis and Gianni Versaces, politely gawking, she twisted herself like a corkscrew, then stood on one leg, a flamingo. "My pussy's frozen," she announced. The strollers slowed. Somebody clapped, someone else called her name. Denise Denise spread herself, splayed and crawly, a crab, and began a vogued rendition of "Cool Water," the fifties Western hit by the Sons of the Pioneers. "*All day I face the barren waste*," she chanted, a halfway Rap, "*in search of torture. Cruel, cruel torture.*"

Through all of this, Sadie had stood off by herself, saying and showing nothing. Now she loomed back to collect me. As if reclaiming a stray mutt, she yanked me by my shoulder, dragged me off down the street. Her hardscrabble face, exposed to direct light, looked old beyond age; the pulse in her throat kept jumping like a trapped bird thrashing blindly. "It happens," she said. She hid herself in a doorway, laid her forehead against the cool stone wall. "You should be home," I said.

"Jesus God," she said, "the dumb male things you say."

"I am a dumb male."

"Dumb, anyway." She started to walk away, stiff-legged. Then she realized she had left her purse, came shuffling back. Another Winnebago pulled in, another truckload of goddesses tumbled out. "Jesus God," said Sadie again. Her black nails went scrabbling in the dark; she fished out a half-smoked cigar. "See you in the morning," she said. Her cheek was soot-smudged from the stone; she brushed my mouth with her own. "Sleep tight," she said.

Next day came up tepid. "Seasonably mild under partly cloudy skies," the weatherman said. But it felt and tasted like last week's bird's-nest soup. Sadie's meeting was somewhere in the West Twenties, where she lived. Afterwards, we kept a date in Madison Square.

This was the most imposing of all Broadway's gardens, felt almost like a park. Before the Civil War, it had been a staging post on the Bloomingale Road, ringed by the country estates of the Empire State elite, and it had never quite shed their imprint. "Privilege, proportion, and a sense of the fitness of things," one nineteenth-century guidebook had said, greasing the landed gentry. A hundred years on, the privileged were Metropolitan Life and Santa's World. Still, the proportions had held up fine. It was the gentry that did not look so well.

Nod Acres was the streetname. Junkies were woodland creatures, automatically drawn to all parks and playgrounds; and Madison Square was both. Its size and depth gave it privacy, its fine trees camouflage: "And then," Sadie said, "there is the southeastern exposure."

"Oh, the arbors! Oh, the bosky dells!" the old guidebook had marveled. And oh, the used hypodermics. Pram-pushing matrons, taking the morning air, now time-shared their benches with smack and crack, angel dust, delaudids, moonrock. From time to time, the law paid a token visit, hauled off a few bodies at random. Then it went away again, and nothing material was changed.

From one angle, this was no great leap. The square had been created expressly to celebrate pleasures; dope was simply pleasure's new form.

To begin with, it had been open grasslands used for hunting, military training, and young bloods' gallops. Downtown fashionables used to ride out in their carriages to shed the city, take their ease over long rustic lunches. But Broadway would not be cast off so lightly; it caught them up over cigars and brandies.

As ever, Phineas T. Barnum led the charge. At Fourth Avenue and Twenty-sixth Street stood Union Depot, the sheds of Commodore Vanderbilt's New York Central and Harlem Railroad. After the Civil War, as the area turned chic, Vanderbilt moved the sleeping trains uptown, and their sheds lay empty. In 1874, Barnum took them over and transformed them into his Great Roman Hippodrome. Seven years later, the Hippodrome became the first Madison Square Garden, presenting the Barnum and London Circus.

Its opening, heralded by a mammoth torchlight parade up Broadway, was the most splendiferous of the showman's whole career: "A half million people, many paying from five to ten dollars for views from windows, stood dazzled by the golden chariots and tableau cars, some drawn by teams of zebras and deer, the barred cages of leopards and hyenas, the glassed wagons of serpents, the 338 horses, 20 elephants, 14 camels, and the 370 costumed circus performers who marched past in review. Then followed General Tom Thumb and Lavinia, the 8-foot

Chinese giant named Chang-Yu Sing, the baby elephant Barnum had once tried to buy from Bailey, the harnessed giraffes, the bareback riders, the wire-rope walkers, the daredevil trapeze artists, the drilling elephants, the Japanese jugglers."

It was Barnum's crowning fantasia; in essence, his last. Afterwards, he spent more and more time with his family and estate in Connecticut, and there in 1891, aged eighty, he expired.

His work was done, and well done. A line of succession—Tony Pastor and Oscar Hammerstein I, Ziegfeld, Frohman, and Ringling—was already rising up behind him. Madison Square was the Garden of Earthly Delights. And Broadway was launched on its Gilded Age.

These period labels were tricky affairs. The Gilded Age, not to be confused with the Golden Era, began obscurely, somewhere in the 1880s, and ended quite distinctly on the night of June 25, 1906, when Harry Thaw shot Stanford White.

White was the Gilded Age's figurehead. It was a period of great wealth and confidence, of aesthetic striving and ostentation, real grandeur and vulgar display, elegance, garishness, and just plain foolishness, and White was all of it in one. He was both artist and city slicker, a gentleman and a player. As an architect, a beaux arts blend of classicism and bombast, he defined and dictated public taste. As a *boulevardier*, he set more private styles.

His energies were volcanic. For twenty years, a massive and rufous presence, six feet two and 240 pounds, with an all-devouring eye, superb moustachios, and a thatch of flaming barbed-wire hair, he seemed to be everywhere at once, at every opera premiere and theatrical gala, every restaurant and regatta and celebrity trial. He built mansions for the Vanderbilts and Astors, the Players Club and the Century, the Mall in Washington, the Lincoln Memorial, most of the Chicago World's Fair, and, to counterbalance so much worldliness, the Church of the Ascension, Madison Square Presbyterian Church, the porticoes of St. Bartholomew's.

Publicly, he reached his apogee with the second Madison Square Garden. In private, his greatest conquest was Evelyn Nesbit. At the end, the two became inextricably mixed.

The Garden came first. By 1890, Barnum having retired, the old Hippodrome site was losing money. New and enlarged quarters were needed, and McKim, Mead & White got the call. For some $4 million, a blocklong Palace of Pleasures arose, with a main amphitheater seating seventeen thousand, two smaller theaters, the city's largest restaurant, an arcade of shops, and a rooftop cabaret, all crowned by a tower modeled after the Giralda Tower of Seville; and, topping that, as a sort of glacé cherry, a nude statue of *Diana*, the work of Augustus Saint-Gaudens, some three hundred feet above the sidewalk.

Old photographs convey the elephantiasis but not the lunatic profusion: "A riot of loggias, niches, girandoles, cartouches, carved flora and fauna, columned belvederes, shielded colonnades," wrote Michael Macdonald Mooney, the best of White's biographers.

The Garden's roof was topped by eight domed cupolas. Sheltered by their Byzantine shade, White could labor by day in his new studio, then climb by night to his theater beneath the stars. From there, seated in solitary state at his private table by the stage, he commanded all of Broadway, as no man before or since.

The world over which he presided was idyllic, entirely unreal. New York in the 1890s, far from gilded, was in general a hell. The millions of immigrants who poured through Ellis Island and filled the Lower East Side endured some of the most abject conditions that viciousness and neglect had ever contrived anywhere. But White's Broadway, not five miles away, might have been on another planet.

From his Garden rooftop, looking north, he saw only incandescence. Electric streetlights had replaced gas, and now the nightly blaze reached clear to Forty-second Street. O. J. Gude, a publicity man, had introduced the phrase *Great White Way* and put up the city's first electrical sign, BUY HOMES ON LONG ISLAND SWEPT BY OCEAN BREEZES, right across the park from the Garden. For block after block, the colored lights flashed and glowed, intertwined, drifted apart, and the carriages paraded, and the dice rolled in Richard Canfield's Casino, and Diamond Jim Brady wolfed down lobsters and champagne in Delmonico's, and the great hotels—the Fifth Avenue, the Hoffman House, the Brunswick, and the Gilsey House—flushed the sidewalks with music, dazzle, the promise of certain magic.

Evelyn Nesbit appeared in 1901. She was then sixteen, a chorine in the hit show *Florodora*, recently arrived on Broadway from Pittsburgh via Philadelphia. She was most exquisite, with heart-shaped face and copper hair flowing to her waist, a delicate Pre-Raphaelite style of beauty ideally suited to the moment. Photographers lined up to pose her as a shepherdess, a water nymph, an Undine with lilies entwined in her hair and two striped tigers painted at her flanks. So she came to the notice of Stanford White, and he fed her champagne in a loft studio on West Twenty-fourth, well away from public gaze. At one end there was a red velvet swing, with green smilax wound around its ropes. White swung her in it, higher and higher, till she could kick her feet through a paper Japanese parasol hung from the ceiling. Later, he dressed her in a yellow satin kimono embroidered with festoons of wisteria, and seduced her in a room filled with mirrors.

Afterwards, when she woke up and started crying, White petted her and kissed her. "Don't. Please don't. It's all over," he said. "Now you belong to me."

There was the whole age, caught in a single encounter. Enshrined as Stanford White's new mistress, Evelyn sat in the red velvet swing stark naked and kicked her feet even higher; posed, in the most famous photograph of the era, as *Tired Butterfly*, curled up in another kimono and sprawled on a polar-bear skin. When her course was run, she moved on and married Harry K. Thaw, a crazy person but heir to $40 million.

The marriage was not a success. Thaw force-fed his wife on uncut cocaine, beat and whipped her at will, but did not cease to resent Stanford White, *the big yellow brute who drugged and wronged her.* At last, on the opening night of *Mamzelle Champagne*, Thaw made his way to the Madison Square Roof Garden and put three bullets between Stanny's eyes.

With White's death, and the death of his time, Madison Square lost its cachet. Already the coming of the Flatiron Building in 1902 had introduced the first smack of vulgar commerce. And vulgar lust with it. The skyscraper's sharp profile and prow-shaped tip had the side effect of whipping up sudden gusts and windflaws liable to upend a maiden's skirt and expose her stockinged ankles. At which revelation, the passing populace would invariably disgrace itself. Talus-crazed, the mob raised such Cain that a special police squad was required to keep it at bay.

Twenty-three Skidoo was the cant phrase then. But nowadays the law did not rate a "Cheese It, the Cops!" When I showed up for my tryst with Sadie, two men were splitting a deck of powder beneath the obelisk to General Worth, smack in the middle of Broadway, while an officer passed, eyes tactfully averted, a few yards away.

The site she'd appointed was Saint-Gaudens' monumental and angel-swathed statue to Admiral David Glasgow Farragut, he of *Damn the torpedoes. Full speed ahead!* "Another dumb male thing to say," Sadie crabbed, but her morning mood was light, almost blithe. She had exchanged her black night uniform for bluejeans and a white T-shirt scrawled with DYING FOR A DRINK. She wore it over a faded blue workshirt, buttoned to the wrists to cover her tracks; and her scrubbed face glowed naked, a too-bright pink, as if she'd made penance with a pumice stone.

"Wanna see something sick?" she asked. She gave me no time to reply. Behind an infants' playground filled with slides and climbing bars, she led me to a blackened tree trunk. Someone had gouged out a hunk of the bole with a blunt knife. The ravaged wood showed jaundice-yellow, carved roughly into a heart, and inside the heart, etched in green ink, were the words *Tired Butterfly*.

"S.O.S.," Sadie said. "Same old shit." She drew me back towards the admiral, sat me down beneath a great oak. Her black nail polish was chipped, beginning to fade, but the nails were newly bitten, her thumbs ripped raw. "This morning I witnessed. Gave evidence," she said. "I never do; I never say a word. But I did today."

"What did you say?"

"The usual." She picked up my hands, inspected my own thumbs. They too were raw. "Passing out. Throwing up in the soup. Waking up in the mornings with someone I never saw," she said. "They like that stuff, they lap it up." She let my hands fall. "But it isn't what I was thinking."

"What were you thinking?"

"Cocks," Sadie said.

Her head hung so close to mine her black hair brushed my cheek. It felt lacquered, as stiff as a bootbrush. "That's what I was thinking," she said. "But you can't say what you think."

"Why not?"

"Everyone else would start."

She had been sober for eighteen months. Before that, she'd been an addict for eighteen years. She had come out of Babylon, Long Island, where her father was a fireman and her mother had taught her that men were gods.

In this world, women existed only to serve and service, keep men satisfied. And Sadie had believed that. Or rather, she had not questioned it. When her turn came, she spread her legs without fuss. It felt good, so she did it often. Too often, her father said, and kicked her out of the firehouse, one hot August morning, right after her period hit. He called her a whore, a *roundheels*, in front of everyone, the fire chief and all. Sadie, Sarah Johanna then, was bleeding and she had no tampons, the blood was leaking out of her, she could feel it ooze, and her father kept on yelling, and she just could not move. *Slut*, he called her. *Tramp*. She was wearing white hot pants, it was that time, and she was standing by one of the firetrucks, shiny red just like the picturebooks. She put her hand flat against the paintwork, to get support, she guessed, and her father went bug-eyed, he screamed as if she'd told him she was pregnant and the Pope was the lucky man. *Get your hand off that goddamn truck*, he screamed. *We keep those goddamn trucks clean.* So she snatched her hand away, the red paint was misted, damp from her sweat, and she felt her blood come down. *Clean*, her father was screaming. *We keep our firetrucks clean.* And Sadie looked down, her white hot pants were all blood. Everybody could see. The fire chief and everybody. *Chippy*, her father called her. *Go pull a train*, her father said.

She moved into the city; she came to Broadway. She lived up and down the boulevard, in TriBeCa, on the Upper West Side, in Washington Heights, and the train she pulled was rock and roll. Just hanging out, getting high a lot, shacking up with a lot of musicians, serving them and servicing, keeping them satisfied, like her mother always told her. She was a waitress, she kept bar, she worked in a used-clothing store, she sold a few drugs and turned a few tricks, nothing heavy, just to stay housed and high. And ten years went by, the way that ten years do. "A decennium," Sadie said. And she was still hanging out on Broadway, *a Broadway baby*; she had two rooms on Eighty-fourth, crummy rooms really, a sewer, but her sewer. And this one day, it was fall, she was tripping on mescaline. She was with three guys; they were screwing on the floor. That's where she always slept, it kept her ear close to the ground. "Ho Ho," Sadie said. And her and these three guys, they were all everywhere, bodies tangled and twisted, it looked to her like a train-wreck. And then it just stopped. She looked down herself, and there were these three cocks, and Sadie thought *Ohmygod*, she thought. *Sweet suffering Jesus*. Because they looked just ludicrous. These dicks, pricks, joysticks. These mighty swords. *How quite bizarre*, she thought. *Three pickles left out in the rain*.

It was not the cocks' fault. They did their best. But their nature was absurd. *Little bits of sticks, if you didn't laugh you could cry*, Sadie thought. And yet the fuss they caused. Her whole life, it seemed, had been spent soothing them. For what? A few minutes' pleasure, a kiss, a pat on the head. *The staff of life*, she thought. *Is that all?*

She spoke in one great rush—it seemed in a single breath—gaining pace in the straightaways, disdaining to break for the turns. But she must have hit a wall. Whatever, she stopped dead. "I forget," she said.

The pulse in her throat was jumping again. She lit one of her cigars, set off towards Broadway, where the Toy Center stood. The pathway was lined with warning signs saying CAUTION: RAT POISON, but an old man in spotted pants and a houndstooth jacket was scrabbling in a rhododendron bush. "The women feed the pigeons. Bread pellets," he explained. "Sometimes the pigeons drop them." His voice, hoarse, indifferent, seemed to calm Sadie down. Breathing deep, she sat down again. "Where was I?" she asked.

"Cocks."

"Oh," said Sadie. "Them."

There wasn't much else to tell. Her lease had run out, so had her twenties, and she'd drifted back to the Island. She got married to a carpenter; it didn't work out. She came back to St. Mark's and took up with a dealer. Heroin, mostly, and a few pills. She got hooked, and the dealer got busted. So then she got another dealer, she stayed stoned for another four years, almost five, but she couldn't remember them, not a lot. And then? Then she stopped.

It was funny the way it went down. All those years that the CIA had sponsored and nurtured drugs. Then one day Washington turns around, just ups and decides that dope isn't nice.

"Just say No." But, of course, it wasn't that simple. When the new word filtered down to the street, there was just chaos. So the same cop that had been Sadie's dealer for years now upped and busted her, threw her ass in jail: "To save his own, I guess. And saved my life on the side."

She was not sorry he had. She was not thrilled to bits, exactly, but she was not complaining. She went to her meetings, and she went to work; she walked down Broadway in the morning and back up Broadway at night. There were no drugs, not much sex, but in the time of AIDS, who was counting? "Not Sadie," she said. Sometimes, like last night, she'd loiter outside Cafe Society or the Palais de Beauté. Dry humps and simulated blow jobs, sex-change goddesses, *Satan: The Real Deal*—she did not feel so deprived. "Bored maybe, but not cheated," she said. "I would not say I pine."

All that she missed was herself. There were moments—how could she express this?—when she thought of another Sadie and really wished she'd met her, maybe even got to know her. "Does that sound sappy?" she asked. "Or only sick?" She hated self-pity; it made her puke. She had just picked the wrong time and place. "Why Broadway? What's it to you?" she asked. She did not wait for an answer. "All I know," she said, "it hates women." She ground out her cigar; she chafed her raw hands. "To death," she said. "Just hates them to death."

I thought of EmCee Marie. I thought of Ellen Fogarty and Enid Gerlin, of Lush Life, of Sadie herself. But she had already rushed on. In some club downtown, in the ladies' room, there was a graffito she could not forget: "*In the country of the castrate, the one-eyed snake is king,*" Sadie said. It gnawed at her, enraged her. "Jesus God," she said. She turned away, then she turned back. In that moment, she had got old again. "Shut up," she said. Her white hand whipped back, black nails poised to scratch and claw. "Just shut the fuck up." The hand fell back. "Why don't you?"

Through the trees came Sasha Zim.

It was his first week out of the hospital; he still wore the badges of honor. One bandage angled rakishly above his left eye, another covered his ear. Otherwise, he looked depressingly fit. "*Vsegda gotovy*. Always ready," he said, clicking heels, and we set off walking again.

The morning's duty was light. Just a quick surge towards Herald Square, through the blocks of the Gilded Age, and a slow fall back to earth. But even that felt too far. The hallowed turf of Delmonico's and the Brunswick Hotel was now a global K-mart, the junkyard of the nations. There was Taiwan crockery, cheap Burmese rugs and Indian jewelry, Japanese home computers, Korean gloves, and Hong Kong everything. There was even a Sasha Handbags. *Trade north of toy belt is widespread as corners of earth that has sent its merchants,* the Soverican read. *But still are reminders of more elegant, if more parochial past.*

Not many. What traces survived of Stanford White's day were fair-to-middling hideous. The Gilsey House, a favorite of Oscar Wilde and Diamond Jim Brady, had recently been refurbished, made over into a beaux arts Liquorice All-Sort. *Perspicacious developers. Juxtapositions of architectural anachronisms,* Sasha droned on. His bandages gave him a pirate look, a man of loot and plunder. *Enduring is comparative word in city that rarely looks back. When even newer money comes along, it builds its own monuments on ruins of old.*

The monuments in question were South of Lebanon Fashions, Dong Jin Trading, Nageena Indo-Pak. Somewhere among them had stood the Hoffman House, its bar inflamed with *Nymphs and Satyrs*, the monumental William Bouguereau nude. There Jubilee Jim Fisk had sheltered from the Hell's Kitchen mobs in the Orange Day riots of 1871. There Maurice Barrymore had brawled with Howard Burros in the Great Blizzard of 1888. Now it sold black awareness T-shirts: *By Any Means Necessary; Knowledge Is the Key.* Sprawling in the doorway, a body-double for Big Daddy Kane was spitting sunflower seeds.

When he saw Sasha's bandaged skull, his upper lip curled. "Whitemeat," he said, "I am not deflowered by your veneer."

It was not a negotiable verdict. Big Daddy spat again, examined his knuckles, and we scuttled down West Twenty-eighth Street, the original Tin Pan Alley and, before that, Satan's Circus.

Deflowered by veneer. In 1900, the currency on Broadway itself had been red velvet and Bouguereau nudes. But just yards away, down the side streets, sex had dealt in a cruder coin. Underneath the Sixth Avenue El, wreathed in gaslight, was the Tenderloin—Satan's Circus—*the grossest guignol of gallimaufry and moral gangrene under God's canopy.*

In the 1880s, deadfalls like the Haymarket and the Cremorne, Dan the Dude's, Paddy the Pig's, and Worth's Museum, where the pickled head of President Garfield's assassin was on permanent display, had been among New York's greatest tourist attractions. The Reverend Talmadge, having cruised here undercover, called down the Lord's burning rain. Satan's Circus, he thundered, was "a Cotopaxi, a Stromboli, a Vesuvius, ready to bury us in ashes deeper than that which overwhelmed Pompeii or Herculaneum." But no plague came, just the wrecker's ball.

It was a tame strip now. Pickled heads and woman's flesh had been replaced by pocket calculators made in Taiwan. Only one small kiss of the past lingered. "No part of Man is not for purchase here," the *Herald* had declared. Sure enough, a discreet door advertised SOUL SALES.

Perhaps it was the fumes of dead vice, perhaps just the exercise. Whatever, Sasha began to flag. When we dropped back to Madison Square, he started fussing for gewgaws and baubles. But all the toymen were either locked up or defunct. Only one House of Fun, a bright-blue playpen called Gordon's, stood open. MASTERS OF MERRIMENT, its sign proclaimed. CANES, GRAB BAGS, LANTERNS, WIGS, BEARDS. "And rude noises, I bet," Sasha said, perking up. "Invisible ink. Rubber spiders for dropping down collars. Red noses lighting up in dark, buttonhole roses pissing mud in eye." He pushed in the door like a born-again Baptist storming Heaven's Gate. "Codpieces. Fright masks. Exploding pies," he cried. "*Yob tvoyu mat!*"

Behind the counter stood a lone salesperson. She was not young, not large, but she did not need to be: Her eye was a lance, a steel-tipped harpoon. One glance at the babbling Zim, and it impaled him as he stood, knee-deep in Mirth and Novelties (Miscellaneous). Gordon's was strictly wholesale, the lady said. Street persons and lunatics, the implication was, need not apply.

Sasha wheedled and cajoled, he blustered, he pleaded. When none of these bore fruit, he asked to see the management: "What is happen to Master of Merriment?" he demanded.

"He got a goiter."

We walked on sadder, slower. At Coffee Shop, a Brazilian rookery full of Scandinavian models and the Monegasque unemployed, Sasha sat down groaning beneath a Day-Glo voodoo goddess. "Novokuz," he said. His *cafe con leche* had the color and consistency of a sperm sample. It matched his mood. "Bad day at Black Rock, worse on White Way," he said. The mugging had dented his bone, but it was his psyche that stung. "Is most hurt my feelings," he said.

How to explain? It just seemed wrong, was all. A case of mistaken identity. Beatings and robbings, street horrors—that was stuff that happened to strangers, outsiders. But Sasha, who so loved Broadway, was surely exempt. "Like marrying Miss America and you go to bridal suite, she's taking off wedding gown, veil, everything, beautiful in mirror like Princess Grace, then she turns round, ta-da, oh brudder, is Madame Brezhnev." He shoveled sugar in his cup, four spoons. "Is breaking spell." He added a fifth. "Giving pause," he said, "for concern."

At the very least, it was a watershed. He had given up his taxi—"Once shy, twice bitten"—and was mulling his future. In his hospital ward, the next bed had been occupied by a part-time magician, a senior citizen called Max Gambon, who'd worked forty years in a bank but now performed at parties and weddings, bar mitzvahs. He'd shown Sasha a few easy moves, and Sasha had been entranced. Maybe that was a sign. The Great Zim. It had a ring. Or maybe not.

Sugar and froth overflowed the cup, started drooling across our table. At this, Sasha spread his hands palms up, as if divining a bad omen. Hastily rising, he scattered loose change like witches' salt, strong to unjinx hexes, and drew me back towards fresh air. "Too careful to be," he said. "You can't."

On Broadway, the scenes of last night's roisterings were now blindfold, shut up tight. Postcoital melancholia hung on the street like bad breath, a sour seed. *Cruel, cruel torture. In the country of the castrate, the one-eyed snake is king. Tired Butterfly. Mamzelle Champagne.* "What of you are thinking?" Sasha asked.

"Cocks," I said.

From an upstairs rehearsal room, an old woman's voice drifted down, halfway between speech and song, to the tune of "Kerry Dance." "Time goes on, and the happy years are dead," it said. The phrasing was hesitant, infinitely weary. "Oh, for one of those nights of madness," it sighed. "Oh, to think of it. Oh, to dream of it." The voice cracked, trailed off, tried again. "Dream of it. Dream of it." There was silence. Then the voice rose again. "Oh, to dream of it." A beat. "Fills my heart. My heart." Another. "It fills my heart with tears."

Outside the Hotel Martinique, corner of Broadway and Thirty-second, a woman screamed. Across the street, something large and heavy was hurled into a newsstand. A young white man stumbled out blindly into traffic, blood running from a head wound, dripping through his fingers onto his Keith Haring CRACK IS WHACK T-shirt. Then a pack of black youths came wilding through Herald Square in hooded tracksuits, and a Greek pushcart was overturned. Souvlaki kebabs and cans of soda scattered every whichway. The black youths began to pound on car roofs and windows. A rock smashed into a taxi windshield. Inside, Bert Randolph Sugar chewed wetly on a Black Watch cigar. "Would Tyson have beaten Ali? Not a chance," he said.

"A lucky punch?" I hazarded.

"Forget it," said Bert. "Ali would have been too fast, too ringwise. He'd have boxed Tyson dizzy, drawn his sting, then put him away around the eighth, maybe sooner."

A few yards ahead, a black child with a shaven skull lay half on the curb, half in the gutter. His left leg was drawn up and twisted beneath him, and he was mouthing words that we could not make out. When another rock came flying, Bert paid off the taxi, stepped out on the sidewalk. He wore a chocolate-brown fedora, brim furled, with a wide black band. Beneath it, his cigar hung soggy, obscene. "Joe Louis, of course," he said. "Now that's a different matter."

Inside O'Reilly's Pub, it was Happy Hour.

Bert's office—a table, a well-worn banquette, a picture of the Killarney Lakes—was in a side room, where Irish sausages and mash were served. Here he laid down his burden, a heavy satchel filled with Xeroxed articles on Bert Randolph Sugar, and he picked up a double Cutty Sark. "Gentlemen, start your engines," he said. So the long voyage began.

He was a famous man. His own publicity called him the Guru of Sports, and he had published some fifty books, among them *100 Years of Boxing, Baseball's 50 Greatest Games, Hit the Sign and Win a Free Suit of Clothes from Harry Finklestein, The Life and Times of Harry Houdini, The Horseplayer's Guide to Winning Systems*, and *The Baseball Trivia Book to End All Baseball Trivia Books, Promise!* Above all, he had edited *Ring*, the Bible of Boxing. Under his aegis, it had been a model of everything that fight magazines should be and never were—fast, funny, devoutly disrespectful. So he had been fired: "Dismissed," he said, "with obloquy, ignominy, opprobrium."

For some years thereafter, his fortunes had stood at low tide. He'd kept himself afloat by churning out trivia books and dealing sports memorabilia; he had plotted lawsuits; he had dreamed of his return. In those mean times, O'Reilly's had been his Elba, this table his safe harbor. "They carried me longer than my mother," he said. Now the first of his lawsuits had been heard and won, and he was back on high. He was editor and publisher of *Boxing Illustrated*; he starred on cable TV. He even paid his bar tabs.

It was much to celebrate, and celebrations were what Bert was best at. A large, wet man, his face all mouth and bloodshot eyes, he was possessed of very great hungers, even greater thirsts, and his acts were scaled to match. When he sang, he caterwauled; when he danced, he dervished. And when he laughed, which was virtually nonstop, he would unleash a Godzilla roar, a widemouthed juddering blast that ripped through brick walls and plate-glass windows, drowned all that stood in its path. At its coming, strong men dove for cover, else they were mowed down in a machine-gun hail of spittle, cigar ash, used whiskey.

On this night at O'Reilly's, however, the killer laugh was stilled. Instead, holding up a frayed patch of newsprint, Bert mopped himself with the red foulard kerchief that he always wore plumed in his breast pocket. Cursing, he spat out pellets of chewed cigar like dead mosquitoes, his big mouth screwed tight with disgust. "This is the saddest story," he said.

"What story?"

"They're closing the Harmony."

I knew the place of old. Formerly the Melody, upstairs on Broadway at Forty-eighth, it was the last of the old-style burlesque clubs, where the girls still had dimples and tassels, "The Stripper" was the one true anthem forever, and the darkness was warm, all-embracing. "Would a pilgrimage be in order?" I asked.

"Nah," said Bert. "Let's just go see the old dump."

Sentimental journeys were his stock in trade. Sometime back in the fifties, when still an undergraduate, he'd been let loose on Broadway for just one night. That night had ended with him and Jerry Lewis, arm in arm, tap dancing down the Great White Way, the *Stem.* They'd followed the white traffic lines all the way from the Winter Garden to Forty-second Street, past the Latin Quarter, past Lindy's and Dempsey's, the Paramount and the Capitol and the Palace, the *Times* Tower Ribbon, Bond's with its lingerie Amazons, the Automat and Schrafft's Spanish Garden, the Astor Hotel and its roof garden, the Orpheum and Honeymoon Lane, Siegmund Klein's Internationally Famous Gymnasium, the Paddock Bar and Grill, the Tango Palace and the Brass Rail, the shooting galleries and penny arcades, the dime-a-dance ballrooms, the tattoo parlors, the magic shops, the orange stands and the pineapple stands, and the movie billboards much larger than any life, *I Was a Teenage Werewolf,* *The Incredible Shrinking Man, East of Eden, And God Created Woman*, and Douglas Leigh's Camels sign, its eight-foot mouth blowing smoke ring after perfect smoke ring, and the Pepsi-Cola sign with the electric waterfall, and the golden peanuts raining down, and the Budweiser Clydesdales prancing, and the neon hands waving and neon feet dancing and neon mouths roaring, kissing, chomping, laughing, the whole crazed tumult and incandescence, the hundred million lightbulbs flashing, the hucksters and panhandlers, the hipsters and tipsters, and the women, the women, the women. "So *that's* it," Bert had thought, and he'd been tap dancing ever since.

The greater part of his life's work and passion had been spent in freezing and reproducing that moment. To aid him, he had created a second self: Broadway Bert; the Hat.

Of his first self, Herbert, he spoke but grudgingly. Under interrogation, he would yield up that he'd been raised middle-class in Washington, D.C.; that the Randolphs were a first family of Virginia and the Sugars, the *Kukars*, Hungarian peddlers of pots and pans; that his grandfather had been a Southern merchant baron; and that he himself had once studied law. He had even done time on Madison Avenue. But none of this had signified. At the age of eight, he'd heard a radio thriller starring a tough-guy sleuth named Bert and had changed his name by law, forging his mother's permission. He was not designed to walk straight, he'd always known that. The only question was where and when he would go askew. "Broadway," he said. "The name of the cankered rose."

For years the two selves cohabited. Herbert earned his living, got married and sired a son, and in time moved upstate to Chappaqua, a suburb east of the Hudson; Bert took over after dark. But a time came when off-hours weren't enough. He wanted to wear a hat. He knew that all the great writers—Damon Runyon, Walter Winchell, Jimmy Cannon, even the young Red Smith—wore hats. The composing rooms at their newspapers were situated directly above their desks. If their scalps were not covered, printers' ink would drip through the cracks in the ceilings and spill into their eyes, blinding them to proper syntax. Or so he had heard. So he quit his job in advertising, took over *Ring*. He bought himself five fedoras for winter, five panamas for summer. Only then, he began to write.

It suited him. On his own admission, he was not built for stamina, so that his work ran strongest in wind sprints. But the best of his leads were deathless: "The first time I saw machismo die a little came when, as a kid seated in front row of the old Savoy Theatre in Washington, D.C., I saw John Wayne kiss a girl instead of his horse. The second time came when Roberto Duran told the whole world to *kiss off* in the eighth round of his fight with Sugar Ray Leonard." Or again, "It was as unbelievable as Santa Claus suffering from vertigo, as Captain Bligh dying from sea sickness, as Mary having a little lamb. . . ."

First and always, the key was celebration; pure blood pleasure. To Bert, Broadway remained the Great White Way forever, its fascinations infinite, its lures unfailing. He loved its ratty sidewalks and its poisoned air, its decomposing temples, its crypts and cenotaphs, its epics, its monstrosities, its farces. He loved its denizens, he loved its stories, and he loved its lines, the more bewhiskered the better. First and last, he loved the word itself: "Broadway," he said. "If you have to ask, I can't tell you."

It was a split life. Up in Chappaqua, so live witnesses claimed, Herbert Sugar was a modest man, of shy and retiring habit, his bald head covered with freckles and his laugh dry as burned toast. With his hats safely locked in the trunk of his car, he did not even drink much. His wife owned a flower shop; his son was in college. On Sundays, the family attended Episcopalian service. Afterwards, Herbert dozed in his den, stretched out in his La-Z-Boy, or read an improving book. At dusk, he tended his garden.

Come the dawn, however, he would rise up singing and

drive on three wheels to the station, dressing and shaving as he went. Unleashing the hat du jour from its captivity, he'd angle it low above his left eye, pat its dimple and smooth its brow, furl it once, furl it twice, then give it one last tug for luck and, bounding up the station stairway two steps at a time, hit any carriage that would have him. Before the train doors were even shut, a deck of cards would appear in his left hand, a silvered hip-flask in his right. "My deal, I believe," said the Hat.

So he Broadwayed. Up and down the Rialto, from saloon to saloon, from gymnasium to coffee stand to walk-up office to naked street corner, he did his rounds, told his tales. Half the citizens bowed at his passing, the other half ducked. Either way, his passage was ceremonial, a one-man parade.

Now we journeyed towards the Harmony.

When we left O'Reilly's, it was getting dark of an April evening and a light rain fell. Outside the Hotel Martinique, all was quiet except for a few stray lawmen idly rounding up the usual suspects.

The Martinique itself was a bastardized Loire chateau, topped with mansard roofs and bottomed with a fast-food joint. Originally, it had been a Broadway showpiece, a *swankery*, much favored by military brass on leave. More recently, it had been a welfare hotel. Now it was between incarnations, stood unoccupied. Security guards hung glumly in the lobby. A dumpster filled with plaster and broken glass blocked the door. "Used to be a ballroom upstairs. A fine romance," Bert said. "First dose of clap I ever caught."

He pulled me indoors. "Just follow the Hat," he said. At the top of a crescent stairway, there was indeed a ballroom, but the way in was barred by rubble. Behind it lurked a man with a toy gun. "You can't come in. You can't," he said. "You can't come in."

"Wasn't a great dose. Average at best," said Bert. "Still, it was the first—you never forget your first."

The man was neatly made, perfumed. He wore the remnants

of a brown suit, double-breasted with wide lapels and a high pinch waist. His yellow hair was waved and oily, and he had the whitest false teeth. "This isn't my job. I don't have to do this," he said. The toy gun shook in his hand. He looked on the verge of tears. "I told them. It isn't my job," he said. "I told them that."

"Laura, her name was," said Bert. "Good field, no hit."

We went back down the stairway. Waves of perfume, simultaneously saccharine and carrion, pursued us. When we touched bottom, the security guards were playing cards, three-card monte for pennies, on top of a dead TV. At the top of the stairs, the neat man still stood amid the rubble, watching us watching him. "Her brother was a featherweight," said Bert. "Couldn't fight worth a damn."

Out in the street, the rain had hardened, we loitered in the doorway of J. J. Hats. Its windows were riotous with Stetsons and Borsalinos, porkpies, derbies and deerstalkers, slouches and wide-awakes, and, of course, wide-brimmed fedoras, stingy-brim panamas. Bert Sugar lit a fresh Black Watch. His face beneath the furled hatbrim was swollen, fat with glee. "Don't you just hate cheap perfume?" he said.

For the first few blocks, headed uptown, we trod water. Herald Square had once been the heart of all things showbiz. This, not Times Square, had been the original Great White Way. Tin Pan Alley was just below it, the Metropolitan Opera House, *that yellow-brick brewery*, just above. Great newspapers, the *Herald* and Horace Greeley's *Tribune*, stared each other down across the square; Macy's rose monumental to the west; while straight ahead, stretching all the way to Times Square, was an unbroken line of theaters and hotels, mauve cafés and scarlet saloons, perpetually at dazzle in this night that outshone any sun.

The names alone made a psalmody: Frohman's Empire and Browne's Chop House, the Hotels Albany, Continental, and Knickerbocker, the Weber and Field's Music Hall, Daly's and

Garrick's, Palmer's and Miner's, sky-gouging electrical signs for Budweiser and Edison Phono, the Kid McCoy Saloon, the original Real McCoy, and gaudiest, most fantastical of all, *The Fiery Chariot Race in New York*, a construct of twenty thousand light-bulbs, so artfully disposed that the pre-neon chariots seemed actually to circle, the horses to gallop, the dust and sand to fly.

Among the theaters, the palm went to the Moorish-turreted Casino, at the southeast corner of Thirty-ninth. There, on November 12, 1900, *Florodora* had opened, featuring the Florodora Sextette, and made Broadway BROADWAY, a synonym for the stage.

According to Allen Churchill's *The Great White Way*, the fuss was all about one "brief scene built around a gentle tune called *Tell Me, Pretty Maiden*. To the first easy strains of this, six girls trip from one side of the Casino stage. Each is identical in height and weight, attired in matching black ostrich-plume hats and frilly pink walking costumes, with parasols gracefully over shoulders. Simultaneously, six exceedingly handsome young men in gray frock coats and gray top hats saunter from the other side of the stage. Politely doffing silk toppers, the young gentlemen melodically inquire, *Tell me, pretty maiden, are there any more at home like you?* In charming unison, the six pretty maidens chorus back, *There are a few, kind sir, and pretty girls and proper, too.*"

Hardly a hanging matter, one might think. But there was yet more to come. At the end of their number, the maidens smiled and exited. As they did so, they winked. And this—the wink—drove the audience to delirium. The Sextette was hauled back for an encore, then a second, then a dozen more. Within the hour, they had become the most famous and desirable sirens in New York: "They are goddesses," one critic wrote, "the first of their class to immortalize the chorus girl."

That was just the beginning. The maidens married millionaires, and so did their replacements. Some of the millionaires wore titles, others Wall Street ermine. Stanford White attended forty performances running. Diamond Jim Brady had a minor stroke. So Broadway's Golden Era was launched.

The dogs had long since barked, the caravan moved on. Long before the Great War, the theater district had relocated uptown, and its old neighborhood became the Garment Center.

By the 1940s, only the Met remained. After dark, when the garment factories had shut down, it offered a lone splash of light in the wilderness. Stage props lined the outer walls, there being no space to store them within, and arriving operagoers would find themselves plunged directly from their taxis into a Spanish bullring, Prince Igor's court, a garret in old Montmartre.

Now the yellow-brick brewery was long gone as well and, with it, the last vestige of romance. By day the side streets teemed, not with Egyptian eunuchs and Spanish *zingari*, but with sweated pushboys hauling handtrucks full of frocks and frillies. And even these were being driven westwards, defeated by rocketing Broadway rents.

The Bridal Building, stuffed with an estimated hundred thousand wedding gowns, was an heroic exception. Increasingly, its splendors were being despoiled by dross and gimcrackery. Still, the building remained Lush Life's especial favorite: "Paradise at cost."

Marriage was much on her mind these days. Tommy Blalock had not popped the question yet, *not in so many words*. But he spent much time in reminiscence, mooning over his mother and sisters and all his old friends, who were married now, who had family and home: "I can read the signs. The handwriting on the wall," said Lush Life.

"And what does it say?"

"Hot diggity dog," she said.

At her behest, I'd sought out a man named Fred Silver, who ran JoElle Bridals and was revered inside the industry as one of the last classicists. His gowns, floor-length with ten-foot trains, had been superb. When he fluttered them and spread them wide, they soared and spun like great white birds, tumbled against the light. But he was not happy. True beauty came expensive, and these days people would not pay. They preferred cheap gewgaws, Hispanic razzle-dazzle, all sequins and plunging necklines. That way, if they got stood up at the altar, they could go directly to the disco without having to go home and change.

Even white was on the outs. In this age of trash, a wedding day was no longer sacrosanct. More than likely, after all, it was merely the first of several. So why not save time and trouble, buy something in pink or baby blue, more amenable to reruns?

"A marriage mart, that's all we have today," Fred Silver said. He was a lovely man, as courteous and melancholic as the sacristan of a desecrated shrine. But he was glad that he was not young, just starting out. "Who wants to be a used-bride salesman?" he asked.

In this bone orchard, Bert's laughter rose up fanfaring, a trumpet involuntary. "It's better to be a good liver than have one," he said. "All horseplayers die broke. Don't look back, something might be gaining. Barely a man is now alive who paid the mortgage at three to five. It's not over till the fat lady sings."

Where the Met had stood, there was a bust of Golda Meir and some blow-ups of French-cut bikinis. Reeling out of the shadows, a drunk flew in our faces. He was singing *Send in the Clowns*: "Which reminds me," said Bert.

The saloon he chose was a McAnn's, deep, dark, and anonymous, with a steam-table reek of corned beef and cabbage so rank that our mouths clogged with grease by osmosis. The Irish bartender's face was full of nose or, more properly, of bandages, tape, and safety pins where a nose should have been. "I got bit by an owl," he said.

We did not ask.

Down along the bar was a grinning, hard-muscled man bursting out of a Black Sabbath T-shirt. "The Hat!" he cried. "It's Charlie. Charlie DeVoe."

Of an instant, Bert was transmogrified. His face went slack and passive, his mouth sagged half-open, his shoulders hunched in remembered defeat, and he was Terry Malloy in *On the Waterfront*. "Charlie," he mumbled. "It wasn't him, Charlie. It was you. Remember that night in the Garden? You came down to my dressing room and said, 'Kid, this ain't your night. We're goin' for the price on Wilson?' You remember that? 'This ain't your night.' My night—I coulda taken Wilson apart. So what happens? He gets the title shot outdoors in the ballpark, and what do I get? A one-way ticket to Palookaville."

At the first words, Charlie DeVoe took on the hurt, avid look of a golden retriever that senses it's being teased but can't think how or why. His grin wilted, froze; he started to back off. But Bert pursued him, his flat whine more deadly than any shouted abuse. "You was my brother, Charlie," he said. "You shoulda looked out for me a little bit. You shoulda taken care of me just a little bit, so I wouldn't have to take them dives for the short-end money."

"I had some bets down on you," the bartender provided, not looking up from his pouring. "You saw some money."

"You don't understand. I coulda had class. I coulda been a contender," Bert ran on, relentless. "Instead of being a bum, which is what I am, let's face it."

He drained his Cutty Sark. Spent, he stared down his own reflection in the backbar mirror: "It was you, Charlie," he said.

Back on the street, we turned our faces uptown, plunged on into the weather. "Who's Charlie DeVoe?" I enquired.

"Never saw him before in my life," said Bert.

So we came to the Deuce.

Since I'd moved into the Hotel Moose, this had become my corner store. Daily use had begun to blur it, dull its edge. But now I stood on Amen Corner, outside the La Primadora Quality smokeshop, and saw it all again for the first time: the hookers in hot pants and lacquered wigs; the bodybuilders and midnight cowboys; the tattooed sailors in leathers; the evangelists with their bullhorns and sandwich boards; the butches, the bitches, the faggots, the femmes; the teenage runaways, and the children standing, staring; the movie marquees pimping *Brain Damage* and *Genital Hospital, Slave Girls from Beyond Infinity* and *Creepozoids* and *Blood Sucking Freaks*; and the men in plastic raincoats, and the men with brown paper bags; the hooded tracksuits, the combat boots and fatigues; the Polaroid photographers, two shots a buck; the three-card monte hustlers; the Mantan All-Americans, the Vampirellas, the Sons of Satan; and Bert.

Close behind my left ear, he quoted Washington Irving, recalling this same vista: "A sweet rural valley, beautiful with many bright flowers, refreshed by many a pure streamlet, and enlivened here and there by a delectable Dutch cottage, sheltered under some sloping hill and almost buried in embowering trees."

A fat lady sang hallelujah. She wore white and she must have weighed three hundred pounds, the rich brown meat jumping on her bare arms, the sweat jumping hot off her forehead at each stomping of her big left foot, each shake of her tambourine. "Jesus loves you," she roared. "Why don't you love Him?"

Her name was Sister Pearl; she had worked this corner for years. The first time I'd seen her, ten years before, she had waxed so ecstatic that she choked on her tongue and all her words got garbled, lost. But lack of coherence had not fazed her. "What's the use in making sense?" she'd told me afterwards. "Far better just to burn. Fan the flame or the fire will die. Then the Lord spews you forth from His mouth."

These were words that had bitten deep. When her preachment was done and she took a break, leaning up against the subway rail, I asked her if she still lived by them. "Middling," said Sister Pearl, and she gave a quick birdlike nod, oddly finicky in one so monumental. "Sometime the flame burn up more fiercer than ever. Only sometime it don't." But that did not break her faith. "I do not weep and moan," she said. "I study God's Grace and contemplate the soaps."

Across the street, Bert was visiting with Lenny Schneider, the Fighting Newsboy. Lenny had been a journeyman welterweight in the forties, and when he retired, he'd taken over this newsstand, Manhattan's most esoteric. It not only stocked the out-of-town papers but *Novoye Russkoye Slovo* and *El Diario La Prensa* and *Il Corriere Della Sera*, the *Haiti Observateur* and the *Gaelic American, Riskarbitrage Monitor* and *Conscience Weekly*, as well as Flash Gordon's boxing newsletter, racing tips, dream books: "You want what to read, we got it," said Lenny. "Or else it's coming, it's coming."

A sturdy soul with no neck or nonsense, he was the last link with an older Forty-second Street: "When the people here was still human beings. Most of them, anyway."

Bizarrely, this block had once bespoken *tone*, civic pride. When the original *Times* Tower went up in 1904, the *Times*'s editor, Charles Miller, had made a dedication speech that I'd long treasured: "The shadow of these walls, with the coming and departing suns, shall fall upon uncounted myriads of men, whose tread shall echo round them, whose eyes shall become wonted to their harmonious proportions, and whose voices shall swell the note and hum of the busy city through generation after generation until where we now stand a gray and time-stained pile shall stir the passer-by to reverie by its venerable and historic interest."

That was the stuff. Inside ten years, however, the *Times* had moved out and sex moved in. Flo Ziegfeld brought his Follies to the New Amsterdam, and soon the whole block was filled with pleasure palaces—George M. Cohan's Candler, the Eltinge, the Liberty and the Lyric, the Victory and the Apollo. Some featured vaudeville, others musical comedy. But showgirls were the staple, and the Deuce had been peddling flesh ever since.

The New Amsterdam still stood, long since converted into a movie palace, a few yards from Lenny's newsstand. At the same time that I'd first met Sister Pearl, I had spent a night there. The experience had not been forgotten.

The movie had been *Looking for Mr. Goodbar*. It was a slow night; I was idle. So I paid my money and entered, and I found myself plunged into an epic madness.

The New Amsterdam had fallen on scuffling times by then; the decor was much scarred, and so was the clientele. But the magnificence was indestructible. There were massive carved-bronze elevators; sculpted stone frescoes of scenes from Shakespeare and Wagner; green marble stairways, soaring to the empyrean; floors of patterned marble; nymphs, satyrs, wizards, elves; walls gilded or bronzed; a granite fireplace the size of a small house. Every inch of available space, it seemed, had been embellished, in some way transmuted. Door handles turned into centaurs, and light holders became Egyptian goddesses. Junkies slumped on baronial thrones.

I went upstairs and sat in the balcony. Discarded hot dogs, cigarettes, and sodas formed a swamp underfoot. Somewhere far above me, I could just discern a vast vaulted ceiling. But the aisles were rank and claustrophobic, and I sat down right at the back, where I could feel solid wall against my back.

Mr. Goodbar was almost over. For reasons which escaped me, everyone on the screen kept screeching and yelling. I took refuge in the bathroom.

When I returned, my seat had been usurped. In the darkness, it was impossible to make out the intruder in any detail, but I sensed something female, white. Too spineless to argue, I took the seat adjacent and dragged my attention back to the screen. A hand touched my knee, paused for a moment, then started to climb my thigh, very soft. It disturbed my concentration, so I moved away. Shortly afterward, the film ran out.

The lights went up; I looked along the row. Sure enough, my neighbor had been female, white. From this distance, she looked about forty, small and well dressed, essentially demure.

She wore white gloves, and she looked straight ahead, as if I no longer existed. She seemed to be waiting.

All around her were men at jive. But she did not move, and she did not seem to notice. After a few moments, a large white person appeared at her side. He was tall and muscular, and he wore a dark uniform, complete with peaked cap, like a chauffeur. Reaching out his right arm, he placed it behind the woman's back. Then, without the smallest sign of effort, he lifted her up, cradled in the crook of his elbow. Her head lay against his shoulder, and he carried her away.

She had no legs.

In the years intervening, the place had fallen yet further. It had been a porno and kung-fu house; had even been reduced to snuff films, live footage of live deaths. Currently it stood empty: "Excepting the ghosts," Lenny said.

He meant this literally. According to derelicts who'd slept there, the shade of one of Ziegfeld's showgirls, identified as Olive Thomas, was in the habit of floating down from the vaulted ceiling onto the deserted stage, where she stood silently watchful, as if waiting for the evening's curtain to rise.

None of this was the Hat's speed. He was not easy unless laughing, safely walled behind his one-liners. Under fire from legless ladies and long-dead ingenues, he spat out the dead stub of his Black Watch, sought refuge in Lenny's stock. "It's *déjà vu* all over again," he said, neck-deep in *Jugs*. "He can run but he can't hide. Kill the body and the head will die. All life is six to five against. Never play cards with a man called Doc."

After Olive Thomas and her Follies had come burlesque. By the thirties, all the showgirls had turned to strippers, *ecdysiasts*, and Forty-second Street was a midway, another Coney Island. Apart from the skin palaces, there were shooting galleries, penny arcades, freak shows. They reached their apotheosis in Hubert's Museum and Flea Circus.

It opened in 1920, west of the New Amsterdam, and for the next five decades, it defined the whole territory. At street level, it was merely a glorified romper room, packed with pinball machines and Wild West gunslinger games, Jap-zapper torpedoes, and Hidden Secrets of Sex displays, shipped direct from the Academy of Medicine, Paris, France. But the real wonders lived in the basement. There you could witness Sealo, the boy amphibian; and Estelline, the three-hundred-pound sword swallower; and Congo, the jungle witch doctor. There Grover Cleveland Alexander, the great baseball pitcher, gave lectures on his career. So did Jack Johnson, *Li'l Arthur*, the first black heavyweight champ. Tiny Tim appeared as the Human Canary; Princess Wago and her Pet Pythons competed with Madame Catalina of the Sixteen Serpents. But the greatest show of all, which ran for thirty years, was Professor Roy Heckler and his educated fleas: the Sensational Siphonapterae.

The Hat remembered it well. The Deuce of his first explorations had been a world of bearded ladies and belly dancers, midget wrestlers, two-headed calves and mule-headed boys, mermaids, gorilla girls, a thousand tassel-twirlers. It was a labyrinth, a sexual Arabian Nights. "You didn't walk it, you got lost in it," Bert said. "If you got lucky, you were not found again."

But now the word was *hard core*, and no secrets were left unexposed, no mysteries whatever. Inside the Sex Shoppe, next door to *Love Slaves Tortured to Blood Dripping Death*, there was a multicolor portrait, many times lifesize, of Superslit, the World's Smartest Pussy. Hand-tinted, it looked as gaudy as sunset in the Painted Desert, as bottomless as the Grand Canyon. According to the Lebanese in charge, it had also been trained to perform party tricks: "See for yourselfs, gentlemens. With your own eyes and ears behold." By his father's beard, it could smoke cigarettes, swallow golf balls and putt them out, even suck in banknotes and make the correct change. "But will it fetch your slippers?" Bert asked.

"How much you wanna pay?"

We stumbled back onto Broadway. The theater crowds were

converging, and the sidewalks were jammed solid. Pinned against the entrance to the Geraldo Rivera show, we looked up at the neon, Coca-Cola and Casio and Citizen Quartz, Toshiba and Minolta, Movieland, the Mardi Gras; and the giant billboards, Mamma Leone's and Solid Gold, *A Chorus Line, Cats*, and the monstrous hand dipping into the jar above Nathan's; and the news squibs flashing, the arcades, the movie signs, the liquor ads, the whole of Times Square ablaze, and all of it had changed, changed utterly, and nothing had changed, never would.

Dazzled, we floated with the tide, let ourselves be punted uptown. "The social ramble ain't restful," said Bert. "In the big inning, God created heaven and earth. He had larceny in his heart but his feet were honest. He might step on your shoes but he don't mess up your shine. Cadillacs are down at the end of the bat. The graveyards are full of irreplaceable people. Even Napoleon met his Watergate."

Between Forty-third and Forty-fourth, the Paramount Building still flaunted its fourteen setbacks and glass globe on top. But its great theater, where the young Sinatra had sung and the bobby-soxers swooned, was destroyed. It was either here or someplace else, said Bert, that *Snow White* had premiered. To publicize the opening, seven dwarfs were flown in from Hollywood and installed, fully costumed, above the neon. They had a long afternoon to pass there, and nothing to do but play cards, so they smuggled up a few fifths of rye concealed in their padded stomachs. The rye proved good, the afternoon humid, the costumes stiflingly hot. When the world's press and the TV crews arrived, they found the dwarfs mother-naked and incontinent, showering the crowds with abuse, empty bottles, and much, much more: "Which reminds me," said the Hat.

On the lip of Seventh Avenue, we ducked into the Metropole. It used to be a shrine to jazz; now it had gone topless. Inside a deserted ballroom, there was a bar as long as a bowling lane, and a strawberry blonde danced on its top in a G-string and glitterdust scarlet pumps, snapping gum, her green eyes fixed on infinity.

"Long, lissome, luciferous," Bert murmured. It was a phrase from Colonel Stingo, beloved of A. J. Liebling. Six feet two, the girl must have been, all legs and no breasts, and she was flexible as raw rubber. When her stint was done and she came down amongst us, she said that she was from Texas. Her name was Katy Freeway.

The Hat and I had comprised her entire audience. With a small frown, she copped a stool between us and called for water, Jack Daniel's back. "You guys writers?" she asked. "Or is it something I ate?"

She was in supreme condition, a racehorse on the muscle. Across her bone-white stomach ran a scar like a pink slashmark, and it flexed and flurried with every sleekit motion. A tangerine wrap was slung loosely across her shoulders. Through one of its cigarette burns, her left nipple flirted with the tip of Bert's cigar. "Jack Dempsey, I loved that man," he said. "He used to sit out in the window of his restaurant, right there on Times Square, with the George M. Cohan statue in front of him and the great James Montgomery Flagg oil painting of him getting knocked clean out of the ring by Luis Firpo behind, 1923, the wildest heavyweight brawl in history, and he must have signed a million autographs and posed for a million pictures—he was on display his entire life, every minute, but never once did I see him lose his poise, his *presence*, not once. Oh, he was just marvellous." Bert rescued his cigar, contemplated its pulped and sopping remains with a dreamy, if raddled, eye, and he raised his glass. "The Champeen," he said.

"Tuna melt," said Katy Freeway.

"You spoke?"

"That was the something I ate."

We had another round, then another. As the Cutty Sarks worked the body, Bert cast off the liquid laugh, waxed analytic. "What I love. No, let's just make that what I enjoy the hell out of," he said, "I get to play. At my time of life, I am still licensed to exceed and carouse, throw my toys around the sandbox."

I remembered Ellen Fogarty's childhood billboard, the one at South Ferry that had read DON'T GROW OLD—GROW UP. But Bert Randolph Sugar, he spit on that sign. "On Broadway, you don't *have* to grow up," he said. "That's its whole secret and beauty."

"Men will be boys," said Katy Freeway.

"They'll never take me alive."

Back on the street, it was raining again. As we crossed Times Square towards the Harmony, Bert paused at Jack Dempsey Corner. Where the restaurant had been, there was now a coffee shop, a Chinese fast-food joint, and a porno house. "The Manassa Mauler," said the Hat, and there on the street corner, in the slashing wind and spittle, he quoted himself verbatim. *He was the picture of the warrior,* he declaimed. *Approaching his opponent with his teeth bared, bobbing and weaving to make his swarthy head with the perpetual five o'clock shadow harder to hit, his black eyes flashing and his blue-black hair flying, Dempsey took on the look of an avenging angel of death.*

When was Life not Life? When it was More. At the threshold of the Harmony, we wavered just a moment, then plunged in blind, hard up a long, steep flight of stairs to a small wooden kiosk. Behind the ticket window sat a wizened body ancient beyond calculation. It had no teeth, no expression, no visible means of support. "Wingbing Toth Arbody, Appyomo Bollocks," it said. "Zattleby Zenbugs."

"Ten bucks?"

"Maky Thive. Andavan Arbodyus Nye."

The big room had fallen on stony times. The place we'd cherished had been darkling and musky, a superior style of womb. What we found this night, however, was stygian gloom and the sick-sweet reek of Roach Motel.

The Harmony's proud claim had always been that it offered

burlesque *legit*, meaning cheesecake rather than gynecology. In a debased age, when its rivals featured acts like Pregnant Polly, the Enema Queen, and Tina Toilet Tonsils, it alone had stayed faithful to All-American womanhood.

"Petals of Pulchritude," the vintage skinzines had called them. "Torrid Temptresses of Tease and Terpsichore." And in the flush times, they had been nothing less. But those times were clearly past. Presently at toil on the runway was a red-haired lady of a certain age. We did not catch her name, but "Black and Blue" was her theme song. It matched her varicose veins.

At the close of her act, she toured the audience. It was a sparse crowd and those few punters that were still breathing, dimly visible through the murk, were widely scattered. To these, the old lady offered up her sex, to be touched or kissed at choice, according to tariff.

As she passed close and creaking above us, her middle fingers disappeared. When they emerged, she licked them clean, then blew us kisses off their tips. The neat man at the Hotel Martinique had favored the selfsame perfume.

Across the lobby was the manager's office. A lean and olive Italian named Robert Anthony Francis Roedere—Bob Anthony—answered my knock. At first he did not wish to speak with me, but then I mentioned Bert Sugar. "The Hat," said Anthony. "Bert Random Slobber. Of course."

He was just recently out of the hospital. Business was down, he said, and so was he. But he had had a prodigious ride. He had been a singer, a bandleader, a Broadway personage. More, he had grown up in Hoboken with Frank Sinatra—they'd been childhood chums. "The Chairman," he said. "I owe him all I got, everything I am today. I used to be his secretary and his driver, belt out guys for him and everything."

It was Sinatra who'd got him his first job as a singer, in 1944, when he got out of the navy. "I worked with the best, believe me. Get a load of the names. Ida Ray Hutton's All-Male Band,

Eddie Duchin, Bob Chester. And I'm still working to this day. I play Las Vegas. I even got a record out. *Angela.* My biggest hit."

As for the Harmony, he did not say that it was terminal, only that it was going through a quiet phase and that Broadway rents were obscene. "This town, I tell ya, when they gave it away to the realtors, they handed us our heads on a golden fuckin' platter," he said. "A golden fuckin' platter."

"It isn't politics," said Bert. "It's just who you know."

"Legit businessmen, tried and proven operators, we don't got a look-in. This ratrace, I tell ya, it's a fuckin' ratrace."

Still, there were consolations. From a desk drawer, he fished out a form letter. It came from the White House, was signed by Ronald and Nancy Reagan. In part, it read: "Our heartfelt thanks for your friendship and support. With your help and prayers, we can reach our goals and demonstrate that America's best days are yet to come. God bless you—and God bless America."

A miniature Stars and Stripes fluttered from the top of a filing cabinet. Reverentially, Bob Anthony refolded the letter, replaced it in its drawer. "You get a tribute like that," he said, "you know you haven't served in vain."

The theaters were just disgorging; the night beginning its next shift. Crossing Broadway, Bert essayed a few tentative tap steps on the white lines, but his forehead was clammy, his gills distinctly green. "My stomach disputes me," he said.

"Avoid fried foods, which angry up the blood," I answered him. "Avoid running at all times."

"I am wishing I'm never born."

The answer sat waiting on the farther shore, in the shape of a health-drink stand. For many years it had traded as Orange Julius. Under new management, it had lately turned into Orange Morris. "So give me an orange something, whatever," Bert said.

"Orange no got," came the grim reply.

Papayas they had. A grisly concoction was slid across the

counter, yellowed and frothing, a liquid lead balloon. Nothing loath, Bert downed it at one swallow. For some seconds, he stood smacking his lips, a man reborn. Then lightly, politely, he sank to his knees. "Just follow the Hat," he said. And he slept.

Interval

IN DONEGAL, the summer that I was nine, Broadway was the ha-ha where the twins took off their clothes and danced. Their names were Sarah and Serena; they were almost thirteen. They were *artistes*, they said.

I saw them first at the lily pond, fishing for tiddlers with a tea-sieve and a pencil box. Their mother had dressed them in matching whites—white organdie blouses, cream boaters with faded rose ribbon, long white tulle dresses—but their cropped hair was black and their flesh a deep earth brown. To go wading, they'd tucked their dresses high about their hips, and the dark limbs that slithered below made me think of night creatures, furtive, sly.

What was I doing there, spying? It was my right. During the term I lived and schooled across the border, but my holidays I spent in the Free State. Buried in the hills above Lough Swilly lay the carcass of an Edwardian estate. My family rented the gatehouse.

The estate had not always been tumbledown. Between the world wars there had been fancy-dress balls in the big house, garden parties on the lawns. There were three brothers then, goodly stout men who lived to shoot duck and fish salmon, each waiting to inherit from their crippled mother.

Came a beautiful stranger, name of Stella, to steal and break their hearts in turn. By the time she was through, so was the inheritance. Now one of the brothers was dead, and the others were old men, skimbleshank ruins, but their mother, past ninety, remained. The big house creaked and echoed; the gardens were deserted. Beyond lay wilderness.

This wilderness was mine. Spread over a thousand acres, there were birch woods and larch woods and pine woods, moors of heather and gorse, purple-headed mountains and unfished tarns, mile upon mile of lost avenues. If I roamed free from dawn till nightfall, and I did, I could not cover all my lands.

The ha-ha was my headquarters. Sometime back in the age of Stella, the eldest brother had had it dug as part of an ornamental garden, a labyrinth of sunken lanes and *trompe l'oeil* bowers, consecrated to his love in all her mysteries. But when that siren played him false, he let the whole affair rot. The walkways and arbors went back to jungle, the grottoes to crumbling rockpiles. Only the ha-ha survived.

It was nothing grandiose, just a brambled grass fosse, some six feet wide by four feet deep. Still, it was the mainstem of my domain; the central artery between the lily pond and the kitchen garden, strategically all-important. Crouched inside its tangles, I commanded a clear view of the big house. Nobody that passed escaped me.

So the twins. In summer, each afternoon sharp at four, high tea was served on the terrace; tea and scones and iced lemonade, wafer-cut cucumber sandwiches. The old lady and her sons sat huddled in their wheelchairs, shivering under mounds of tartan blankets, skulls wagging like dandelion clocks. Minor worthies—the doctor and the dominie, assorted clerics, spinsters, and gentlefolk in distressed circumstances—passed by in half-hourly shifts. But the twins were different class. Their father had been a judge, so they got to stay a whole week.

It was a strange season. Most years, Irish summer meant only that the rain felt warmer down the back of your neck. But now it ran dry; there was heat. In shock, the land went into withdrawal. The fields cracked wide open and the wells failed and no birds sang. Inside the ha-ha, the grass turned to scorched straw and scratched my face where I squatted, too torpid to brush the flies off.

Everything just stopped. Up at the big house the taps coughed up a brownish slime, and there was no ice for the lemonade. Prisoners under siege, the guests clustered round a wind-up gramophone and played the same damn song, over and over: "Begin the Beguine."

The water in the lily pond was tepid, stagnating. Late afternoon, when the twins went in wading, they roiled up clouds of purpling sludge at every step, turned the whole surface thunderous. Fireflies danced attendance. So did armies of midges and gnats. "My titties itch," Sarah said.

"What tits?"

"My twin thrones of desire."

Hidden in the weeds, I did not rightly know what a tit was, still less a desire, only that both were forbidden. A foundered rowboat lay festering in the slushy mud and I crawled towards it on my belly; I crept. The long grass squeaked, a duck flew in my face. Out in midstream, the twins were playing I Spy. "Something beginning with *M*," Serena said.

"Midget," said Sarah, not unkindly, and the twins dragged me out from hiding, splashed me head to toe with warm mud.

They were not identical, not even close. Sarah was longer and lither, more like an otter, while Serena favored a seal. But both were water animals, sleek and slippery, forever secret. "Wet things," I'd heard a housemaid call them. So they were.

They'd come here from Kilmacrenan. It was only a crossroads, a hole in the hills, but crossroads were places of power, always had been. Their father lived in a castle and owned racehorses, their uncle had a wooden leg. A few short years, and the twins would also be stars, "supernovas."

"Blazing meteors."

"The brightest new gems in the showbiz firmament."

At home their bedroom closet was stuffed to overflowing with back copies of *Photoplay* and *Broadway Babies* and *Hollywood Confidential*, and they'd learned the argot by rote. Now it was their native tongue. "How do you do?" I said.

"Enchanté," the twins replied.

They sang, they danced; they entertained. In Kilmacrenan, the priest played ragtime piano, one of the grooms had been a juggler, and their own mother knew how to yodel. Performance ran in their blood and bone. As far back as they could remember, they had known this for their destinies, to tread the boards, to star. "Broadway," they whispered, a mystic and awful conjuration, full of dread, like God. "The Great White Way," they said.

It was the gaudiest sunset. The lily pond, stirred to liquid flame, became a tropic lagoon, and the twins ordered me to punt the ruined rowboat out into its heart. At the dead center we stopped, trapped by the last rays. Water ran in through the cracks, the boat began to fill. "What now?" I asked.

"We sink."

And we did. Like bridesmaids, perfect in repose, the twins sat up straight, kept utterly still, and slowly we went under. At first the pond felt clammy and unclean; alien. But by the time it covered our thighs and our laps, all sense of strangeness was gone. A thick green broth, rich with weeds and darting silver fishes, it sucked me in unresisting, drew me down.

Lulled, I shut my eyes. And when I opened them again, I was underwater. The twins' legs, greenish yellow in the half-light, twined and untwined like streamers. Idly kicking, they danced of their own accord, a slow pagan strutting. I reached out to touch but their flesh slid away, escaped me. I understood that I was drowning. It felt good.

Then somehow I had surfaced. White dresses spread wide, cream boaters just so, the twins sat still upon the waters, stately as two swans.

Afterwards, drying off in the ha-ha, they stripped to their

slips and their skins, and they performed. "Sisters" was the song they sang. They waggled their arms and flirted their eyes, they kicked their brown legs up higher than their shoulders. Then their mother called them in to their suppers, they were gone. I did not see them again.

Three

We all did," said Aggie.

"Had to," said Tess.

"Or else."

They were not twins, just sisters. Aggie Doyle was seventy-seven, Tess seventy-four, and they had come to Broadway from Dublin in 1936. "On a wet Thursday," said Aggie.

"In March," said Tess.

"And dark."

Their first stop had been Times Square. "We had to count the lights," Aggie said. "The last thing before we left home, Father told us we were free to go and show all our legs in the pit of Sodom if that was our notion of duty, only please to remember, pert misses, that we went with his eternal curse on our heads, and if by chance, in the giddy round of fleshly pleasure, we paused long enough to remember those we left behind, perhaps we'd spare an instant to look up and count the lights."

"Because there was," said Tess.

"A broken heart."

"For every light."

"On Broadway."

They never were good at sums. Before they'd even reached

a hundred, they had gotten hopelessly muddled. "So we shared a hot dog instead," Aggie said.

"With mustard and sweet relish."

"But no kraut." Aggie folded white hands in her lap, drooped her eyes in girlish submission. "Father hated the Germans," she said.

His power had not withered with time. Half a century on, perched like schoolgirls on the high stools of Nathan's Famous, the sisters slavered their lunch with such heaping mounds of onion and yellow mustard, ketchup and sickly green relish, that the hot dog itself was buried without trace. But not one strand of sour cabbage ever soiled their bright-painted lips. "Respect," Aggie said. Ladylike, she dabbed her chin and powdered cheeks with a lace handkerchief, then she reached for the Tums. "Filial obedience," she said. "You can't beat it; you can't lick it."

She was sturdy, firmly anchored, while Tess twitched and flittered. But it was Aggie who poeticized, Tess who shot to kill. No matter, they were troupers both: "The Emerald Doyles," Aggie said. *"A Song, a Sigh."*

"And a Saucy Smile."

It was not the act that they themselves had intended. In Dublin, growing up in the Liberties, the hillside slum between the Christ Church Cathedral and the Guinness Brewery, they'd hungered for elegance, artistic distinction. The name of Doyle had seemed unworthy: "Too suggestive of gross endeavor," Aggie said.

"Sweat and navvies, she means," said Tess. So they had called themselves Les Sylphides, gone in for water ballet. But the three McManus girls—they lived just up the street—had them beat. The janitor at the Glasnevin swimming pool was Caithleen's fancy man; he let them practice in chlorine for free, while Aggie and Tess, just because they were virgins, must do their splits and entrechats in Dublin Bay: "January to December," Aggie said, "in the slimy green dawn, in the naked salt sea."

"And us," said Tess, "with no mother living."

So they had come to America. They had traveled to Times Square, and its glitz had hooked them forever. When they got through counting the lights, they became the Vesuvio Sisters, hot stuff from old Napoli; ZiZi and ZaZou, those Frilly Fillies from Chantilly; at last, the Emerald Doyles. Vaudeville was already in its death-throes. That left burlesque: "Ten shows a day, six days a week, three hundred dollars a month, and all the free gum you could chew," said Aggie, "showing everything God gave you."

"Or didn't," said Tess.

They were not built to play New York. Back in the Liberties, they had pictured themselves on the Keith-Albee or Orpheum circuits, nestled among true *artistes.* "We thought to rise on winsomeness and grace, inner beauty," said Aggie, "but all that sold was the big bazooms."

"Udders. Dugs," said Tess.

"Water wings."

"And artistry my Aunt Fanny."

The Doyles, however they sang and danced, were more the willowy type. "Creatures of mist," said Aggie, "of gauze and gossamer."

"Flat as pancakes, she means," said Tess. And that, in turn, had meant Kalamazoo. For seven years, until Pearl Harbor, they'd toured the outback, living out of one shared suitcase. "Chickasha, Waxahachie, Kosciusko, Palmyra, North Platte," Aggie intoned, singsong as a railroad conductor. "Las Animas, Laredo, Jerk, Chatahoochee, Chincoteague, Eufaula, Cut 'n Shoot, Anaconda, Xenia, Uvalde, Alamogordo, Snowflake, Big Timber, Thermopolis, Calipatria, Calexico, McMinnville, Effingham, Crystal City, Tallulah, El Dorado, Eureka Springs."

"And Butte," said Tess.

When the war came, it left them stranded in Gallup, New Mexico, with forty-two dollars and a Claddagh ring. They made their way to Phoenix, went to work in the factories, *Rosie the*

Riveter and partner. It was the first time they'd stopped still since childhood. Within six months, they were both married; by D-Day, both divorced. Aggie had two sons, Tess a baby daughter, and they came East in the back of a lumber truck, direct from Durango, Colorado, to the Father Duffy statue, Times Square.

When the truck set them down, it was late of an August night. The whole square was one solid mass of sweating flesh, parading and exulting, just showing off. The moment the sisters touched ground, two GIs swept them up, started dancing them in circles. "What happened? Did your horse come in?" Aggie asked. "Our horse, damn right," her soldier shouted back. He looked about fifteen. "Our horse came in at last," he yelled, and then he yelled a lot more, only Aggie couldn't pick up the words, the noise of the crowd drowned them out. So the soldier stopped shouting, just hugged her and whirled her around. Above their heads, the *Times*'s ticker tape was spooling, an unbroken ribbon of News. AXEMAN SLAYS THREE, it read. JAPAN SURRENDERS. The soldier fed Aggie Four Roses whiskey. SINATRA TO GO HOLLYWOOD. He kissed her lips. VICTORY, the ticker tape read. TAX HIKE IN WORKS.

The Claddagh ring was long lost, but they had saved five hundred dollars, almost six. It was enough to stake them in a rooming house: "Liberties Hall," Aggie said, "catering to the Profession."

Off-Broadway, in those years, was full of such retreats. With vaudeville deceased and burlesque on life-support, the whole West Side overflowed with workless performers: "Acts at Rest," as Aggie called them. Their home housed tattooed ladies in distress, illustrated men, blackface minstrels, talking dogs, and midgets that had had their day.

All of this made for convivial company, but not much rent. The Doyles, who stipulated "No Ethiopians, No Houris," went broke inside a year. Escaping north to Inwood, an Irish conclave off Upper Broadway, they took a sweetshop and *poste restante* beneath a bookie's office, and there at last they stuck.

Now retired, they were left with few wants, only one complaint. "Time weighs," Aggie said, and she quoted Emerson's Journals: "The days come and go like muffled and veiled figures sent from a distant friendly party, but they say nothing, and if we do not use the gifts they bring, they carry them as silently away." Wiping the last ketchup from her whiskers, she gazed mournfully at its stain in her lace handkerchief, like Camille reviewing her poisoned lifeblood. "We find ourselves languid, inert," she sighed.

"Bored spitless, she means," said Tess.

That's what had brought them downtown. Whenever the sweets of idleness grew too glutinous to stomach, they'd ride the Broadway Local, renew their struggles and triumphs. The lights might now be Japanese, the burlesque houses reduced to porn palaces, and Liberties Hall was a parking lot. Still, Times Square itself did not dim. "Baghdad on the Subway," O. Henry had called it. To the sisters Doyle, though, it was not so exotic by half. "Just our old neighborhood," said Tess. "The place."

"Where we."

"Come from."

Their visits were off-hand, unstructured. Sometimes they'd take in a second-run movie on the Deuce, sometimes sip Shirley Temples in the Marriott Marquis Skybar, and sometimes they'd just walk: "It does not import," Aggie said. "The air alone rejuvenates, revivifies."

"Stirs up the old tripes."

"The Pause That Refreshes."

"Great gas."

Back in Inwood, their lace-curtain neighbors shrieked in affected horror. To hear them squawk, you'd think a day-trip downtown was suicide guaranteed—"the hara-kiri or the kamikaze," said Tess. "One of them dead yellow things, anyway."

But the sisters were not troubled. No bad behavior or gutter language could touch them. To them, Times Square remained inviolate, eternally stuck at August 14, 1945: "Not the best place," said Aggie.

"The only place," said Tess.

From underneath her long woollen skirts, a pair of well-scuffed sneakers peeked, green and orange with Mercury wings. Now outdoors, shaking off the air-conditioned stagnance of Nathan's Famous, she breathed in deep, filled her lungs with fumes and May Day heat, the sweet aching filth of Times Square: "You want to know the secret?" she asked, and when she received no answer, she told it anyway. "Don't stop," said Tess.

"Whatever you do," said Aggie.

"Just don't stop."

Around the corner and up the stairs, inside the Times Square Boxing Club, Emile Griffith laughed with his mouth wide open, his big jaw flashing gold. He was a man in middle age, short and stocky, in a knitted woollen cap. "Who stopped?" he squealed. "I discontinued, was all."

Even that had come bitter hard. By the time he retired from the ring, in 1977, he had fought pro for twenty years, won and lost five world titles, waged over a hundred bouts and headlined more cards at Madison Square Garden "than any other man living, dead, or not."

As welterweight and middle, he had been *the* New York fighter of his time: "The last of the hometown heroes," Bert Sugar said, "from the age when the Garden was still the center of fistic creation, not an outskirt of Atlantic City."

When Emile Griffith turned pro, the Garden had meant Sugar Ray Robinson and Willie Pep, Rocky Graziano and Jake La Motta; by the time he quit, it meant Pedro Soto, Edwin Viruet, Diabolito Valdez. "The place turned into a microwave," Bert said. "Just take the flesh of one couldabeena contender, fatten it up on tomato cans, then shove it under the ringlights, ınt Pumpkin, served horizontal, on a bed of ripe

e survived the curse. As welterweight and middle, the most ballyhooed of warriors, nor the flashiest ᴏʀ ʜ...)sive, just the slickest, the most enduring, and Bert's prose still purpled at his name: "In his prime," wrote the Hat, "he was a Y-shaped youngster with a pinch waist and shoulders big enough to support water buckets, with a sparkling style of fighting to match the sparkle that danced and played in his dark eyes."

"My biggest fight?" Emile said now. "The most famous was Benny Paret. The third time." He laughed again, his eyes young in an aged face. "Right there," he said, "in the Garden."

It was not a fight that a man forgot. Griffith had come from St. Thomas, Benny "Kid" Paret from Cuba. Between them lay mutual loathing: "He never liked," said Emile, shrugging. "I didn't like even more."

All of the epic ring rivalries were in some degree a rematch of Ariel/Caliban; the clash of elemental opposites. So with Griffith/Paret. The Kid was a gladiator, battle-hardened and austere, but Emile was a laughing boy. He worshipped his mother, his own body, and the power of mockery. Before he turned fighter, he had worked as a milliner, designed picture hats. And he approached the ring in the same spirit, as a mortal game, terminal but not serious. When Hurricane Carter once knocked him kicking, over and out in the first round, he welcomed the press to his dressing room, not with tears or alibis, but with a brisk chorus of *Merry Christmas*.

For Paret, that was blasphemy. A dark and brooding man of primitive gods, he spoke little English, did not say much in any language. His whole expression was in fighting. Fast and flashy, a natural mover, his style held a mirror to Griffith's own. Their three battles were all flair and movement, swift hands and swifter reactions. Griffith won the first, Paret the second; the third, for Paret's welterweight title, arrived on.

By that time, Paret's hatred of Griffith had come to him. He was a warrior; he followed a warrior's code. Griffith, by clowning, dishonored that code. He had no dignity, no sense of *gravitas*. When he should have glared, he only giggled, a girlish squeal that flayed Paret, pursued him everywhere, in the gym, at press conferences, down the echoing Garden corridors to his dressing room, till he could stand no more and snapped. *"Maricón,"* he said. "You faggot."

He only wanted Griffith to stop laughing. And he succeeded. In the night, when they met in the ring, Emile did not crack one smile. He was knocked down early, took a beating. But, late in the twelfth round, he trapped Kid Paret in a corner and would not let him out. Normally, his right hand was for ornament. Now it turned into a jackhammer. Like John Henry driving steel, he drove Paret down in wedges. With his back jammed tight against the ringpost, the Kid could not duck or turn away, could not even fall. Perhaps a dozen, perhaps twenty blows blackjacked him. He tried to collapse, but the turnbuckle held him up. So the blows kept raining, and Paret kept sinking beneath them. His face did not change, showed no fear or pain, nothing, but he slowly slid down the ropes. At last he sank to his haunches. "He was dead when he hit the floor," Bert Sugar said. But it took him ten days to expire.

Griffith did not say much. In the ring, when the fight was done, he just looked dazed. And afterwards, in his dressing room, he did not care to discuss the thing. "He took a gamble. He lost," Emile said. He pouted, he ducked his head. "Sometimes I get too excited," he said.

Twenty-seven years on, he did not often think of that fight. The only reason he recalled it now was that some researcher was here from a Stuttgart TV station and kept on dredging it up. A glum and bespectacled sort, heavy on the literal, the German's name was Horst, and his questions filled three foolscap sheets on a legal pad. "What it was? When Kid Paret he died?" he enquired. "What was your exact feeling?"

" 'When do I get paid?' " said Emile.

The Times Square Boxing Club was a long, narrow chamber above a cut-price tuxedo store. It had used to be a movie studio specializing in X-rated loops. Stag classics like *Porker's Delight* and *Anal Dwarf* had been created in this stark space. Now it sheltered the hard core of New York fistiana.

Floor to ceiling, right behind the ring, there was a massive plate-glass window, thickly smeared with the grime of years, and at its foot, ranged in a row like a hung jury, sat managers and trainers, ex-fighters, cut men, shills. In season, they warmed their haunches on the hissing radiators, or they soaked up what pinched sunlight seeped through the blanketing murk. They watched, they watched, and then they watched. Sometimes Jimmy Glenn, who owned the gym, would do the rounds, collecting gym fees. Like pigeons disturbed, the watchers would go through the motions of rising and dispersing. Then they'd settle back, untouched, and watch some more.

It was an august and hushed gathering. No ritual on earth was more solemn than the schooling of prizefighters, and the Times Square was the Game at its most austere. The walls were papered with posters of champion alumni—Duran and Tyson, Boom Boom Mancini, Edwin Rosario, Rocky Lockridge. Beneath their blinkless gaze, present hopefuls skipped rope and worked the speedbags, shadowboxed, sparred. The shuffle of their feet and the slap of gloves, the hissing and grunting of breath, were the only sounds allowed. From the window, the old men watched, shook their heads. Only Emile Griffith made noise. His high girl's voice careened off the boards and canvas and the smeared glass like a trapped bird, and he laughed and laughed. "My feeling? Exact?" he cried. "*When do I get paid?*" he said.

The Y-shaped youth of the Kid Paret fights had been replaced by a pleasant plumptitude, its torso swathed in a patched sweater, bald pate concealed by a woollen cap. Pulled low, the cap cut off the face an inch above the eyebrows; from beneath, the sweater's rolled neck devoured both throat and jowls. All that had survived, it seemed, were teeth and a bright pink tongue.

The teeth flashed white and gold; the pink tongue darted. The eyes, still bright, tried dazzling. But Horst from Stuttgart was not to be distracted. "And afterward?" he demanded.

"After what?"

"When you have been paid?"

"I fought Ralph Dupas."

Dupas, said Emile, *and Denny Moyer*. He paused a moment in mid-giggle, cast back his mind. *Denny Moyer*, he said. *Tacoma. Won ten. Scrappy kinda fight.* He scratched an itch on his nose. *Denny Moyer*, he said. *And Jose Stable, and Don Fullmer*. With each name, he picked up a little speed, a bit more certainty, like a rusted caboose, long idled, getting shunted into service again. *Don Fullmer, right*, he said. *Jorge Fernandez and Manny Gonzalez. And Luis Rodriguez.* He rolled his shoulders, threw a feint. *Rodriguez three times.* He balled his right fist. *Tough bastard*, he said. *One tough mother son.* Between his Caribbean singsong and the giggling, it was not easy to keep pace. Names and places got tangled up, came out fractured. With each remembrance, the tempo increased, the lurch and piston-shudder. Soon the words and thoughts flew by in a wild blur, too fast to track. And the names. So many names. *Dick Tiger.* A warrior. *And Nino Benvenuti. And Gypsy Joe Harris and Indian Red Lopez. And Stan Kitten Hayward.* Slick, slick. *Mantequilla Napoles.* Smooth like butter. *And Willie The Worm Monroe.* Slippery like dogshit. *Carlos Monzon twice, and Vito Antufermo. Caveman Lee.* After the night with Paret, there were fifteen more years and eighty more fights, twenty-three in the Garden. *Good nights. Big nights*, Emile said. *Whole lotta big nights.* In Hamilton and New Orleans, in San Juan and St. Thomas and Saratoga

Springs. *Holley Mims, won ten. A good boy*, he said. *Only I was better.* With his sneaky fast left and his flapping right, with his great legs. *Stan Harrington, Honolulu, won ten*, he said. *I put a good whipping in him.* And his mother shrieking like a banshee from the box seats, three hundred pounds of womanhood, in floral hats and feathered hats, Lillie Langtry hats and Carmen Miranda hats. *My mother, she is my sweetheart, I mean my own heart*, he said. And Emile in red satin, Emile in leopardskin, Emile in solid gold, and Emile in virgin white. *Gabe Terronez, Fresno, KO four. Don't remember.* The waist thickening with the years, the muscle-tone dulling, the punches he used to land solid just missing, the punches that used to slip by him just connecting. *Nessim Cohen, Paris, draw ten.* His hair gone, *that was a good friend of mine.* And his legs going too. *My legs*, he said. *My bread and butter. Those were the legs I ate on.* And still he fought on. *Florentino Fernandez, some left hook, you feel you been hit by your own past life.* And still there was that subliminal radar that never quite deserted him, kept pulling his chin back just a millimeter from that final right hand. *Art Hernandez, Sioux Falls, won ten. Tony Licata, lost twelve.* That punch that wouldn't just fell him but kill him. *Jean-Claude Bouttier, lost seven. But that doesn't count.* So he clutched and clinched; he stole points; he flurried. And even when he lost, he entertained. *I was cute*, he said. *I always had the ring smarts.* Right up to the very end. *I was a good show.* On his best night, and his last night. *Alan Minter, London, lost fifteen.* Out on his feet, but still standing. *What you want to say?* he asked. *A fighter's life*, he replied.

Now, in his years of leisure, he did some training, worked a few corners, a little this, bit of that. He tried to teach, pass on his own understanding. But what he knew, he could not put into words. And these young studs today, what the hell, they didn't care to listen. They lacked the patience, the smarts. The ways things were, all that big TV money, two million for this fight, three million for the next, they did not wish to pay the price: "Just flybynights, flibberybibberies," said Emile. "And others."

"So what to do?" Horst asked.

"A man can laugh," said Emile. "Can't he?"

Jimmy Glenn had heard that one before. "It only hurts when I laugh," he said, "and I only laugh when it hurts." But he did not have time for either. When he was not running the gym, he was minding his bar, Jimmy's Corner, on West Forty-fourth. It meant a twenty-hour day: "Make that twenty-one," Jimmy said.

He was another of Bert Sugar's heroes. "If Times Square had a soul, he'd be it," said the Hat.

"Soul don't pay the rent," said Jimmy Glenn.

He was built big as a down lineman, a sleeping bear. Left in peace, he was benign. But it did not do to push him. Under threat, every pound of him hardened. *Don't Mess with Jim,* the message flashed. And no one did.

Still, strength did not buy rest. Every morning he climbed out of bed and into his clothes in his sleep; ate breakfast and caught the subway, read the paper in his sleep. Sleeping, he opened up the gym. Sleeping, he checked the equipment, ran through the accounts, thought about washing the windows. At the fifth cup of coffee, he roused himself sufficiently to throw a few bums out and let a few more in, shoot the shit before it shot him. Sometime in the afternoon, he'd somnambulate the two blocks to Jimmy's Corner. In the back room, he collapsed into a decomposing armchair, allowed himself to drift. Only rest never came. A drunk started shrieking, or a woman began to weep. "Somebody need something," he said. "Somebody always does."

After ten years on this treadmill, his eyes stayed permanently ajar. Great purpled circles like bone bruises surrounded them, giving him the look of a jet-lagged panda. All about him, Times Square seethed and burbled, muggers pounced, psychotics ranted, and sirens screamed, but Jimmy neither saw nor heard: "Do not disturb," he said, "I got my living to earn."

This day, traveling from gym to bar, he was suddenly hit by a whirlpool of hot air. May had blown in on a sirocco. In one night, all trace of spring was expunged.

Sweeping in off the Hudson, a parched wind whipped through Times Square like dragon's breath, bearing trash and loose talk, Lush Life's false eyelashes. Yellowed light backlit the crossroads like a movie set ripped apart by a dustbowl simoom. Everything not nailed down went whizzing past the ears. And with it went all restraints. Under Father Duffy's statue, a gaggle of street urchins lay flat out on their backs, jeering and leering up dresses. Since most ladies hereabouts wore glitter-shorts or microskirts, the gesture was symbolic: "But apropos," said Lush Life, "in the context."

The context was that she was upping sticks. She wore her favorite Debbie Reynolds, *Tammy and the Bachelor*, a frilly confectioner's frock with matching pumps and a pink-veiled toque, and her suitcase sat fat in her hand. Down the street, at Tad's Steaks, Tommy Blalock was waiting with the tickets. Together they were booked, train and bus, all the way through to New Iberia. He was taking her home to meet his mom.

The night before, packing up her trousseau at the Hotel Moose, she had kept playing an old Frank Sinatra record: "Love and marriage, love and marriage," Lush Life sang along, "go together like a horse and carriage."

It made her sad; she did not know why. Long as she could remember, she had yearned for this style of romance. But now that she'd achieved it, all she felt was estrangement: "Like it happened to some person else."

Her suitcase was full of flimsies. The way she had it figured, a honeymoon lasted four nights. So she'd packed four colors of negligees—"White for Ingrid Bergman, black for Cyd Charisse. Scarlet satin for Mamie van Doren. And amber forever"—and four silk teddies. Four wigs, push-up bras, and sets of false eyelashes. And four lace handkerchiefs, for waving hello and good-bye.

In the dark of her room, she laid out her earthly possessions. The clothes she packed, and the rest she left. "Dead letters," she said. "Take your pick."

There were back copies of *Glamour* and *Cosmopolitan*; there were three empty bottles of Night Train. There were Polaroids of Lush Life with Velma, Lush Life with Denise Denise, Lush Life with International Chrysis and Vanessa the Undresser. There was a dog-eared copy of *1001 Diseases*, a burned-out coffee pot, a cardboard box full of Christmas decorations. And a child's doll in a baby-pink ballet dress.

Down the hall, Petros Kassimatis was rhythmically bouncing a guest back and forth off the garden wall. The guest, a small brown man, did not protest, didn't utter a sound. As I passed, Petros paused in mid-bounce. "Unseasonably hot for May," he said, and dropped his guest on the floor. The brown man lay still, his left leg bent back double. "Smells like rain," Petros said. Wearily, he spat against the wall. Yellow spittle, thick with phlegm, clung to the vines. "Hard to say for sure," Petros said.

I had done with *Struggles and Triumphs*. Now I was immersed in *South with Scott*. I had reached the part where Captain Scott's Antarctic Expedition of 1911 arrives at the South Pole only to find that Amundsen, the Norwegian, has beaten them to it. Heartsick, they take a few snapshots and share a can of seal meat, then start on the endless trek back to home base. But the weather worsens; the world is blotted out by blizzards. Captain Titus Oates, most faithful and beloved of Scott's followers, comes down with frostbite. Soon he knows that he must die. He also knows that his prolonged suffering is holding back his comrades. Unless he dies faster, the whole party faces doom. So he rises up from the nightly writing of his journal, and he drags himself to the tent door. Each step is a crucifixion, but he does not flinch. His colleagues regard him in mute dismay, half-starved themselves, too sick to protest or even stir. Outside is eternal night. Quietly, Titus Oates raises the tent flap: "So ask," said Lush Life.

She was dressed as a man.

Or a schoolboy, rather; a tenth grader. She wore a wine-colored blazer with a wine-striped tie, a button-down cream shirt, gray flannels, and lace-up brogues, and instead of glugging Night Train, she was chomping on Juicy Fruit gum.

Scrubbed free of makeup, her face glowed pink and white, an ad for the virtues of milk. "So how do I look?" she asked.

"Very nice," I replied.

"But I'm not."

Hitching up her flannels at the knee, she sat on the edge of my bed, let her legs dangle free. "I'm not a sissy. I'm not," she said.

She never had been. Back in Paterson, in elementary school, a boy called Juan Negron had called Geraldo Cruz that name and worse. "Dollface. Crybaby. Cocksucker," Juan Negron had called him. "Mamma's boy." But Geraldo had changed Juan's mind.

Three blocks down the street from school, between a pizza stand and a pawnshop, there was an alley that led to waste ground. Juan Negron used it for a shortcut home, slid through it every day. So Geraldo waited in a doorway. Around him, there were garbage cans full of pizza trash, puddles thick and black with goop. In one puddle was a busted half-brick. And Juan Negron came walking.

When he passed the doorway, Geraldo felled him with the half-brick. Then he rubbed his face in a black puddle; then he dropped him in a garbage can. Bits of pizza clung to Juan's clothes and face, strands of melted cheese, globs of unbaked dough. He was not unconscious, just stunned. His mouth was stuffed full of anchovies and mushrooms, extra pepperoni, but he did not move. He never made a sound. Not even when Geraldo cut him.

Outdoors, the wind had begun to rise. In the airshaft beyond my window, there were noises of whipping and howling. I tried to return to my book, but the storm sounds kept distracting me. When I looked up, Lush Life was crying.

She did not weep like a woman but a child, a small, bullied boy. She ground her knuckles in her eyes. Snot came from her nose, got mixed with her tears. But she made no move to wipe herself; she only sat and cried.

When the sobbing and snuffling stopped, she turned away, lay down among the marigolds. There was a hole in the sole of her left brogue. "Don't look," she said. Then she turned back again, showed her face of her own accord.

The pink and white was smeared black and gray. The eyes were swollen half-shut; the mouth hung loose and sodden. "Go ahead. Look all you want," Lush Life said. She wiped her nose on her wine-striped tie. She chomped her gum. "You can look," she said. "But you can't see."

But that had been in the night, inside the Hotel Moose. By daylight, windblown in Times Square, she was tremulous, ecstatic. "I left you *Madame Butterfly*, Ladybeard," she cried. Her voice against the dry wind was a siren's wail. "I won't be needing it."

"And *South Pacific?*"

"Goes with me."

As she wiggled across Forty-fourth Street, her hips roller-coasting at each step, a construction worker dropped to his knees before her. Hands clasped and eyes upturned, he cartooned the ardent swain. "One kiss. Just one kiss," he begged. But Lush Life, dimpling, only shook her platinum head. "I am promised," she said, "to another."

A redoubled gust sent her scudding downwind, tossed chaff. Cardboard boxes and aluminum trashcans chased each other down the sidewalks, and streetlights gleamed, malevolent sulfurous eyes, in the middle of the afternoon. HOLD ON TO YOUR SOUL, an evangelist's placard proclaimed, IT IS PERISHABLE GOODS.

So was all Times Square. It had been conceived on the fly, with a frontier-town's haphazardness. After dark, neon masked the joins, washed all flaws in instant glamour. But by daylight it stood stripped, a pasteboard mess, all girders and pitprops, false fronts.

It had been a shantytown always. In the nineteenth century, when it was called Longacre, it was a place of blacksmiths and stables, the center of the harness trade. The corner of Forty-second Street, where La Primadora Quality now stood, was then known as Thieves' Lair. Period pictures show wide unpaved streets like pig wallows, shacks of loose board and kindling, and ragged men in doorways, at watch for the unwary. "So what all changed?" asked Jimmy Glenn. Just the scale, and the choice of weapons.

Easy money had come with the 1890s. Broadway as Rialto was now moving northwards at such a lick that the stretch from Thirty-fourth Street, deserted twenty-five years before, was already wedged solid. Unable to squeeze in below, Oscar Hammerstein I jumped the Deuce. At Forty-fourth Street, he opened the Olympia, three theaters in one plus the Paradise Roof Garden. The rest of the wolfpack followed close at heel.

For the collector of farces, the Olympia's opening in 1895 was a gem. Hammerstein, a portly little party with a Prince Albert frock-coat, a Van Dyke, and a long black cigar, was an inveterate practical joker. Perhaps that was why he opted to launch his dream in late November, with rain and sleetstorms forecast.

At the hour appointed, the five thousand first-nighters began to debouch from their carriages, resplendent in full evening fig. Mysteriously, they found the doors locked, their entry barred. Then the rain began. Soon it was a deluge. Milling around the sidewalk in their top hats and furs, the swells began to panic. "With the strength of a dozen catapults," wrote the *Times*, "they banged at the portals of the new palace of pleasure and sent them flying open." But their travails had only started. The stairwells were choked, impassable; the walls, freshly painted, were not yet dry. So the mob was striped red, yellow, and green. "Never mind. It's only water colors," Oscar Hammerstein said, as they went stampeding over seats, stormed the empty stage. Yvette Guilbert had been announced as the opening attraction but, on the night, she was replaced by marionettes, a female impersonator, and a troupe of one-legged acrobats. Outdoors, as the sleet turned to hail, "puff sleeves wilted and crimped hair became hoydenish in the crush. Trousers were splashed, dresses were torn and still the crowd pushed on." In his private box, Hammerstein drank champagne. Having supped his fill of lobster, he lit up another cigar as the army of five thousand, defeated, "slid through the slush and mud of Longacre back into the ranks of Cosmopolis."

The following day, a pipe-joint burst open in the theater's cellar, killing two and scalding many others. Times Square's debut was complete.

Unamazingly, the Olympia went bankrupt, and Hammerstein with it. But he bounced back in good order. By 1900, he and his son Willie had opened the Victoria, home of the Cherry Sisters. Billed as the worst act in America, the sisters sang and danced behind a proscenium net, to ward off the fruit and veg. Supporting them were, among others, Sarah Bernhardt and Charlie Chaplin, Lillie Langtry, the Marx Brothers and Fannie Brice, Houdini, W. C. Fields and, of course, Armand Kalisz, *He with the Savoir Faire.*

Now the Hammersteins were unstoppable, and so was their neighborhood. For the next two decades, Times Square *was* Broadway, and Broadway seeming paradise. Marian Spitzer, the biographer of the Palace Theatre, wrote an aching description of herself as a small girl taken by her father to see Mary Pickford and Lillian Gish in a Forty-second Street matinee. Afterwards, they had hot chocolate at the Knickerbocker Hotel, where Caruso lived; then they strolled up Broadway through the glimmering dusk: "It was the day before Easter, and cold; fair but cold, and the wind whipped the ladies' skirts way up above the tops of their eight-button shoes. The year was 1913 and no nice girls wore slippers on the street."

The stroll stretched only five blocks, but in that space they passed the *Times* Tower and the Victoria, Shanley's lobster palace and Consodine's Metropole, George M. Cohan's and David Belasco's, and the Paradise Roof Garden. And the Astor Hotel, its sidewalk lined with private carriages; and the Cadillac, where Eugene O'Neill was born; and George Rector's at Forty-third, unmarked save for the illuminated griffin that hung above its doorway: the *famous* Rector's, where Diamond Jim Brady and Lillian Russell dined, and John Drew and the Barrymores, and all the *Florodora* maidens, each reigning beauty in turn posing by the revolving doors, then prancing to her table to the tune of her latest hit.

It was an idyll inspired by Europe; a transplanted dream of *boulevardiers*. The world of Rector's was essentially the world of Maxim's or the Café Royal, a champagne-and-lobster playground in which the blue-blooded, the louche, the financial, and the artistic could wine and twine at random, and there was only one rule that did not exist to be broken: "Appearances must be observed," George Rector dictated, "or else Society founders."

That age had vanished with Prohibition. Once driven underground, Broadway had no more need to keep up fronts. The same peccadilloes that had once been hushed—nude showgirls popping out of birthday cakes at Sherry's, Evelyn Nesbit on her red velvet swing—were now glorified. Far from guilty secrets, excess became a rallying point, a gesture of righteous defiance. Every night that Texas Guinan, Longacre's new avatar, greeted her patrons at El Fay with her trademark cry of "Hello, Suckers," she stuck her tongue in Rector's stately ear. "Appearances? In a pig's eye," she was saying, more or less. "Society went thataway."

In one form or another, the sentiment had been echoing ever since. "What does Times Square mean? The freedom to say 'Fuck You,' " Bert Sugar said now. He considered his dead cigar, chewed idly at its corpse. "It is the American way."

At Jimmy's Corner, he hung on the ropes, most horribly battered, but refused to take a count. May 1 was the date reserved for the Changing of the Hat. Lunch completed at O'Reilly's, Bert stepped outside, ceremoniously removed his winter fedora and gave it to the first passerby in need. Then he crossed Broadway to J. J. Hats and selected a summer panama.

This day his choice had fallen on a creamy wide-brim with a plain black band, brand-name Napoli. Inwardly rejoicing, he wore it outdoors, only to find the street rushing by in headlong panic, put to flight by the sirocco. Before he could get himself planted, a passing lamppost had unseated the new panama, sent it spinning and cavorting down Thirty-third. It had taken Bert three blocks to catch it up. When he did, he wished he hadn't.

The sodden remnant now sat on the bar. Smeared and bleared with toil, a ragged hole punched in its crown, it looked like nothing so much as Judy Garland's stovepipe in *Easter Parade*. "See Naples. See Naples die," Bert said. Pouring him a double, Jimmy Glenn unlocked one owlish eye. "Lampposts," Jimmy said. It was a one-word history of grief.

"A good man," Emile Griffith called Glenn; in boxing, there was no rarer praise. Jimmy's father had been a preacher, and Jimmy had been raised to minister, to tutor and provide. As a young man, he had run an amateur gym in Harlem, pulling gang kids off Lenox Avenue. When the city took his building away, he traveled downtown.

Apart from running the Times Square gym, he trained his own fighters there. Sometimes they had serious talent, the gloss of potential headliners. Then he was their surrogate father. He fed them and clothed them, schooled them, developed them into contenders. Two of them, Howard Davis and Terrence Alli, even fought for world championships. And then they left him. "Happens every time. The same old softshoe shuffle," Jimmy said. "Some wiseguy gets in their ear, promises them the world in a jug. So they walk. Forget where they come from, how they got from there to here. Stop training right, stop listening. Stop every damn thing but playing the fool. So soon they get their clocks cleaned. Then the wiseguys don't know their right names, and they come back crawling. But what could I tell them? *Too late*, is all. *You had your time. Now it's not your time any more.*"

Outrage made his eyelids quiver. They soon subsided, relapsed into their usual bloodhound folds. But the poison remained. "You think betrayal doesn't hurt? Let me tell you," Jimmy said, "it hurts." He had six children from his first marriage, and he'd put all of them through college. His son by his current marriage showed gifts as a cartoonist. Still, the lack of a champion, this sense of unfinished business, would not give him peace. "Giving up," he said, "that's not something that impresses my mind." He had a new kid in hand, John Wesley Meekins, *a good boy*. A junior welterweight, good jab, good work habits. No drugs and no women troubles, no bad company to steer him wrong. "The total package. He's got it all," Jimmy said. Twenty-one and one, sixteen KOs, with a wicked left hook: "And smart. Real smart," Jimmy said. His eyes were closed, his head lolled on his chest. "Can't miss," Jimmy said. "He just can't miss."

Jimmy's Corner had become my uptown headquarters. Handy to the Hotel Moose, it also sat just three blocks from Hannah Sophia, the latest caretaker of Sasha's drums. A muscular Teuton, and perhaps the only legitimate masseuse in Times Square history, Hannah outweighed the Soverican by a good twenty pounds, kept him tamed and close to heel. Only when she was busy, breaking backs and cracking necks all over Central Park West, did he get to come out and play. "Too old I am to be cutting mustard," he confessed. But he looked well-fed, at peace. "I'm thinking perhaps, in heart of my hearts, I am just pussycat," Sasha said.

Jimmy's Corner was the Times Square bar generic, a thin dark tube extending backwards into nothingness and the latrines. The surface of the bar was covered with Polaroids of roistering clients; there were old fight pictures on the walls; the barmaids wore hot pants and thigh boots. Christmas tinsel hung from the lowering ceiling twelve months a year.

The block it looked out on, West Forty-fourth between Broadway and Sixth, was among the meanest in this mean neighborhood. But the Corner was sanctuary. "Anyone has trouble on their mind, I ask them please to reconsider," Jimmy Glenn explained, "and they have no trouble on their mind."

Whosoever entered here—hookers, messengers, taxi drivers, junkies, waiters, steeplejacks, scribes—checked their weapons at the door. While they rested, they murmured, genteel. Then, zealots refreshed, they went back into their trenches.

Sasha's spot was halfway down the long bar, foursquare in front of the Stolichnaya. He himself did not drink much, never had, because it made his nose bleed. Still, he liked the thought: "Is very Broadway, no?"

"To get drunk?"

"To be great star," he said, "and throw up on boots."

His head had healed fine, but the rest of him remained dubious. Before his mugging, he had seemed replete. It was enough for him just to be on Broadway and praise it all his days. But cheerleading had ceased to suffice him. He was worn down; he felt the need of something more.

"To sleep, perchance to drum," he said. There was a band called the O'Fays, white boys who wished they were black. They rehearsed in a disused synagogue, way down in Loisaida, revamping old Stax and Volt hits from the sixties: Otis Redding, Ann Peebles and King Floyd, Booker T and Solomon Burke. Two of them came from Marseilles and two from New Orleans, one from Cracow, one more from Jakarta, the lead guitar from Elephant and Castle, the singer from Jersey City. And the drummer? "Novokuz."

Were they any good? Good enough to pass, it seemed. A booker for some Southern club circuit had heard them and mumbled wet air: "Is praising with faint damn," Sasha said. "But not to give up day jobs."

Still he hoped. The moment had come, he sensed, to draw back, take his act on the road. Then, when he returned to the Main Stem, he would come to it refreshed, without scars. The second time around, he would conquer. "This I know," he said. It might be as a drummer, it might be as a magician. But he was fated to wind up a star, his name in lights: "And spelled right," he said. His scar lit up at the thought. "This I know," he said.

The mention of magic was not cheap rhetoric. "Affordable, yes, but not cheap," Sasha said. Since his first lessons with Max Gambon, he had been practicing, practicing. Of late, when Hannah wasn't watching and the weather suited his clothes, he had even turned street performer, working outside Broadway theaters.

His proficiency was still erratic, a thing of rags and patches. Juggling and fire-swallowing escaped him. So did telepathy. But he had a drummer's gift for sleight-of-hand. He worked harmoniously with playing cards and silken scarves, tumbling dice. In particular, he was skilled at turning coins into notes, then causing both to vanish: "Like Liberty Booster," he said. "Then for encore, I make trousers to fall down."

"Not here, you don't," said Jimmy Glenn.

"Of course not here," said Sasha, shocked. "Only on Great White Way."

It was a Wednesday afternoon; matinees were his best speed. Retiring to the bathroom, he went in a nobody and came out the Mad Monk Rasputin, complete with beard, black robe, and black-tinted contact lenses, which turned his eyes into Darth Vader zap-guns. "Is stinging like ten thousand bitches, but what hell, is for art," he said.

"Bitches don't sting," said Jimmy. His eyes stayed shut; his big hands did not move. "Bitches bite."

"Not *these* bitches," Sasha said.

Gathering up his robes, he swept outdoors, stage right. West Forty-fourth was still lashed by the chinook, but he braved its blast head-on, Rasputin's beard gusting over his shoulder like a schoolboy's scarf.

At Shubert Alley, we were joined by a juggler in a Bugs Bunny suit; outside *Les Misérables*, two blind boys from Alabama sang hymns *a cappella*. Otherwise, Sasha held the field unopposed, for these were lean times in the busking trade. Street performers were not corporate. In New York City these days, that made them a health risk.

Ten years before, the policy had been different. Before the Clean Up Times Square campaign, magic men were not proscribed. On the contrary, amusement was encouraged. There were intermission shows outside every Broadway theater, and the top acts, like Mal Cross, grew into curbside celebrities: "Stars of street and subway."

Cross was a Cyrano de Bergerac figure in flowing silk cape, waxed moustaches, and furl-brimmed chevalier's hat, who had been working theater crowds since the early seventies. His father, once a big-time Broadway gambler, had left him "profoundly broke, exceptionally witty and charming, but with no way to make a living. Rather like a defunct duke." So he had paid his dues by running a penthouse poker mill, then adapted his dealer's touch to street magic. And the magic had been good: "Oh, you should have seen me," he sighed, "I was a galaxy."

At his peak, he'd averaged a hundred dollars a night. But the glamour had long since soured. "There used to be romance. The old sock and buskin," he said. Now he surveyed the remnants—one rabbit, two blind boys, and Sasha—and he raised his eyes to heaven or the Minolta sign, whichever came first. "A galaxy," he said.

In these hard times, old magicians took shelter inside the Edison Hotel on West Forty-seventh, where they could be found huddled around a back table in the coffee shop.

Every weekday lunchtime, the table filled with mages—conjurers and closeup men, masters of misdirection, drop stealers and flat palmers, purse framers and imp passers, all-purpose *escamoteurs*. Their average age was somewhere past seventy; around the Edison, they were known as the Merlin Mob.

By consensus, their grand wizard was Mike Bornstein, né Kolmar, the Magical Mandarin. A brisk and pragmatic man, he did not seem born to hocus, but he had been turning tricks for half a century: "Had my own magic shop, right on Broadway at Fifty-first," he said. "Next door to the Capitol and half a block from Lindy's." He paddled in his soup du jour, stared fixedly at the ripples. "Of course," he said, "that was before the plague."

It was the universal Times Square lament. The name of the plague was uncertain. Depending on the plaintiff's generation and/or line of work, it might be war or Prohibition, gangsters, blacks or realtors, welfare hotels or AIDS. But the basic tale never changed. Once upon a time on Broadway, there had been a magical world. And now it was lost, gone to dust.

At its memory, Mike Bornstein's bald skull crinkled, glowed deep red like embers. "There was a carnival; it ran night and day," he said. "Any hour of the twenty-four you could take a walk, you'd see wonders. What I'm saying, *amazements*. And characters! Don't talk to me! All the big-time comedians at Lindy's. Walter Winchell, Milton Berle. And the hoodlums, the wiseguys. Some maybe murderers, or maybe just bad actors. Of course, they kept to themselves back then, didn't bother nobody that didn't want bothering. What I'm saying, they were just part of the show. *Your Show of Shows!* And the crowds they had, the motley I guess, you never saw such crowds. Day and night. The thousands and the millions. Three, four in the morning, they'd still be up and down, up and down. Get out of the theaters and take a stroll, never get home till dawn. And on every block almost, there'd be a magic shop, some kind of novelties. Tricks and mystifications. Just foolish things. Innocent. Like rubber snakes, false noses, that manner of stuff. Or harmonicas. A whole lotta harmonicas then. People look in the window, they see something silly. So what the heck? It tickles their fancy. So they buy, what the heck? They pay good money; they have a few laughs. And they're not scared of nothing. Nothing! Because they're out here on Broadway, see, and not a thing can touch them."

And the name of the plague? "Minorities," he said. Before the war, like all downtown Broadway, Times Square had been strictly vanilla. Harlem jazz musicians, if they were good, were let out to play Fifty-second Street: "And shoeshine men, porters, maids," Bornstein said. "But only in line of service, see. There was no confusion. No fuss."

Fuss was putting it mildly. Quite suddenly, people who had always known their place, *Negroes and so forth and such*, started sweeping down Broadway, a flood tide. And these people were upset. *Just kids, most of them, but mean. A chip on their shoulder as big as the Empire State Building*. In the past, their sort had seemed content to drift, live on hope. They'd had a Broadway of their own, 125th Street, jammed solid with theaters, night clubs, fine restaurants. But the city had abandoned Harlem, let it die. The theaters and hot spots were boarded up, and the crowds, dispossessed, spilled downtown. They acted outraged, *like someone done them wrong. What I'm saying, a bad attitude*. As if, whatever they wanted, they'd better grab it themselves: "Which they did. With both hands," Mike Bornstein said, "and then some."

The wind change came after the war. Up till the late forties, he kept his store open till three in the morning and used a simple padlock. By 1950, he was closing at midnight and using bars. Then it was ten and rolldown gates, and then he just gave up: "I'm out of there on a bagel," he said. "So long, sayonara, farewell."

Since then he had worked magic shows all around America, given private lessons, published books such as *Money Magic* and *Mike Bornstein's Triple Threat Reverse*. But jobs came and went;

these daily lunches at the Edison, so close to Broadway, were constant: "A center. A core," he said. He crumbled bread-crumbs in his soup. A strong-built man, with capable hands, he frowned. *"The still point in the circle,"* he quoted, "Tony Slydini said that."

He spoke of Slydini often. All magic men did. As the great maestro of modern closeup, Grand Master of Misdirection, cre-ator of the imp pass and the revolve, he was a magicians' ma-gician: "The essence," said Mike Bornstein.

The reverence was not for his physical skills. Strictly as a sleight-of-hand artist, he was rated as just average. His genius lay in psychology: "The magic of the mind," Bornstein said. "What I'm saying, he'd give you just one look and you were an open book, he could play you like a pipe organ."

Slydini was now in extreme old age, confined to a home upstate. Till recently, however, he had endured in a West Forties apartment block. It was there that I'd gone to meet him.

He had lived in half-light. Behind double-draped blue cur-tains, his demonstration room was bathed in a dim roseate glow. Soothing music played, off; there was a faint scent of cedarwood. Overall, the effect was not unlike an undertaker's chapel.

Slydini himself was then eighty-eight, stooped and very frag-ile, his eyes already filming. He had been the most elegant man, and grace was on him still. His features, always fine drawn, had worn away to silhouettes, his flesh thinned to a silver-blue trans-lucence. In repose, his face against the light, it gave him the look of a death's-head. His long hands, with nicotine-stained fingers, shook uncontrollably.

His English was halting, heavily accented. Born Quintino Marucci in Italy, he had grown up in Buenos Aires, only came to America in his thirties. For ten years, he got nowhere. In 1940, while staying in Boston with a sister, he was reduced to taking a five-dollar date at a local church: "Just to buy some present," he said. "And, believe me, I am feeling sick. Always I am a failure, nothing it ever breaks. But the church is beautiful.

This I must say. It is plain but white and shining, and the dressing room so clean."

Having got there early, he practiced his act alone. Then another man arrived, a man with a heavy suitcase, which he sat upon, looking angry: "Like the world gives him the pain. The big stink in his nose," Slydini said. "I'm asking him when the show starts, how many will be in the audience, dumb questions all like that, just to be friendly, you understand, and show I am the good fellow. But all the man does, he stares and talks very gruff, not nice." Remembering, he shut his eyes. The lids were frail as butterfly wings. "A very rude man," he said. "Believe me."

The man's name was Sayso; he was the show's comedian. When Slydini went on stage, Sayso watched from the wings, but he still did not smile, gave no sign of approval: "Afterwards, back in the dressing room, all he said was, 'Meet me tomorrow, twelve noon. The corner of Tremont and Boilstone.' "

Next day came up a blizzard. Ploughing through the snowdrifts, Slydini showed up a half hour late. "But Sayso, he is still waiting. Without he speaks, not a word, he takes my arm, he leads me to an agent; the agent is waiting with a contract, fifteen dollars a day, the Queens Theatre in Quincy. Then after I'm playing Joyland, a night club, twenty-five dollars, and then all over, everyplace. I am, what you like, a headliner. A made star."

The word gave no seeming pleasure. Fastidious, the thin lips curled, the eyelids drooped, as if at an unseemly odor. He was no braggart, his look implied, no man for cheap vainglory. "If fortune does not send me one good angel, believe me, I am not going nowhere. Forever I am just sitting," he said, "waiting for Sayso."

This type of mystical intervention had marked his whole career. According to Mike Bornstein, who had once shared an apartment with him, Slydini had always been a man of gentleness and quietude, *a child within a man, lost in wonders.* So a whole series of angels—Sayso, Nat Bernstein, Blanca Lopez, and Murray Celwit—had orchestrated his fame, while he himself was left free to ponder mysteries: "Pure magic of enormous cerebral content, 'Intelligence made magic,' " wrote Ascanio, the great Catalan illusionist. "A magic of repeated and repeated destroying impact, visual magic, spectacular with unending surprises, with effects that disarm one and again, always in crescendo, always more astonishing. . . ."

These effects, *direct and sharp as a rapier's thrust*, were achieved with the simplest tools—a cigarette, some coins, a few paper balls. The secret, said Slydini himself, lay purely in the timing. "Picture a murder," he said. "A gun goes off; a dead body falls to feet. So the audience, the watching men, what are they to think? The gunshot killed the body, no?"

"Makes sense."

"Sense, yes. But maybe not truth." His rheumy eyes crinkled; his spatulate yellow fingers sat shaking in his lap. "Suppose if the death comes before. Only nothing announces it. No movement, no sound. What then? In effect, it does not exist."

"Until the bang?"

"The misdirection, yes." He smiled then, very faintly, with the most civilized regret. "Illusion, magic, what you like, all the secret is the moment. Not how or why, only when," he said. *"The anatomy of time."*

On a plain white table sat a plain white tablecloth. Behind it, Slydini sat slightly askew. His fingers spasmed, stark against the white. Then he picked up a cigarette, made a pass. In an instant, he was steady as a metronome.

Quietly and at ease, with an unbroken flow, he began to move his hands. They opened, they shut, they fluttered. The cigarette hovered in mid-air, then it passed through the table. Then it was broken in the middle. Tobacco spilled loose on the tablecloth. Then the cigarette was whole again. It was lit; it was extinguished. The hands rose once and fell, and the cigarette was a coin. It disappeared into Slydini's closed hand, a single quarter, and came out as three. Then one was in my breast pocket, a second behind his ear, and the third jumped out of his mouth. The hands fluttered, and there was just one again. They fluttered once more, and it was a cigarette. Then Slydini smiled, inclined his head. He spread his hands flat, palms up, and then there was nothing at all.

Afterwards, he was exhausted. A very old man, he mopped his face with a silk handkerchief, licked spittle from his lips. When his hands dropped back in his lap, they were shaking again, worse than ever. "So you writing a book on magic?" he asked.

"On Broadway."

"What's a difference?"

Now, at the back table in the Edison Hotel, Mike Bornstein drank fresh coffee, crumbled another roll. "What I'm saying, the man was a pro," he said, and the subject turned to the New York Mets.

The coffee shop had once been the Grand Ballroom, for the Edison's past was sumptuous. Even now, flaking gilt ceilings and marble balconies overlooked the blue plate specials. Rumor had it a major facelift was planned. For the moment, however, the great lobby was drab as a carpark, reeked of with stale disinfectant; and two doormen in unpressed maroon uniforms stood disputing. "So tell me this," said one. "Who killed Izzy Grove?"

Izzy Grove! At that name, the glum present vanished and Broadway past, in all its raucous splendors, rose up renewed. I had not known he was gone. But if it was true, it was like the passing of the Automat or Dempsey's. For Izzy Grove, alive, had defined Times Square.

Like so many of its veterans, he had started out a prizefighter. In the 1920s, a middleweight billed as the Ghetto Avenger, he had scored the first KO ever at the second Madison Square Garden and beaten three world champions. Afterwards, he'd turned booking agent, handling Duke Ellington and Cab Calloway. Then he had run singles' dances out of the Edison Theater, which now showed *Oh! Calcutta!* Most important, he had hung out at Lindy's.

It was the new Rector's, the bedrock of Broadway Cafe Society. As such, it symbolized everything that Prohibition had changed. Rather than theatrical deities and Wall Street tycoons, it served newspapermen and gangsters, comedians and racetrack touts, Tin Pan Alley, burlesque, and the fight crowd. Champagne and stuffed lobster was not their speed. No orchestra piped them to their tables. Instead, scrunched into booths, they lived on sturgeon and knishes, cheesecake and strudel.

To be Jewish at Rector's had been wolfbane. A lifetime's striving might not suffice to overcome the curse. At Lindy's, however, it was a free pass. Strudel was a quarter, *a dime if you were Kike*, said Izzy Grove.

This was the Hebrew halfworld that Damon Runyon chronicled, the hometurf of Harry the Horse and Regret, Little Isadore and Spanish John. In deference to his mass readership, Runyon toned down both the Jewishness and the harshness. But Izzy Grove and his ilk felt the fallout just the same. Of a sudden, they found themselves called Runyonesque. Like all generic labels, it was an idler's word. "Whatever I am," Izzy said, "*esque* I'm not."

The originals of Runyon's heroes—Gyp the Blood, Dago Frank, Big Jack Zelig, Lefty Louie—were not exactly the lovable lugs of the stories: "They didn't like your face, or the way you handled your knife, you went home to the wife on the installment plan." Arnold Rothstein, the man that fixed the World Series, was lured from Lindy's to be shot. Herman Rosenthal, another regular, took eighty-three bullets outside the Metropole. "But the sturgeon was out of this world."

Broadway's machine-gun phase had carpeted two decades, stretched neatly from war to war. The Volstead Act turned it loose in 1920; Fiorello La Guardia pulled its plug in 1939. In between, to hear Izzy tell it, Times Square was hell on the halfshell.

On January 16, 1920, the last wet night, he had been in short pants but already working on Broadway, a message boy at the I. Miller Shoe Corp. "They let me off early—*get safe home, kid, case it might be some trouble.* A course, I just nip around the corner, try to catch the action."

The night came in like a witch. "A bitterly chill wind swept around the corners," Stanley Walker wrote in *The Night Club Era.* "Derelicts huddled in hallways, and tried to sleep under piles of old newspapers. The blanketed horses arched their backs and hobbled along on the icy pavements. After midnight the temperature in the city went down to six degrees above zero."

In Izzy's remembrance it was even colder: "Twenty below easy, thirty maybe. Your breath turned to icicles any time you breathed out." So he breathed in and drifted with the crowds. Outside the Café de Paris, formerly Rector's, there was a figure on stilts, done up like Rollin Kirby's newspaper cartoon of Prohibition—Abraham Lincoln turned mortician's mate, with a high stovepipe hat and red boozer's nose, a bottle peeking from his hip pocket. He started to swing up Broadway. And Izzy Grove traveled with him.

They journeyed out of Times Square past Automobile Row—its showrooms aglint with De Sotos, Pierce-Arrows, La Salles—and the American Horse Exchange till they came to Evelyn Nesbit.

She was not in a good mood. Divorced from Harry Thaw, she now ran a small tearoom in the West Fifties. She had spent years in vaudeville, demonstrating novelty jazz dances like the Castle Walk and the Grizzly Bear. That was finished, and she was resting—a weary, overstrung woman, described as *a whipped race-mare,* with a budding morphine habit.

On Prohibition Eve, slouching outside her tearoom, she drank gin from a stone hot-water bottle. The street was full of horses, not a car in sight. That's what stuck in Izzy's mind, the dry-ice steam rising off the horses' rumps, the warm reek of their turds. And Evelyn Nesbit was drunk; she kept shouting

out *It's over. Everything is finished*. And the Prohibition man
on stilts started mocking her, bouncing back the phrases like
an echo. *It's finished. Over and done.* Then the crowd took it
up. *Everything is finished. Tutta e finito.* They crushed in around
Evelyn Nesbit, jeering in her face, and she was still a lovely
woman, big eyes like beacons in the fog and chestnut hair running wild, just scared, a little strange. Like she couldn't grasp
what was happening. "Outta touch with reality, you could call
it," Izzy said. So she was shouting and cursing, the gin slopping
down the front of her dress and the ice-steam billowing, the
streetlights haloed with mist, the smell of fresh horseshit: "Like
a stage set or some movie. And this lost woman, but beautiful,
crying *Over, it's all over*. And me, I'm just a kid, I bust out
crying, too."

Enter Bat Masterson.

The old Dodge City gunslinger now served as a boxing writer
for the *Morning Telegraph*. Ancient but still straight-backed, he
was a familiar Broadway figure. "Long tailcoats, high-heel boots,
a ten-gallon hat," Izzy said. "Looked like he was wearing fancy
dress. But he was good to kids, whatchacallem *street urchins*,
always tossed us loose change. He wrote me up one time; I was
still in the amateurs. The paper never printed it." And now he
hove up through the icy mists, the Bat. To find a lady in distress.

He did not hesitate. Swiping freely with his cane, he parted
the drunken mob, pushed through to Evelyn Nesbit's side. The
man on stilts, Prohibition, blocked his path. Twelve feet high,
and his swaying shadow, a monster's shape, playing over the
tenement walls. But the Bat flicked his cane, and the figure came
tumbling down. "Just a halfpint runt he was, at that. Laying
out in the gutter, squealing he was killed." Right on cue, a
hansom cab appeared. Evelyn Nesbit wrapped the hot-water
bottle inside her shawl; Bat Masterson handed her up. "You
are kind, sir," she said.

"Ma'am, you honor me," the Bat replied. He raised his hat,

she lowered her veil, they went their separate ways. Through the biting cold, Izzy Grove felt a sudden warmth against his thigh: "Goddamn horse was pissing down my leg."

It was a tale often told; the details varied each time. Only the central image was fixed—the gunslinger and the scarlet woman, both down on their luck, still flawless in gallantry, grace: *"You are kind, sir. Ma'am, you honor me,"* Izzy said. "Two years of Prohibition, and all you heard was *Oh, you kid!"*

In those years, the center had moved east. Most of the fashionable speaks were clustered round Madison and Fifth, and Broadway was left with the honky-tonks. Instead of lobster palaces, there were night clubs and bottleshops, blind pigs, discreetly tucked off the square; instead of Diamond Jim Brady and Lillian Russell, there was Owney Madden.

Soon Jimmy Walker was mayor, and boodle was in bloom. Following Madden and Larry Fay, whole tribes of mobsters came pouring out of Hell's Kitchen, which festered two blocks to the west. Graduates of street gangs, the Gophers and the Hudson Dusters, they carried .32s and names like Shuffles Goldberg, Skush Thomas, Big Frenchy DeMange. By Chicago standards, they were pinochle players, but they played rough enough for Broadway. Suddenly, there were clubs called the Silver Slipper and the Cave of the Fallen Angels. Two dead bodies headlined at Legs Diamond's Hotsy Totsy Club. At Porky Murray's, there were two more.

Survivors of the Golden Era glanced once at the new Broadway, then fled. "The slaughterhouse of Moronia," Stanley Walker called it. "There are chow-meineries, peep shows for men only, flea circuses, lectures on what killed Rudolph Valentino. An old army sergeant, aided by fast-spieling salesmen, lectures on health soap, psyllium seeds and reducing belts, with dire threats of the toxic poisoning habit. Another lecturer, armed with vials filled with chemicals of many colors, pleads for the buying of real estate near the Muscle Shoals development, Alabama. Haberdasheries are closing out at reduced prices; a fire sale is going full blast; an auction sale of fantastic gewgaws draws enough people to block the sidewalk; a pushcart pedlar exhibits *100% pure whiskey candies—three for five cents.*"

The depression only quickened the fall. Movie houses had already driven the theaters into side streets. Now the last plush restaurants failed. Faced by the burlesque houses and the dime dance halls, even the Palace could no longer compete. Self-styled the World's Capital of Vaudeville, it folded its two-a-days in 1932: "Went skin," said Izzy Grove. Of all the square's Edwardian pomps, only the Astor Hotel clung on.

Even La Guardia kicking out the mobsters did not raise the tone. They had been happy as clams, content with their slot machines and penny arcades, the fights, prostitution, and dope. But when the Little Flower declared war, they opted to dim their lights. So they backed off Broadway, regrouped in Brooklyn and New Jersey: "And that's where the crime came in," Izzy said. "When the Mob had control, there might be coupla shootings, unnerstand, between friends. But street crime, you never heard a such a thing. Purse snatching, mugging and such, it just wasn't done. A guy could walk on Broadway at midnight, a thousand bucks sticking outta his back pocket, and nobody would touch it. In case the guy is Dutch Schultz's cousin."

With the mobsters gone, Lindy's reverted to a school for newspapermen, press agents, comics; and in that peaceful strain it remained, till Leo Lindemann sold out in 1969. "A good Broadway man. He knew to make a dollar," Izzy said. But today his memory was desecrated, years after his death, by a chain of tourist-trap slopshops in his name, peddling eye of newt and tongue of toad at $9.95, plus tax.

Izzy Grove, too, had fallen on evil times. By the late seventies, when I met him first, he was no longer active as a booking agent. For the past thirty years, in fact, he hadn't been active as much of anything. His last steady employ had been at the Garden, sticking up fight posters. Through the fifties and sixties, his shopping cart and bucket of glue were Eighth Avenue landmarks. Then the Garden changed management, and his phone had stopped ringing.

Even so, he maintained an office on West Forty-sixth. It was a broom closet in a showbiz building, right up the block from the Edison Hotel. At sixty dollars a month, he'd been there since the Eisenhower years, and there he planned to remain, holed up against change, *till the fat lady sings*, he said.

He was a blocky figure with bottle-bottom glasses and busted hands, his ruined face framed by twin cauliflower ears; and he did not stop talking, not ever. "I got a talking mouth. Born that way," Izzy said. "I see people, I start to gab, it's automatic. Then I don't know to stop. I got so much inside me, unnerstand, it's gotta go get some air."

At seventy, he'd been on Broadway for fifty-eight years. Twice daily, he did his ceremonial laps, a *tummler*'s progress, Fifty-first to Forty-second and back, on the stump from deli to newsstand, luncheon counter to cigar store, shaking hands and waving at every step, blowing kisses, slapping backs, monologuing nonstop. It was as if he was campaigning: "Running for office," he said. "But the office always runs faster."

He kissed his hand to himself. "Everybody knows Izzy Grove, and I know some of them," he said. It was his street, his property. He had been written up by Runyon, by Dan Parker of the *Mirror*. "The day there is no Izzy Grove, there's no more Broadway." He tapped himself on the nose. "They say they're gonna pull my lease, kick my *tuchis* in the street." He punched himself in the guts. "It'll never happen," he said. And it happened.

The day he got his eviction notice, he came into the Gaiety Deli; it was a Tuesday lunchtime. There was an old lady used to eat there every day—her name was Sarah; she used to be a conjurer's assistant. Every day she'd come in at the same time, order up the exact same lunch, egg salad on wheat toast, a celery soda. And she had this dog, some kind of pug, that was even older than her. She called it Bernhardt. Sarah and Bernhardt,

that was her little joke. A disgusting yellow-fang mutt, all slobber
and snuffle and stink. But anyhow, Izzy Grove, he'd come in
the Gaiety for coffee or a knish, and every day without fail, the
old dog would get under his feet somehow, and Izzy would rear
back, aim a kick at its fat butt. This was his sense of fun. Only
this day, this Tuesday, when Izzy Grove came in, he didn't lift
a flat foot. He didn't even see the dog waiting there to get its
kick. He just ordered a white coffee, walked away. "Whatsa
matter?" Sarah asked him. "You get too big a man to kick a
dog these days. It's too much trouble, maybe." She was hurt,
anyone could see that. She took it personally. "Or maybe," Sarah
said, "maybe you find another dog. Not so old, not so fat. Maybe
you're finding some fine young bitch." But Izzy didn't rise to
her. He looked at Sarah, then he looked at Bernhardt. It was
like he'd never seen them before. "I tell you what," Izzy said,
"go kick your own dog."

It was a terrible thing. People were getting evicted all over
Broadway. From the Deuce to Columbus Circle, seventeen
blocks, it seemed no building was safe. The Japanese had taken
over; the mammoth realty conglomerates; and worse than either,
the AGONYS—Americans Gloating on New York Slime. Between them, they had determined that Times Square was a
hellpit—"the national cesspool," said William Whyte, urban
strategist; "a stink in the nostrils of propriety," said a federal
aide—and must be exorcised. All its crazed and shambolic,
insanitary, and wondrous labyrinths must go, to be replaced by
antiseptic tanks and traffic-free walkways, "a Bloomingdale's
atmosphere."

The first step in achieving this shopping-mall utopia was to
rid the area of human rodents. "Scattering them is the first shot,"
said William J. Stern, the chairman of the Urban Development
Corporation. "We fire the first cannonball which scatters them
and then we hunt them out."

Officially, the prime targets were pornographers. But the
smut-peddlers proved too shifty. Flush them out of one foxhole,

they merely nipped around the corner and started over. Izzy Groves, however, were so many fish in a barrel. They had no friends in the right places, no wads to grease the right palms. So out they went, haunch, paunch, and jowl. "They cut my phone; they knock down my door," Izzy told Josh Alan Friedman, a writer for *Oui* magazine. "I live right; I behave myself. My wife, Alice, she rest in peace, always told me that instead of being a tough guy, a shylock, a racket guy, a numbers runner, or a bookmaker, to go into legitimate business." So now he was defenseless. "No leverage, no dice," he said.

When the first freeze of shock wore off, he started to seep, like melting wax. "I don't want to cry. It's just my face is wet," he said. He was the Ghetto Avenger, survivor of a hundred wars, but not fool enough to believe that he would survive this. Take him out of Broadway, and he was done for. "Any other place, I can't breathe," he said. "You can't breathe, you die."

He ran the street in panic frenzy, howling out loud. Prayer meetings were held at the Actors' Temple, and Izzy granted interviews. "It's one of these odd quirks of happenstance that befall mankind," he was quoted in *Oui*. "I got relatives. Where are they? I was in the papers. Where are they? Where? When I made money, unnerstand, *hey, yeah*, free tickets, the fights, afterwards somethin' to eat. But I want to pinpoint one thought. Quote me. Yesterday's cheers have a very short echo—"

Now, less than ten years on, the razing of Izzy Grove's street was almost complete. Block after block had been cleared of detritus—booking agents and song pluggers, dance studios, music publishers. In their place, gleaming new, stood a Novotel and a Holiday Inn, assorted office blocks and construction sites. Ten years more, and the whole strip would be indistinguishable from any other American downtown: "Like Duluth," Bert Sugar said, "only not so much distinction."

The last time I saw Izzy Grove, he'd taken refuge at the

Chin-Ya, a Japanese bar in back of a Fifty-fifth Street halfway house. He was not a drinking man, barely touched the stuff. But this day his hands were shaking; he couldn't stop leaking. "It's all over," he said. "History."

He did not mean just himself. Not any more. For most of his life, it was true, he had been blinkered, half-blind: "All I seen is before my nose. Me, me, and me," he said. "But since this, I gotta new angle. I come to unnerstand how I'm connected. *A constituent member*, you heard that phrase? My wife, she rest in peace, that was her favorite saying." He was drinking kosher wine. Stray droplets clung to his chin. "What it means is, *a piece of the pie*," Izzy said. "Just one small slice, a *sliver*, out of the total totality."

In his new vision, Broadway was no longer *his* street, *his* property. It did not belong to him, but he to it. So his own ruin was just part of a larger crime, a systematic crushing of all proper things. "They're tearing down the world," he said.

"Good for business," said the Japanese barman brightly.

"Not for mine."

These were the last days, he believed. "Lemme tell you about Broadway. The truth," he said. "People think it's about bright lights, this star and that star, unnerstand, the theaters and babes, limousines, the big wheels and cheeses, all that order of affairs." His face was all knots and gnarls, liver spots; it looked like riven oak. "It's not about that," he said.

"Then what?"

"Quirks," said Izzy Grove.

He pushed away his empty glass, a gesture of abdication. "City pols and landlords call them crazies, freaks, call them bums. But quirks is all they are," he said. "Just people a little different, they got some kind of bug in their heads, some kinda notion, unnerstand. It could be singing, dancing, could be fighting, could be selling the best sturgeon, *schtupping* the most broads, anything. Wearing a pink tie with lobsters on it. Dancing the Big Apple in their underwear. Could be nothing wears a name." His eyes behind the thick glasses would not stop leaking. "Just some tweak like an itch, won't let them be. So they don't fit in, they got no place, see what I mean. No place except for Broadway, and now they don't got that." He dabbed at his wet face with a handkerchief the color of dried putty. "Where'm I gonna go?" he cried. "How'm I gonna live?"

On the street, the wind blew harder.

In Roseland, the lights went blue, green, purple, pink, and the couples danced cheek to cheek. At night there were rock groups or salsa bands, but on matinee afternoons the great arena reverted to a ballroom. Again the floor filled with people touching, holding on. Most of them were past sixty, and many were much older. Some had been coming here since 1932, the year that Roseland began. Still they waltzed and fox-trotted, they quickstepped, and they tangoed. The changing lights played over them, clothing them in soft washes. "Make believe," the emcee purred. "Close your eyes, drift away. Make believe."

Up some steps was a long horseshoe bar. On faster numbers, the mambos and *pasodobles*, it filled with old ladies resting. They kicked off their pumps, sat kneading their swollen feet. Spotting me sitting alone, a single man with a tall drink and a notebook, one figure detached itself from the ranks, plumped down on the stool at my side.

"Let me entertain you," it said.

The voice was girlish, slightly nasal, but musical withal. Cigarette-husky, it came from a slim-bottled blonde in a green sheath dress cut tight above the knee and slit up the left thigh. The dress set off showgirl legs in sheer silk stockings and high-heeled silver slingbacks. "My name is Roz, I'm sixty-nine," the blonde said. "My speciality is bringing joy."

Hopping down off the stool, she backed a few steps across the bar alcove, launched herself into a recitation. "Hello, I'm Rosalind Kantor from Roslyn," she began. "Actually I live in Mineola but Roslyn is close enough, so you can call me Roz from Roslyn, not so young in years but younger than springtime at heart."

At the end of each phrase she paused, frozen in mid-gesture, her smile congealed, until my scribbling caught her up. Her diction was crystalline, her delivery button-bright. Where required, she even threw in stage directions. "Roz from Roslyn," she said. "Not so young in years but younger than springtime at heart, and this is my life's story, actually it's just a sketch, but I hope it keeps you amused anyway." She curtsied and set up a time-step, three steps to the left, then back, three steps to the right, then back. "Thank you," she said. "You are a lovely audience."

She raised her right hand to her throat, her ringed fingers curled loosely about an unseen microphone. "It's been a long, long journey my little life has made, and I hardly know where to start. So I'll start right here, at Roseland, that's where it all began. I was just fifteen and all the boys said I looked very cute, actually I drove them crazy, but I don't like to seem I'm tooting my own horn, even though I am. (Laugh.) Well, in those days they had talent contests here, every Tuesday afternoon I think, and one time my friends ganged up on me and would not stop kvetching until I gave it a shot. So I did. I did a little song and dance, a couple of gags, and my impression of Jimmy Durante. *Inka Dinka Doo*, you remember that one? Well, that certainly dates *you*. (Drumroll. Rimshot.) Anyway, I entered, and they booed me off. No, really, it was just horrible. I cried and cried for days. But the showbiz bug had bit me, and actually it never stopped. And the rest is history. (Laugh. Sing eight bars of *Inka Dinka Doo*.)

"Now about my first husband. I met him in my line of work. No, not *that* line of work. (Bump; big wink.) I was a cigarette girl at a club on Fifty-second Street—I'd like to tell you the club's name but I don't dare, today it's such a famous place, the owners might sue me. But it was Twenty-one. That's right,

Jack and Charlie's Twenty-one Club. Well, in those days Fifty-second was the greatest night-club street in New York City, in America even, the world. They used to call it the Street That Never Sleeps, and all the great jazz musicians of that long-ago era, like Duke Ellington and Count Basie, Benny Goodman and Miss Billie Holiday, they all used to play and party there. The whole street was a blaze of lights from dusk to dawn, with beautiful music, oh such beautiful music, pouring out from every open door, the Three Deuces and the Onyx, Jimmy Ryan's, Leon & Eddie's; you'd think you must of died and gone to heaven. And there I was, little me, actually not so little, I'd filled out very nicely, thank you, even though I do say so myself. (Strike pose. Laugh.) Selling cigarettes in fishnet stockings and tails, with a white gardenia in my buttonhole, a *boutonniere* they call it, *très chic ma chérie*. That's Popsy in French. And one night my husband comes in. Of course, he wasn't my husband then; he was a total stranger. But he comes in anyhow, and he takes one look at me, our eyes meet, and how could you put it in words, it's love at first sight, that old black magic, it's like a Spanish earthquake or is that Sicilian, I always forget. (Look dumb but adorable.) Well, he doesn't just buy a pack of cigarettes, he buys the whole trayload and fills up all his pockets, he's bulging out like a Santa Claus, smokes are spilling all over the place, and so is my heart, believe me. *Hubba hubba.* So when I come off work, we cross the street to Mammy's Chicken Koop—they had just the greatest fried chicken then, Southern-style, all spicy and crisp. Like me. (Laugh.) And my husband's name is Jerry, he tells me he's from the Coast—Santa Clara—and he's in the insurance business actually. But I don't hear two words together, I'm so *that way*. I tell you, we just ate up all that chicken, and then we drove down to Atlantic City in the dawn, took our blood tests, and we were married the very next day. That's how hot we were. Hotter than a pepper sprout. (Laugh. Sigh. Stretch like cat.) We had our honeymoon in

Pompton Lakes, up in the mountains, just a simple log cabin with a blazing fire and lots to drink, not much to eat but who needed food, we had our love. Such a love. It was my first, and they say you never forget your first. And it's true, believe me, you never do. (Sing.) *When they begin the beguine, it brings back the sound of music so tender, it brings back a night of tropical splendor.* (Stop sing.) Four days and nights of bliss. *What moments divine, what raptures serene.* And on the fifth day the feds came. Yes, you heard me right, the Untouchables. We were woken from our dream of love by the sound of a bullhorn and a man's voice yelling, 'Come on out with your hands up. We have you surrounded. You don't have a prayer. Come on out.' And then the gunfire started. And Jerry died in a hail of bullets. My husband of five days. They filled him full of lead."

Her voice had grown hoarse, begun to crack. Dropping another curtsy, she came back to the bar and drank two full glasses of ice water. "Why did they shoot him?" I asked.

"They had no heart," said Roz, and went back to work again. Three steps left she paced, then three steps right, up and back, up and back, over and over and over. "They filled him full of lead," she said. "He was my first, and you never forget your first. But a winner never quits, and a quitter never wins. Nobody does actually, but that's another story. So then I came back to good old Times Square. (Sing.) *Come on along and listen to, the Lullaby of Broadway. The hip hooray and ballyhoo, the Lullaby of Broadway.* (Stop sing.) And oh, it was so gorgeous then, it was just everything. These days all the shops are locked up behind those iron gates, they look like prison bars. But it was so gorgeous then. And so was I. (Bump. Girlish squeal.) I went to work for the great Mr. Roxy Rothafel at his fabulous Roxy Theater, right here on Seventh Avenue, they used to call it the Cathedral of the Motion Picture, but movies were just one part of it; they also had the Mighty Wurlitzer and Louis Something furnishings in the ladies' rooms. They gave you a free bar of soap with every handwash, and a thousand stars of stage and screen, and of course the fabulous Rockettes. That was me. (Four highkicks and a split.)

"Now about my second husband. He was just the opposite of Number One, a very quiet man, neat and clean in all his habits; you never saw a soiled shirt on him. Never mind a bullethole. (Laugh.) He was a movie projectionist at Loews New York; you could say he was in show business too, so that gave us something in common right away. We met at Child's, and he just swept me off my feet. A regular Don Juan. Even if he was bald and kind of stumpy. And we had twenty-three years of rapture. Oh, words could not express it—he was the world to me, the sun and stars and the moon at night, my mother and father and lover and brother. (Sing.) *Night and day, deep in the heart of me.* (Stop sing.) And then he died. It was our anniversary, number twenty-three, and we went to Sardi's for dinner, the same way we did every year. My husband—his name was Hubert—he toasted me in a martini, bone-dry, the way he always liked it. And then he choked on the olive. He coughed and looked at me kind of funny, and then he just fell down across the table. The glasses and the flowers, and oh, all the lovely food were scattered all everywhere. And that was that. Heart attack. Right before my eyes. And that was that."

Out on the floor, the lights went blue, green, purple, pink, and the couples danced cheek to cheek. Roz drank down two more glasses of ice water, then she ordered a double gin and tonic and drank that down as well. "So what do you think so far?" she asked.

" 'Begin the Beguine,' " I said. "I always loved that song."

"I told you I brought joy."

Three steps to the left, then back. Three steps to the right, then back. "And that was that," she said. "And oh, I was just devastated. I thought my life was over, you might as well plough me under. But a poet once said, 'Time is the root of all evil.' So I pulled myself off the floor. I said to myself, *Roz*, I said, *when skies are cloudy and gray, they're only gray for a day*, I said, *so wrap your troubles in dreams, and dream all your troubles away*. (Beat.) I have been dreaming ever since.

"Now about my third husband—"

Outdoors, the duststorm swirled unabated, and every block back to the Deuce was a battle hard won. At Father Duffy Square, a twenty-foot red banner said COME AND MEET THOSE DANCING FEET. Directly beneath it, I paid a dollar for a soiled green pamphlet copyright 1985. *Evils of the Elders*, it was called. *AIDS, Sex, Sin and Worse Things to Come*.

The author was Ray Crabtree.

In the blurb at the back, he was described as "a long time impresario, a humanitarian who for many years helped the poor in selling them first class clothing to wear especially in seeking jobs, at very little or no cost."

His words were words of flame.

The argument of *Evils of the Elders* was tortuous, the basic point stark. Modern Man was bad, Woman worse: "These women's lib has simply joined the tyrannical rot of men," Crabtree wrote. "Let's take a look at the things they term liberation, orgies galore, swap parties, abortion, drugs, sex in the schools, gay rights, almost all persons in NYC is gay one way or the other they are doing the same thing, the mouth work. One just have to walk through the streets nightly and will see heads going up and down sucking on lollipops and mushrooms I guess. . . . Watch out miss thing they are stealing and messing up the trade mark."

The pamphlets were being sold out of an orange crate by Ramon, a fourteen-year-old boy. He said he'd found them, he couldn't remember where, but he knew where the author lived: "Everybody knows where that man's at. He abide in the spirit house."

According to *Evils of the Elders*, he was not alone. "This writer lives with cats, dogs and birds so that they may warn and protect him when the plague comes around the house. We live in the dark and are able to see many things and to think. There are peace in the dark also." Still, like all creatures who meant no harm, they lived under constant threat. Evil and foulness swirled everywhere about them, only waiting the chance to strike. "Today this plague is in the form of humans but when they go monster they will be much dangerous. It will not be war weapons necessarily that will devour mankind, it will be human bums, vampires, werewolves and fangs. Yes, the time of the ugly has arrived."

In the section of Hell's Kitchen that realtors now called Clinton, Ray Crabtree's home stood facing DeWitt Clinton Park, infamous for crack and murder one. It was a white house behind a black fence, badly fire-scarred, with boarded-up windows; it had a vaguely Southern look, a whiff of boondocks and poke salad. A supermarket shopping-cart was chained to the gate. Many dogs howled unseen.

Crabtree did not emerge in haste. It took an hour of knocking and calling, sticking messages through the fence. When at last he ventured forth, he was a black man in his sixties, robust in a patched red sweater. His features were high-boned, fine. He spoke without prompting. "I knew you was coming. I was informed," he said.

"Warned?"

"Let's just say *apprised*."

He could not invite visitors inside the house. It was not tidied up; there were too many animals. Three years before, some firebugs had tried to burn him out. The roof had been ruined, the windows blown out, the whole interior trashed. But that was not the worst: "All my dogs burned up," Crabtree said.

In person, he was gently spoken, a man of conscious dignity. Ruminant, his voice was pitched like a stringed instrument, all swoops and scurries, pizzicato stabs, sudden leaps: "The violin. The fiddle," he said. "It was my first wife."

They'd met when he was in grade school, growing up near

Okmulgee, Oklahoma. He was the fifth of thirteen children, the son of a sharecropper. Seeing Ingrid Bergman in *Intermezzo* at the local movie house, he fell in love, bought a fiddle second-hand, and joined a local band: "I even took lessons. It was my destiny. But it didn't work out," he said. So he left home, made his way to Tulsa, then New York. He walked the streets, found out where money went, and followed it. For weeks and months, he sat in the lobby of the Waldorf-Astoria, the Pierre, talking to any man or woman who did not spurn him. He was nineteen years old, an Aries, "the Ram, bold and brazen, not scared of anything or nothing." He knew that he had been elected.

It was 1942. For ten years, he studied composition, read, and practiced philosophy. His models were Aristotle and Spinoza, Voltaire, Wagner and Rasputin, *the greatest man of the twentieth century, the most misunderstood.* He wrote two operas, one of them complete, and songs, trios, quartets. He would have joined the Katherine Dunham Dance Company, only he could not dance: "So I went on with my reading. And it was like magic, everything I read, it was in me already, I knew it before, only I didn't know what it was," he said. "Its right name."

Knowing its name, he was fully armed. And again he went where the money went: "For Solomon says that the feast is made for laughter, wine for making merry, but money answers all things." Finding backers, he put on concerts at the Town Hall, the Carnegie Recital Hall. In program notes, he wrote that he was "attempting to add to the ineversal thought." His compositions included *The Senses—Inspirations from the Readings of Nietzsche, The Will Is Everything,* and the Crabtree Violin Concerto.

"There was more. Always more," he said. Beyond himself, he promoted ballroom dancing and jazz, performers like Noble Sissle, Eubie Blake, and Hazel Scott, and he had his own radio program, *Crabtree's Youth Show.* More gainful, he sold used clothes. He never married; he had no intimates; he lived in one room off Madison Avenue. Around 1960, he began to accumulate spare dogs. "Historically wise, this was the turning point," he believed. "When my bitch, she littered nine pups, I put them in my bathroom—it was a good-size bathroom, a shower and all—but the neighbors, they complained and then I was put outdoors, outcast, and my dogs too."

Since then, he had moved many times. Sometimes, it seemed, he'd been moving on forever. But he had supporters, loyal friends; they did not let him starve. In 1974, he published his first book, *View of Life and Things*. Privately printed, it was subtitled *The Message That Created Watergate*, a collection of prophecies, dreams, meditations, and sold some three hundred copies. On the back cover was engraved the Crabtree crest—a hand erect holding a dagger in pale proper, argent a cross ragulé, sable a chief azure.

On Eleventh Avenue, he and his dogs took shelter in an abandoned rail-freight office. There he sold more used clothes, read more books; he promoted Saturday night dances in a loading dock, which he rechristened the Ballroom. Then the city tore down the freight yard, turned it into the Jacob Javits Convention Center, a $375 million complex of glass and mirrors and steel. "I just wanted to make dreams come to reality," Crabtree told the *New York Times*. "I didn't know anything else."

So he had come to DeWitt Clinton Park. The firebugs crept in the night, and all his dogs burned up. "But that's to be expected," he said. "In the olden days, they killed all my kinds of people. Seers, prophets, and philosophers. John the Baptist and such." But that knowledge did not daunt him. "These people forget one thing," he said. "I am an Aries."

He did not thrive, he got by. Twice a week, he toured the neighborhood restaurants; they gave him plenty bones for the dogs and prime meat for himself. The rest of the time, he studied eternity. "Only one thing is certain," he pronounced. "We're headed for the Fall."

Outside his white house, he stood against the wind and scratched his skull, a gentle man but lost. "Used to be, I dreamed

most every night," he said. "I saw bright lights across my eyes.
I was walking, not running, I was walking from my enemies. I
was falling off a cliff; I dreamed music. I was floating. I dreamed
mid-air." Behind the boarded windows, the dogs did not stop
howling. "These days I don't dream nothing," Ray Crabtree
said.

"Not ever?"

"No nothing. No more."

Hearing this, Richard H. Roffman pursed his lips, shook his
head. "Of course, even humanitarians have their down days,"
he said, doubtfully.

Roffman was Crabtree's press agent. He was also mayor of
Times Square, self-styled, and the patron saint of quirks. His
weekly cable TV show, *The Dick Roffman World*, had given a
free platform to more stateless talents than any Broadway promoter since P. T. Barnum himself. Crabtree apart, his current
roster included Monde, *Genie of the Accordion and inventor of
the world-famous celebrity handshake glove*; Tino Valenti, *Society
Troubadour*, and Adonaiasis, *Singing Psychic*; Morris Katz, *the
world's fastest painter*; Dr. Joseph Yellis, *podiatrist-humorist*; and
Dee Dee Darnell, *Songthrush Who Needs No Introduction*.

This was no gag. A large round personage of the Humpty
Dumpty persuasion, Roffman was a born missionary. If he didn't
believe in all of his clients' talents, he believed devoutly in their
right to a public airing. "The Pied Piper of Broadway," Wambly
Bald, *Valued friend, Close confidant*, called him. "Where seldom
is heard an encouraging word, his voice is the voice of bright
lights."

Roffman himself had no such pretensions. "I am just a flack.
The Woolworth of publicity, not the Tiffany," he said. Eggshell
bald beneath an artist's beret, which he wore rakishly aslant, he
had trouble catching his breath. In his seventies, he was racked
by arthritis and hernias, leaned heavily on a cane. But he did
not abate his pace. In the last year, he had worked 365 days,
attended twelve hundred gala functions, put out some seven

thousand publicity releases. "My job is to hold out hope. This requires stamina," he said.

Among the PR releases, tapped out with two fingers at a vintage Royal, were small masterworks: "The Whirling Dervish Society presented an award to Tino Valenti, the society troubadour, raconteur, character actor, artist, fashion designer, singer, guitarist, bicyclist, lecturer, producer, director for being the Busiest Man of Quality Around."

Or again: "Six vegetarian Dachshunds are available for placement by noted singing psychic Adonaiasis. At a press conference held at the Lotos Eaters Chinese Restaurant, Adonaiasis, a tall, handsome, blond man of muscular physique said: 'I sadly must give up these wonderful dogs, for I am getting so very busy with my consultation and personal advisory services and can only find time to give personal attention to a very few loved ones of the canine world. . . .' "

In return for such inspirations, Roffman was rewarded much mockery, few thanks. For forty years, he had been working out of the same office/living room off Upper Broadway. Painted baby-pink, it was piled ceiling-high with publicity glossies, press clippings, demonstration tapes. Somewhere in the middle, propped up by his sister Malvina, Roffman sat talking on two phones at once, typing fresh releases. His great moon head gleamed stark-white with pain, a sweating cheese. Still he did not skip a beat: "Nat Lehrfeld, *Furrier and Seashell Sculptor*," he said. "Big Eddie Carmel, *Gentle Nine-foot Jewish Giant from the Bronx*. Princess Saint Joan, *Noted Painter in Oils*."

"Your pills," his sister Malvina said.

"Brother Ignatius, *holistic health guru who swears by the miraculous healing powers of the common coconut*. Cowboy Jack Willis, *Prizefighter and Poet*. Harold Blum, *Cookie Wholesaler*."

"Oh, Dick. Oh, Dick," Malvina cried, wailing now. "What did the doctor tell you?"

"Ugly George Urban," said Dick. "*Wears silver suit*."

He averaged twenty puffs and a hundred calls each day.

Then the night shift began. "After my divorce, I swore I would never spend another night of my life at home. I never have," he said.

"Never has," Malvina sighed.

"Nor never will."

His Broadway ramblings went back to early childhood. Maurice Roffman, his father, *Distinguished Orchestra Leader and Composer*, had used to lead the house band at the Elysee Hotel and walk his heir down the Great White Way between sets. Dick himself became a Vitagraph child-star, appeared in a couple of *Our Gang* comedies, then turned boy reporter with the *New York Journal-American*. He interviewed Dutch Schultz and Meyer Lansky, was a stringer for Walter Winchell, did PR for Sherman Billingsley's Stork Club, and hosted his own radio show, *Real Stories from Real Life*. At last he found his vocation: "To be the catalyst."

It wasn't much of a living. He did not charge fixed fees, was leery of legal matters. Sometimes he got paid in dollars, more often in promises. One journalist described him accepting a pair of secondhand gloves in return for a TV spot. But that didn't mean that his clients did not value him. On the contrary, they believed him a true saint. Every year there was a Richard H. Roffman Birthday Tribute, staged by the Friends of Richard H. Roffman. Led by Dr. Murray C. Kaye, *Civic leader and retail beauty-world industrialist—owner of Murray Kaye Way Beauty Salon*, all of his protégés would come together in the banquet room of some off-Broadway restaurant, or in Roffman's basement TV studio beneath an automotive-parts distributor on West Fifty-ninth, and one by one, the genie of the accordion and the singing psychic, the podiatrist-humorist and the seashell sculptor and the society troubadour, the songthrush who needs no introduction, the nine-foot Jewish giant, the holistic health guru, and the cookie wholesaler, they'd sing and dance, tell jokes and recite poetry, do impressions.

When the entertainment was done, there were speeches, and

these speeches always said the same thing: "Richard H. Roffman made me what I am today. He made my dreams come true."

The thought made him flush with remembered pleasure. His eyes were watery; his white flesh mottled with pink. "For such good friends I thank God," Roffman said. *"Noted Supreme Being."*

He was almost the last press agent. In a few years more, the trade would be extinct, another Broadway gone. For as long as there'd been a Times Square, flacks had been its town criers. In a real sense, the place was their invention. It was they, in cahoots with the tabloid columnists, who had first enshrined it as the Big Drag, the *Crossroads of the World*: "A flaming witch who rides high on the wings of promise and brushes blinding siroccos into the eyes of those who would put faith in her."

Press agentry was always a cottage industry, underpaid and short on plumbing. But it had had its own seedy glamour. In the fifties, it had even spawned Tub-Thumpers Row, a cluster of office apartments on West Forty-eighth. Its center, Eddie Jaffe's bedroom above Duffy's Tavern, was then a Broadway landmark. Marlon Brando slept on its floor; Rocky Graziano put his fist through its steel-plated door. And there Margie Ward, *Famed Burlesque Queen*, announced she was going legit, to star as Clytemnestra: "I'm the wife of King Agamemnon," she explained. "He owes me twenty grand."

In that halcyon day, *Cosmopolitan* claimed that more than five hundred flacks worked Times Square alone. Now Richard H. Roffman and Dick Falk were left: "It's sad," Falk said, "but not very sad."

He was seventy-eight, a dashing figure with a white goatee and white yachting cap, a white handlebar moustache. His cubbyhole office overlooked the corner of Broadway and Forty-second, the Crossroads of the World itself: "A grandstand seat," he said. "From my window, I can watch a mugging every fifteen minutes, *buy one, get another for free*, as they say on the TV, and never have to move a muscle. It helps keep me young."

He was Roffman's polar opposite. Where the Pied Piper walked on gilded splinters, Falk strode with cleated hooves. His stride was voracious, his eye lubricious, and his voice a drill sergeant's blast. "The history of Times Square?" he bellowed, brazen-tongued as any Barnum. "It started out a stinkpot, then it went downhill."

He could not speak of the Golden Era, so called; that was before his time. But from the twenties on, the Big Drag had always been what it was right now—a carnival midway, a land-locked Coney Island. "People talk so much folderol," he said. "Gilded this, golden that. Believe me, the only gold worth a damn here was always cash in hand."

From decade to decade, the trappings might evolve, the dialogue and the sound effects. But the basic plot was set in stone. "Guys come here to get laid, gals come here to get paid," Falk said.

A look of false alarm froze his eye. Tugging sheepishly at the upturned ends of his white moustache, he dropped his voice to a medium bark. "Is that a sexist remark?" he asked. "It's true, so it probably is." Then contrition passed, he brightened. "Serves me right," he said. "Flacks and truth don't mix."

Self-deprecation ran through him like a trademark, the name in a stick of rock. Underneath his yachting cap, he was smooth-pated, as glabrous as Richard H. Roffman. But that was the price of admission: "All press agents are bald. They have to be." He sighed heavily. "Their hair gets burned off by the lies."

Falk, who came from Newark, New Jersey, had inherited a fortune in railroad stock and blown it by age twenty-one; had tried and failed to become a Hollywood actor; tried and failed in business; tried and failed to eat: "So I'm thirty years old, I'm living in the Washington-Jefferson Hotel on Eighth, nine dollars a week, I can't even pay that, and I'm eating oatmeal at the Automat, you got a free roll before nine in the morning. So I'm sick, my stomach is killing me, I can't get out of bed most days. So I think to myself, *What's left? What can a guy do that knows*

nothing, has no talent, no prospects, no hope and not a prayer?"
He waggled his fine eyebrows, stroked his snowy beard. "All
answers on a postcard, please."

He'd worked fifteen years for the Shubert Organization, then
struck out alone. Over the decades, his clientele had ranged
from Jayne Mansfield to Norman Mailer, Barbra Streisand to
Salvador Dali. Inspired by Dick Falk and "the pure, vertical,
mystical, gothic love of cash," Dali had once deigned to design
a series of Hallmark greeting cards. "But they didn't sell," Falk
confessed. "Neither did the Great Herman."

Herman—"the smartest, most versatile performer I ever
handled, and the most perfect gentleman"—had hit New York
in the late fifties. Falk reserved a suite at the Waldorf-Astoria,
summoned the world's press. The hotel, warned to prepare for
a Swiss acrobat who spoke not a word of English, sent up
complimentary champagne and canapes, a German-Italian in-
terpreter. Promptly at noon, a rented Daimler pulled up. Flash-
bulbs exploded all over the lobby. And out stepped the Great
Herman, a flea: "But quite a big flea. And really a marvellous
mixer."

This was the soul of flackery; the unsaleable in pursuit of
the unavailable. If you found the chase puerile and tasteless, an
insult to human intelligence, "you show fine common sense,"
Falk said, "and you got no business on Broadway."

His own Broadway had faded somewhere round 1970. Television was making the press agent obsolescent. New York, which
had once supported nine major papers, was down to three and
counting. And the clients, too, had changed: "Suddenly, they
all wanted to play Hamlet. Even the Great Herman." Office
rents skyrocketed, old colleagues kept dropping dead. In the
square below, meanwhile, the Porn Age had come.

In theory, Falk had no objections. "Trade is trade," he said.
"A gal dancing topless on the bar, you stick a dollar down her
panties and cop a feel, what's wrong with that? If only Norman
Mailer had been as honest." But the sex shows came with surplus

baggage. "Pushers, pimps, and psychos. Sickies, skells," said Falk. "Dead flacks."

These days he worked shortened hours, did not ride the subway at dawn. But his crimson banner—Richard R. Falk Associates, Public Relations, 221-0043—still bellied proudly from his second-floor window, and he was by no means inactive. Recently, a nobly white-bearded portrait of him in soulful profile had been circulating America's colleges, announcing that he, Sigmund Freud, *Distinguished Octoganarian and Thinker*, was available for lecture tours. But his greatest passion was flying.

On his desk sat an outsized Quaker Oats box labeled AIR-PLANE ASHES: "I offer a special service, the gift of eternal flight, I like to hope it's unique," he said. For a modest fee, he would collect the ashes of crematees, pack them securely inside the Quaker Oats box and scatter them at sea while reciting the *Rubáiyát* of Omar Khayyám. "*Take the cash and carry, and let the credit cards go*," he quoted, striking a tragedian's pose. "Or something."

Sometimes, when the wind was from the north, he'd catch himself brooding on his own Quaker Oats. The thought did not oppress him for long. "A guy calls me up last week, he says he's got cancer, he's taking the count, and he wants me to handle his ashes. So fine. *You do your bit, I'll do mine*, I say. Only it turns out, the guy's terrified of flying. So what then?" Falk mimed bafflement, consternation. "What could I tell the poor clown? *I'll take it slow*," he roared. He banged his clenched fist on his desk, scaring dust and yesterday's papers, the glossies of dead chorines. "Like hell I'll take it slow," he said.

It was six o'clock. Across the street was a sign for Delicate Touch, Topless Shines. For many years, it had been a Times Square staple. You climbed a long, darkened stairway to a corridor lined with shoeshine stands, polish tins and chamois rags, but no topless shinists. An old black man—"my name is my own"—sat behind a wooden barrier and spelled out the deal: five dollars for a girl and a room for fifteen minutes, all extras negotiable. Or if you preferred, you could stay out front and have a girl shine your shoes. That had happened one time, the counterman said. But he did not recall what year.

Now the old man had vanished, and the shoestands with him. In their place was a girl called Wesley, knocking stolidly at a locked and bolted door. She was seventeen, stark white with flaming red hair; she sought a man named Smiling George. "He said be here by six. Now it's six," she said, "and he's not here."

We walked out together on the Deuce. The shifts were changing, the old men going home, the young coming out for the night. Fresh crowds surrounded the three-card monte games. Cops in their prowl cars oozed by, but did not bother the monte men. What was the use? Cut off one and two reappeared. "I heard they cheat," Wesley said.

She came from Concordia, Kansas; she had been in New York five days. "But I only ate the first three," she said, her face chalky white, her eyes red-rimmed and swimming. At Nedick's, where I bought her a snack, she inhaled four hamburgers and four large orders of fries, four large Cokes, four ice-cream sundaes. "Four is my lucky number. Smiling George told me so," she said.

She wore a green miniskirt with bubblegum-pink tights, a navy blue boy's shirt. That was the reason she was called Wesley, her father had wanted a boy. But her red hair flowed gleaming on her shoulders; it smelled fresh of coconuts. She was an actress, or she was going to be, and actresses did not go sloppy in public. "They wash all the time, every day. They have to," Wesley said. Her gray eyes were painted purplish blue, shaped to slant like a Siamese cat's. "In this business, your personal attractions are your bluechip stock, the one asset you never sell short," she said. "George told me that."

She'd only met him the night before. The way they found each other, it was so strange, it seemed like fate happening. Wesley had been standing on the corner of Broadway and Forty-fourth. It was getting dark, and she was starving hungry; she hadn't slept in her bed for a week. To be honest, she felt lost. The only reason she'd come to New York, there was a boy she knew. His name was Martin; he was older.

She'd met him at Easter, up in South Dakota, the Badlands National Park. She was touring with some girlfriends, they stopped at a picnic ground, and Martin had borrowed their salt. He was into acting, just like her, but he was way ahead of her. He already had a room in Long Island City, a steady job waiting tables. He took breathing lessons, he could tap dance and primal scream. He wore Obsession by Calvin Klein.

The first time they made love, they were inside Martin's Chevy Rambler, and he kept inching their bodies sideways, raising them up, till his left profile was caught in the rearview mirror. "He was just so dedicated," Wesley said. In the morning, she told him she was planning on coming to New York, the Big Apple. Which was kind of a lie in a way, the thought just jumped in her head. But Martin did not blink. *Awesome*, he said. *Mi casa es su casa*. So here she was. Only Martin had moved to Marblehead.

"What's that phrase? Something horny dilemma?" Wesley asked. She couldn't go crawling home, that wasn't her way. "I was brought up to be a Marine," she said. But even Marines could get hungry, feel lost. She'd spent the last two nights in Penn Station, getting hustled from bench to bench; she still had a ten-dollar note tucked in her shoe, but that was her suicide fund. So what to do? "I started to cry," she said. "Well, not cry. Sort of sniffle." And Smiling George happened by.

It was unreal. Just when she was fresh out of hope, she heard this man's voice crying *Jennifer! Jenny! Jenny Feffer!* A white hand grasped her bare arm, and she smelled Obsession by Calvin Klein. But when she turned the man was old, maybe fifty, and looked close to tears. "You're not my daughter," he said.

He made it sound like her fault. People always did. Maybe it was her aura, maybe just her red hair. She'd had a friend in high school, Marianne Tibbs, who was kind of a mystic, and Marianne told her once that all redheads were fated to burn, consumed by their own flame. Elemental fire, they symbolized witchcraft, the forbidden unknown. "The siren's song. Irresistible, yet deadly," Marianne had said. But Wesley did not feel like a witch. She felt like a miscalculation.

"Somebody that should have been somebody else," she said. A boy or some nice girl, a lush tan blonde, a cool mysterious brunette. Anything but this carrot-topped white thing, all arms and legs and an ass as flat as Kansas, who was not this man's daughter, never would be.

At Broadway and Forty-fourth, the man kept walking round her in slow circles, inspecting her from every angle, checking and rechecking. "I can't understand it," he said. He hadn't been gone a moment. He had popped into La Primadora for one fat cigar, and when he came out, Jennifer had simply vanished, gone up in smoke. She was sixteen, just a child. If she fell among thieves, she wouldn't have a prayer. "I am beside myself," the man said.

Wesley looked in his face; it was the saddest face out. Every part of it drooped, the eyes, the ears and jowls, the long hook snout. It put her in mind of a beagle she found once. The beagle's name was Trigger, and it had been abused. "I'm sorry," she said.

"You're not the blame," said the man.

That was nice of him to say; but Wesley didn't believe him. His look was full of hurt, a wordless accusation, and it made her feel so guilty, so rotten deep inside. "I'm sorry," she kept on saying. "Sorry, sorry, sorry." Still he stood and drooped; he would not disappear. "My only daughter," he said.

"Yes," said Wesley, and surrendered. "Yes, I will, yes."

His office was a darkened room beyond Eighth Avenue, where Hell's Kitchen used to be. The doorman wore a green cap trimmed with gold braid and, when he saw them coming, he clicked his heels, he winked. "How's Smiling George?" the doorman asked.

"I am beside myself," said George.

He was a movie producer. Though he was just George to his friends, his professional name was Federico Fellini. "That's the game you have to play. In this business you'd better be Italian or some Jew, or you're dead in the water," he explained. He shook his head, flapped his jowls. "It's sick, but what can you do?" he said. "This is a sick, sick world."

Posters of his old films covered the office walls. Wesley could not remember the exact names—they were all in a foreign language—but George said they had been megahits. "Blockbusters. Global monsters," he said. Still he was not satisfied. True artists never were. He had a new project in the works, guaranteed to tear the roof off the sucker. It was not a total package yet. It didn't even have a title. But every detail was clear in his head. Plot, dialogue, publicity angle: "I even got the advertising slogan. *You've Seen the Rest, Now Catch the Best*," George said. Only the casting remained. "The lead actress," he said. "A movie like this, it could be *Gone with the Wind* or it could be *Blood Sucking Freaks*. It all depends on the star."

The way he explained it, the role required a unique gift. "A Hollywood actress couldn't cut it. She'd be too jaded, too shopworn," said George. What he was looking for was freshness. "An incandescence," he said.

The word was not familiar. Wesley was too shy to say so out loud, but George just seemed to sense it. "*Incandescence*," he explained, "an inner heat, banked fires, just waiting to ignite. A raw sensual flame like paint-stripper, all it takes is one stray match and every red-blooded male in America goes down with scorched eyeballs."

That kind of blaze did not lurk in every cattle call. Smiling George had been seeking it for months, make that years, without finding just the right face and figure. Sometimes he felt like giving up. Perhaps the vision he sought did not exist, perhaps it was just a mirage. "An impossible dream," he said. But he could not help himself. "It is my Holy Grail," he said. "The artist's eternal quest for the divine."

As he talked, he paced his office floor, chain-smoking. Windows black with grime blocked out the light; there seemed no air to breathe. "Smoldering. Sizzling. Simmering. Seething," said George, his face growing longer and more doglike with each adjective. "Sexsational," he said. "Like you."

Wesley was sunk in an armchair, so deep and soft it felt like squatting in quicksand. Right above her was a hooded standard lamp. When George hit the switch, the glare blinded her. "Like you could be," he said. "If only you'd dare to try."

She was not naive. She watched TV like anyone else, so she knew about movie producers. They were not to be trusted. They took young girls' hearts and threw them away like broken toys. But the light in her eyes paralyzed her. "Sexsational," George kept saying. She felt him moving somewhere above her, but she could not see. "Raw sensual flame," he said.

Telling it now, she felt foolish. A stray fleck of ketchup clung to the corner of her mouth; she buried herself in ice-cream sundae. "I was not born yesterday, if that's what you think. I've been around the block," she said. Two bright-red spots like pinlights burned on either cheek. "I just felt I had no choice," she said. "No say."

When Smiling George switched the light back off and she could focus again, the first thing she saw was the wall full of old movie posters. One of them showed a blonde with big breasts in a skintight dress, sort of crawling on all fours like an animal, a jungle beast of prey. *La Dolce Vita*, the poster read: "One of my biggest," said George.

By some bizarre coincidence, there was a similar scene in his next film. If Wesley liked, they could run it through. "Let's see how you take direction," said George. But now he seemed not to care. Suddenly, it felt as if Wesley was canvassing *him*. "Tell you what I'll do. I'll give you a shot, see how the cookie crumbles," he said. "What have I got to lose?"

Riffling through his shooting script, he pinned down the scene in question. It called for Wesley to take off her clothes, climb up on the office desk, and crouching on all fours, bark like a dog. But not just any dog. "A pedigree poodle," said Smiling George. "Miniature. Female. French."

Wesley was not properly prepared. Her only previous speaking part had been the March Hare in *Alice in Wonderland*. That had been in the eighth grade, and her stagecraft had grown rusty.

When she started to undress, she seemed all thumbs. There was a vase full of plastic wildflowers on the desk. Crawling up, she knocked it over, sent the flowers flying. Stale smoke and dust choked her lungs, brought on a coughing fit. "But I did not freeze," she said. As Smiling George directed, she took up her position, awaited her cue. Then she shut her eyes tight, and she barked till she was hoarse.

The take seemed to go on forever. In the darkness behind her, she could feel George watching her, judging. But he did not reach out to touch; he never made a move. At the end of forever, he just clapped his hands once. "Cut," he said. Wesley climbed back down again, began to put on her clothes. Smiling George was standing by the window, still watching her, black on black, but he did not say what he thought; he did not say anything.

"Imagine," Wesley said. There she'd been, bent double, pulling up her new pink tights by L'eggs, and somehow the tights had got snarled, twisted tight in a knot. So she'd knelt down to unravel them; she bowed her head. And when she looked up, George was standing right above her.

Up close, the smell of Obsession by Calvin Klein was so strong, it made her eyes sting and water. George's hand fell on her shoulder, it felt cold and rigid like wax. "You want to be somebody in this business? A serious actress?" he asked. She did not reply, just nodded her head. Her tights were ripped at the gusset. She wrestled them up around her knees, but could not force them any higher. "You want to be superstar?" said George.

"Yes. I will. Yes."

"Then you better learn Rule One."

Fatherly, he cupped her chin in his hand, raised her up. "When the director says French poodle," said Smiling George, "don't give him a damn Pekinese."

She had felt just dreadful then. She'd thought that she was a total failure. But George must have seen something in her, *raw sensual flame*, after all. He had promised her a second chance, a proper screen test: "With cameras and everything," Wesley said. On the strength of that, she had saved $3.30 by missing dinner, $2.45 from lunch, and spent it on fresh makeup, a sachet of coconut-oil conditioner. YOUTH IS NOT AN AGE, JUST A STATE OF MIND, the blurb on its sachet proclaimed.

"He promised," Wesley said. The last lick of sundae had been consumed; the tabletop was piled high with debris. "I wouldn't treat a dog like that," she said. Then she heard what she had said. Her face split and crumpled, she looked about to bawl, but she got the giggles instead. "Smoldering. Sizzling. Simmering. Seething," she said. Among the ruins of her meals lay plastic packets of mustard and tomato ketchup. Grabbing up a fistful at random, she scrunched them tight. Red and yellow glop squirted over her hand, ran together. "Sexsational," said Wesley. "Like me."

Up and down Forty-second Street, the evening sidewalks were filling, overflowing. Outside the movie marquees, the night's trade took up position, selling new sex and drugs, new deaths. "I got crack so good, it make wrong right," said a gray ghost by the Victory, leaning on a poster for *Hot Saddle Tramp*. He was seventeen, the same age as Wesley, but he had lost all his teeth except one, a top left molar, which he'd had filled with a diamond. It winked in his maw like a flashlight in an open-pit mine. "So good, so good," he said, "it certify your soul."

Underground was a whole other city. Between Times Square and Port Authority lay a labyrinth of subway corridors, platforms, and walkways, storage vaults, arcades. Men lived here, had lived here for years. Performers worked the junctions; doo-wop quartets singing "Heart and Soul," saxophonists playing "Giant Steps," mimes and jugglers, one-man bands.

Below the Eighth Avenue exit, there were shinists and plastic-cheese sandwiches, vintage pinball machines. Set between a William's Apollo and a Gottlieb's Jack O' Diamonds, at swim in stale urine, stood a Discover Your Destiny machine. STAND THE TEST OF FATE, it read; and one man did. A salesman clad in sky-blue polyester, he'd come here from Philly, got drunk, and had his wallet swiped. All that remained to him was a quarter and four pennies, but he was still game. He stuck the quarter in the slot and waited with hands upraised, fingers crossed. When Destiny's card emerged, however, he was too soused to read it. "Fortune follows," he began. "Brave fortune follows brave." That much was clear, but the small print defeated him. "Snow use," he said. He tore the card into scraps, he hurled them at the wall. "No way to stand the test," he mumbled, "if the test can't stand you."

Three blocks away, Larry Marshall heard the tale, and nodded. "Tell me 'bout it," he said. His laugh was strident, joyless. "It could have been me," he said.

He sat alone in Barrymore's, a theater bar on West Forty-fifth, sipping chastely at a Diet Coke. He had been testing for thirty years. He would not weep if he never tested again.

It was strange in a way, because everybody on Broadway knew what he could do. Singer, dancer, and actor in one, he'd been in so many shows—*Hair, Jesus Christ Superstar, The Three-penny Opera*, a dozen more. He had sung doo-wop and Bernstein's Mass, the Beatles and Palestrina. As Sportin' Life in *Porgy and Bess*, he'd played the Met and all over the globe. He had even starred in a Broadway musical, *Rockabye Hamlet*. Admittedly, it ran only four nights. Still his name had topped the bill; he had lit up the Great White Way. That was a thing nobody could take from him. Yet here he was, facing fifty, still doing auditions.

"It causes a man to ponder," he said. He was a walking lexicon, a glossary of performance. Perhaps some man alive on Broadway had worn more hats, played more fields. If so, nobody in Barrymore's could conjure the name. "I covered the waterfront," Larry said.

"So what happened?"

"I fell in."

Black, Irish, and Cherokee mixed, his flesh was a light caramel, his wide face dusted with freckles. He laughed a lot, very loud, and told many jokes. His melancholia seemed bottomless.

In his nonage, he'd been rake-thin, a whip, but mileage had blurred the edges: "Scuffed the paintwork, played hell with the suspension," he said. There had been too many years on the road, too many rough nights in Jericho, and much too much to drink. Booze had hurt him, and hurt his work. In its thrall, he had grown bloated, lethargic: "A carcass," he said. But the drinking had stopped now; the weight was off. Inside Barrymore's, Diet Coke in hand, Larry looked like an aging greyhound, race-scarred and a little lame, but a purebred still, styled to run.

"How I got here from there? A very fine question," he said. He'd begun in Spartanburg, South Carolina, thirteen pounds at birth. His grandfather had run away from a Cherokee reservation and married a black woman. He had a farm and a big old roomy house painted white, with chickens and goats in the yard, a horse, a cow. But he did not fit in the black community. He was a Catholic convert, a man of education. Priests said mass in the living room. Larry was named for St. Lawrence. His mother was fifteen. For many years, Larry could not sleep unless he held her breast. His father, a sergeant from a nearby army post, had vanished overseas. Larry was told he was dead. Then his mother went away to Atlanta, to study in hair-dressing school. The house was full of aunts and uncles, massed cousins. Everybody talked at once. There was noise night and day. Out in the yard, alone, Larry killed baby chicks. Nobody could work out why. "Because they walk behind their mother," Larry said.

He grew up circular, insatiable. He could not keep still, couldn't seem to stay out of trouble. His mother married a man who worked in a funeral parlor and recoiled when Larry called him Daddy. More aunts and uncles appeared, a fresh batch of cousins. For Sunday lunch, Larry roasted his pet kitten in the oven. He was four, turning five. The weekend of his birthday, he wolf-whistled at a white woman outside the Palmetto Theater. His family decided he might be better off elsewhere.

He had an aunt in New York, his mother's elder sister. She'd married into a family of Cubans and Barbadians, they lived in Hamilton Heights, and Larry was sent on a visit. The visit never ended.

"My aunt's whole existence was a sigh," Larry said. She tried to keep Larry a baby forever, washed him and dressed him till he was ten. But not everyone was so pampering. In his life, somewhere in the neighborhood, was a man he would not name; and this man lived to punish. All week he worked and kept count of Larry's sins, totting up the whippings due. Friday he got paid; Saturday he whipped. And on certain Sundays, for variety, he'd hold a pillow over Larry's mouth, smother him till he turned blue.

"An education," Larry called it. Hamilton Heights today was crackhouse heaven, but back then it was genteel, a symbol of black progress. Duke Ellington lived down the block, Mary Lou Williams around the corner. Larry's uncle, a postal clerk, owned a four-floor brownstone, weighty as a citadel, all scrubbed and gleaming with dark-red woods.

Locked in his bedroom, Larry lived in front of the full-length mirror. He was skinny now, a baggage of bones. A snapshot of him as an altar boy showed a Belsen child, sunken-cheeked, head lolling, with only the eyes left alive. At school he wore a West Point uniform and saluted each time a nun passed by. In his mirror, he was Captain Fantastic; he mimed to the Make-Believe Ballroom. He had two ambitions—to be a priest, to play the tenor sax—and could not choose.

In a sense, he never had. By the time he entered his teens, he was a soloist with the Corpus Christi choir, performing Gregorian chants and Fauré's Requiem; and smoking reefer and drinking Thunderbird and singing falsetto with a doo-wop quartet, *a cappella* in a local graveyard.

The quartet was led by a smooth operator named David. They called themselves the Del-Chords and wore matching high-school sweaters with D–C logos. *Jet* magazine wrote them up; they seemed set for stardom: "Only thing wrong," Larry said. "We sang too good."

Too schooled, too clean—they did not sound black, but they couldn't pass for white. It was 1960, the high summer of the rock and roll gold rush. At the Brill Building, 1652 Broadway, every office and broom closet held next week's Elvis, last month's Platters. You got in the elevator, and the Crests started singing *Sixteen Candles*. You stepped out in the lobby, and Jackie Wilson sang *Lonely Weekends*.

At the corner, Broadway at Forty-ninth, was a coffee shop called the Turf. Its legal capacity was 83 but, one Monday lunchtime, Larry counted 226, all scatting and riffing at once: the Skyliners and the Spaniels, the Jesters and Chantels, the Ravens and Falcons and Flamingos and Crows; and the Cadillacs and the Impalas, the Eldorados and the Edsels; and Ben E. King and the Drifters; and Leiber & Stoller, and Goffin & King; Doc Pomus and Mort Shuman; and Neil Sedaka and Frankie Valli; and Little Eva, Lavern Baker, Clyde McPhatter, Sam Cooke; and one small squirt with thinning hair and bad skin, who never picked up a tab. Phil Spector, his name was.

The Del-Chords were lost in the crush. They did a hundred

auditions, stood a hundred tests, but always somebody sang louder and dressed flashier. Besides, David's true dream was to be a gangster. When the group's break came at last and they appeared on a Martha Raye telethon, he found he'd run out of cigarettes. So he robbed a drugstore. Next morning, when Larry woke to read the review in the *Daily News*, he found instead a front-page picture of David in handcuffs, screaming abuse from the back of a Black Maria.

"Martha Raye did not book us back," Larry said. With the Del-Chords kaput, he moved to the Sierras. They made a record, "I'll Believe It When I See It," that reached ninety-eight on the Billboard Hot Hundred. Then the girl singer, Cassandra, got pregnant or married, the Sierras broke up, and Larry could never again hear an Oldies but Goodies show without he felt sick to his stomach. "The Dubs, the Silhouettes. Lee Andrews and the Hearts," he cried. "It could have been me."

The saxman rebuffed, it was the turn of the priest. Even while he haunted the Brill Building, he had been conducting choirs, studying classical voice. Now he won music scholarships to Xavier in New Orleans, the New England Conservatory.

He was twenty-one. In his life, he had never spent one day out of reach of mothering women: "Females trying to make me female, too." As long as he could remember, he'd ached to break free, be alone. And at last his chance had come. In New Orleans he played Beatles songs and hootenanny on Bourbon Street, got drunk every morning and laid every night; in Boston he played drums, sat in with John Coltrane. "I was my own man. Alone," Larry said, exulting. And his first trip home to New York, he got married to his high-school sweetheart: "Not to be alone."

His wife's father was Avon Long, self-styled the Great Avon. He was a cornerstone of the black theater; had been, after John Bubbles, the second man to play Sportin' Life in *Porgy and Bess*. Thirty years on, he was playing him still. The next time he went touring, Larry understudied him.

"He tutored me the world," Larry said. For ninety days, the company rode America, pent up in a bus with a broken-down driver called Wrong-Way Wally. They traveled Tennessee and Georgia, Texas and Alabama, sharing seven-dollar rooms in Holiday Inns; snatching breakfasts in carparks while hating white faces stared in through the bus windows; playing cards all day, shooting craps by night; cheating, lying, pulling knives; hunting pigs' feet and deviled brains in the Bottoms; rolling and racing, never sleeping: "Drinking, doping, just dying," said Larry. "I wished it would never end."

It was the first time he had been black. And the first time he'd had a father. "Avon Long?" Larry said. "A piece of work." A man in a lavender suit, with accessories in green and gold, Avon played Sportin' Life as a black leprechaun, mercurial, serpentine, all slick-sharp angles and hissing venom. "Picture Ariel as a motherfucker," Larry said. But off-stage, on the bus, Avon had been more like Prospero. "Cantankerous, capricious. A total egomaniac," Larry said. Yet a great magician withal. "That was the key," Larry said. "Everything else about him contradicted. He was a braggart, a blowhard, but he loved silence. He lived in bars but craved solitude. He'd been a Communist with Paul Robeson, he was a rebel always, but his hobbies were playing solitaire and watching reruns of 'Perry Mason.'" Only the magic was constant: "The sorcery of performance."

This was his great gift to Larry—the sense that performers were born special, a breed apart; that if they took care of their art, somehow God would take care of *them*. In his blood, he'd always believed it. But Avon made it law: "A life sentence," Larry said. *"You got the gift. Go use it."* He sighed a heavy sigh; he called for more Diet Coke. "I was not given a choice," he said.

That was twenty years ago, rising twenty-five. In that span, theater life had changed utterly. When Larry first came to Broadway, there had been a kinship, a sense of shared excitement. "You didn't just show up, do your stuff, and go home," he said.

"You were part of something living. You belonged." Performers who worked together drank together, stayed up too late, talked too much, and got too loud together. They knew how to celebrate, and there was just cause for celebration: "You were alive, you were talented and working. You were on Broadway," Larry said, "and Broadway was the world."

Not anymore. In these last years, the theater had shrunk in on itself, grown grudging and hard as a shriveled walnut. Soaring overheads, Equity wars, the fifty-dollar ducat, the Japanese invasion, and the triumph of size over substance, special effects over special performers—the list of causes was tedious to recite, drabber still to contemplate. Broadway shows were now the province of corporate fatcats, all expense accounts and muffled snores. If you truly loved the theater, odds were, you couldn't afford to go.

"It used to be *the Business*. Now it's just a business," Larry said. He himself had survived, just about. But it had been a split decision. He'd worked with Joseph Papp at the Public Theater, with Leonard Bernstein in Washington, with Allen Toussaint in New Orleans. He had worked clubs, cathedrals and casino lounges, La Scala and Covent Garden; played Cab Calloway in *The Cotton Club*, and Simon Zealotes in *Jesus Christ Superstar*; served fourteen years as Sportin' Life. Yet always, even in his flushest times, he had felt himself teetering, scrabbling for footing and balance, one step away from a fall. "Petrified," he said. "Scared stiff to be alone. Scared worse not to be."

He seemed to have no safe niche. He was too light to be dark, too black to be white. On Broadway these days, there were plenty of roles for mail-order brothers. If only he'd looked more street, he could have played the pimps and dope pushers that honky producers craved. *It could have been me*. But he was not the type, couldn't pass: "Not the right degree of nigger," he said.

Nothing changed. In Spartanburg, when the big house filled

with family, he'd gone out in the yard and wrung chickens' necks; on Broadway, he hid in Barrymore's and wrung his own. He punished himself with cognac, so long and hard that his heart went bad. Sometime later, he found himself in detox, strapped down to a steel-frame bed.

"I figured I made my point. Whatever it was," he said now. At the bar, he was toasting three years sober. Work, which had grown scarce, was trickling back again. He had just finished one show, was about to direct another. The Met was staging a revival of *Porgy and Bess*. There was his new club act to rehearse. Come the fall, there would be Europe: *"The Larry Marshall Story,"* he said, "coming to a cinema near you."

Out of Barrymore's, we strolled east towards Broadway. The theaters were just emptying, the crowds scuttling for safety. Years before, a leisurely post-curtain stroll had been integral to every Broadway night out. "Times Square was code for pleasure," Larry said. Now it stood for fear.

"Strange," Larry said. If there was one thing that Broadway could not abide, it was Broadway, and *vice versa*. Everywhere outside New York, theater and street were synonymous. On the spot, they were mutual poison.

The feud had its roots in the twenties. When the motion-picture palaces hit Times Square, theaters had been shunted off into side streets. The Gaiety and the Globe were swept aside by the Paramount and the Roxy. Then came the night clubs and dance halls—Billy Rose's Diamond Horseshoe and Sally Rand's fan dance at the Paradise, the International Casino, the Palais Royal. Times Square turned honky-tonk, and the insult was never forgotten. "The ingrate unwashed," John Barrymore called the rabble. "A bunch of pinko twinkletoes," Izzy Grove called the Stage.

On Times Square this night, the crowds walked stooped and crooked, knocked crabwise by the windstorm. The blast had held steady all day; still the multitudes swarmed. As midnight neared, the howling seemed to grow hotter, more intense. Venturing out into Broadway, we found ourselves picked up bodily, hurled back where we came from. A palmist, a young black girl wrapped in shawls, grabbed my arm. "I save you," she said. Her name was Irish Eyes. "You have a deadly enemy. He plot your damnation," she said.

"Who is he?"

"Check your fatty tissues."

Larry took shelter in a cinema doorway. The current attraction was *Make Them Die Slowly*, an everyday story of cannibal folk, and key scenes were flashed on a TV screen. Even as we tuned in, a victim was being devoured alive, up close and personal. One diner gnawed on an arm, another chomped on toes. In bloodsoaked close-up, the cold buffet rolled his eyes. Then one of the eyes disappeared. "Don't say it," Larry begged. But he could not help himself. "It could have been me," he said.

Alone again, I trekked back to Jimmy's Corner. Sasha was sitting by the window, drawing moustachios on a picture of Gorbachev; but the Mad Monk Rasputin had vanished. "Was not all is cracked up to be," Sasha said. He scratched the itch where the beard had been. Then he flashed the day's take. "Eight dollars and forty-three cents," he said. "Is to make mad any monk."

Down on the Deuce, the last civilians were in retreat. Senior citizens from Queens and Staten Island, they'd come to catch the second-run Hollywood features at the Lyric, the Selwyn, the Empire, the same palaces they had haunted in their teens.

In the Grand Luncheonette, an antique Tin Man called Arnold held hands with Mamie, his bride of fifty-eight years. "I had my first orgasm in the Selwyn," he confided.

"The Apollo," Mamie said.

"No, dear," said Arnold. "The Selwyn."

"How could I forget?" Mamie said. "*Red Dust* with Gable and Harlow, Mary Astor as the wife who strays. The tropical typhoon. The malaria, the heat. The second balcony."

"No, dear," said Arnold. *"Camille."*

When midnight struck, they were gone. Then the strip was left to the lifers. The Hotel Carter, where Rashan and his mother had lived on welfare, now catered to tourists again. Still its doorway was thick with peddlers; touts of every stripe. *Check it out, check it out*, the dealers cried. *Fresh pussy*, the pimps replied.

I thought of the passage in Proust where the Narrator lies abed for forty pages and listens to the cries of the morning's street vendors, weaving a choral symphony. *Crack, smack, mescaline*, the dealers rumbled. *Cherry, cherry*, the chickens chirped.

Sweet young pussy. Get your pussy right here.

Check it out, check it out.

Positively no positives.

Enemas. Golden showers. Black gold.

Moonrock. Angel Dust.

Cherry, cherry.

Check it out.

Through the lobby, on West Forty-third, we sought a drink at the Rose Saigon, but the doorman turned us away. No Caucasians were admitted. So we slid up the block to Sally's Hideaway.

Denise Denise was at the bar, toasting Lush Life's departure. "All the best to the bitch. I take off my wig to her," she said, and she did. Underneath was a mess of stubble, a blighted cornfield. "I did it to myself. Tried to take out the kinks with lye, and I burned up all my roots," said Denise Denise. Her eyes filled with mist. "I was only sixteen. A teenage dream," she said.

"A homecoming queen," the bar person supplied.

"And bald as Chicken Little."

The room was full of bad girls. They dressed like the girls that their mothers had once told them to avoid: black microskirts and leather jackets, six-inch heels, slit dresses and push-up bras. On a tiny stage like a Murphy bed, a lady in red sat painting her fingernails. Electrifying Grace, she said her name was. "Wanna see my pussy?" she inquired.

"How much?" Sasha asked.

"I don't got it with me tonight," said Grace. "It's on order, though. Should be in any day."

Across the street were the loading bays for the *New York Times*. From Sally's doorway, we could rerun the opening shots of *The Sweet Smell of Success*, unchanged after four decades: the blaze of lights in the dark street, the backlit shadows blown huge; the great trucks idling in their stalls; the bound bales of newsprint tumbling down the chutes, and the sudden roar of engines. "Cookie full of arsenic. Boy with ice-cream face," Sasha said. *"Gotovy na Zastchitzu Zhop?"*

"Vsegda gotovy," I replied.

Times Square had begun to empty. The fast-food joints were closing, the last troupe of Japanese businessmen heading back to their hotels. Outside Godfather's Pizza, a black man begged in a brown derby hat. "Buddy, can you spare a dime? Or any multiple thereof?" he asked. His smile was sheepish, self-mocking. "The line is old, I know," he said. "Then again, so am I."

So was anyone past twenty. When whites and tourists abandoned the square, sonic youth remained. Black and Hispanic, Korean, Chinese, it ran in ratpacks, ravaging the sidewalks, noise-raping the arcades. Inside Playland, Pac Man warred with Operation Wolf, The Temple of Doom with Stealth. Machine guns and missiles, rocket blasts, exploding mines kept up a nonstop fusillade. Ghetto blasters pumped a dozen clashing raps. But Public Enemy triumphed over all. *"Subject of suckers, object of hate, who's the one some think is great?"* Chuck D roared out. *"I am that one—"*

"Lies, all lies," purred Barkley, a three-card monte man. "I am that one myself."

He was a wisp of a man, blue-black, with a smudge of goatee, a red shirt printed with green parakeets, and fingers like long, fleshless tendrils, trailing. Youths clustered round his cardboard box like first graders round a Good Humor man; could not wait to thrust cash on him. "Softly, softly," Barkley said. "The greatest assassin of life is haste."

Slydini would have loved his touch. His hands, as they moved the cards, were so fleet that the cards seemed to move themselves. Crack-spined and curling, they turned into the nine of clubs, the seven of spades, but never the queen of diamonds. "Don't mope, don't grope. Find the scarlet lady," Barkley chanted, silky soft. "Who fear being damned cannot be blessed." His fingers whirred, the cards flew. A yellow hand, reaching out from the crush, hovered over one, then another. "He who hesitate be lost," Barkley said. The yellow hand descended; the seven of spades turned up. "Nothing venture, nothing gain," Barkley said. "Virtue be its own reward." And he set the cards flying again.

Sasha stood beneath a mammoth Toshiba sign, at work on his neon suntan; but it was an uphill slog. Some signs had been switched off for the night, others dimmed. Instead of refracted orange and passion pink, the air was turned a greenish gray, like a marathon runner out of gas. Still the dry wind crackled, burned. "You want to know one sad thing?" Sasha asked.

"Why not?"

"I'm missing Brooke Shields."

When first he'd come here, at seventeen, her image had been everywhere. Her rump in tight bluejeans—*Nothing comes between me and my Calvins*—had towered forty feet high; her puckered lips, soda-sipping, stretched half a block. "World was her clam," Sasha said. Now the world had gone Japanese, and Sasha Zim was twenty-five. "Those were days," he said.

"UsedToBe?"

"Yob tvoyu mat!"

Arm in arm, two old codgers, we strolled towards Nathan's Famous, where they played a more elderly game. Its doorway was full of uniformed lawmen with drawn guns and walkie-talkies. Three youths, spread-eagled against the plate-glass window, assumed the position. "Don't tell my mother," one pleaded.

"You shot a man," his captor said.

"Just barely," said the boy, a Hispanic. Blood ran down his chin, made stains on his white T-shirt. "You don't have to tell. Why you have to tell?" he whined.

"Who gave you the gun?"

"Idano. Some guy." The boy's voice was shrill with panic, a schoolchild's squeak. "You don't know my mother. She get so mad," he said. His legs began to tremble and twitch, out of his control. "Why for you wanna make her mad?" he asked.

Now the Deuce was half-deserted. Every storefront was padlocked, every window barred. Only the all-night movies ran on: *Mad Monkey Kung Fu* and *Basket Case, Splatter University, Jail Bait.*

Next door to the New Amsterdam was a sign that read CHESS AND CHECKERS CLUB OF NEW YORK. At the top of a steep flight of steps, we entered a large open room, bright and clean, the image of decorum. Beneath a glass counter was a collection of antique cakes and sandwiches, neatly wrapped; coffee was served in white cups. On the walls, there were pictures of sunlit valleys, of grasslands and blue skies.

Scattered about the room, men of all races faced each other over Formica-topped tables, pondering the complexities of backgammon, Scrabble, chess. Most of them wore suits and ties, and none of them was young. Sages, elders, they spoke only when they had to, and then in undertones. Nobody laughed, no one swore. These were serious men.

Close beside the glass counter, a man slouched in an upright chair, half asleep. We sat down beside him, watched the play. Cards slapped on the tabletops, setting up irregular riffs; dice rattled like snakes; the players murmured, droned. "Don't shoot," said the sleeping man.

Startled by his own voice, he sat up straight; he opened his left eye. Stray hairs stuck up angrily on his skull and his Adam's apple jumped, giving him the look of an outraged turkey-cock, old but fierce in pride. "So you got here," he said, seeing us. "It's about goddamn time."

His name was Leopold Fischbein, Leo Fish; he'd been on the Deuce since 1937. For thirty years he worked at the Hotel Carter when it was still the Dixie, *In The Center Of Everything*. Afterwards, he took stock at the Superfly Boutique, sold tickets at the Liberty and the Victory, was a counterman in Nedick's. Six years ago, he had retired, gone to live with his married sister in Ithaca, New York. But the arrangement did not take. "Adele is a bundle of laughs. Always looks on the bright side," he said. "I got disgusted, I guess."

He'd been back in town for fourteen months. Mostly, he stayed at a friend's place in the Village. Mort Raditz, they'd worked together at the Dixie. But that had its drawbacks, too. At seventy-three, after forty years married and eight as a widower, Mort had taken to bringing home boys. "Weekends I don't mind," Leo said. "I figure weekends, a man can do what the fuck a man wants. But Wednesdays!" He shook his head, appalled. "Wednesdays was our bowling night."

In this upper room, he found sanctuary. "They got a nice class of person; you don't get slapped around," he said. "My age, you don't like to get slapped around." He could sit and doze, bum a few cigarettes, chew over a few grievances, reflect. From the high windows, he could look down and watch Broadway die.

"Ashes to ashes," he said. Every time he looked in the paper, it seemed, there was a fresh nail in the coffin. The Urban Development board kept unveiling new architects' models, more Leggo-brick hotels and office towers, merchandise marts, thirty-four-floor parking lots. The Deuce's theaters were being systematically condemned and taken over by the state, to be turned into arts centers and glass lobotomats. Even the New Amsterdam, Ziegfeld's folly, was not safe. Its steel frame had corroded;

rain was pouring in through the rotted roof. "They might save it for a museum," said Leo Fish. "But living people? Don't make me laugh."

The living people were the problem. "You want to turn Times Square into Disneyland, you gotta disinfect it. You want to disinfect it, you gotta kill it dead," Leo said. He brightened at the thought. "Course, I'm half-dead already, it don't make no odds." He cracked his knuckles, and the chess players swung their heads, outraged. But Leo showed no remorse. "I had my time. Take me out of the oven, I'm done," he said. Rising up, he reached for his coat and hat. "So long, suckers," he said.

It was very late; even Times Square was dark. Spent, we rested on the base of George M. Cohan's statue. "The Broadway man has a better idea of life and things in general than any other class of man in the world. He sees more, meets more, and absorbs more in a day than the average individual will in a month," Cohan had said. But no Broadway men were left around. All the arcades were shut, sonic youth disbanded, the neon stilled. Alone with the pigeons, we stared across the wind-driven square. "What of are you thinking?" Sasha asked.

"Carmen Venus Colon," I began. "Ousmane and Ismaila, Stoney Bisonette, Rickey O and Refugio, Maynard Baines, Ellen Fogarty, the Dad, Robert Moses, Dom Parisi, Liquor Jack Young, Lucius Havens, Tony Bruan, P. T. Barnum, Joe Wojcik and Velma, Matty Troy, Donald Manes, George Washington Plunkitt, EmCee Marie, Enid Gerlin, Shaquille Cleamons and Lionel Ward Justice, Mercedes Purissima Vargas, Sam Wing, Uncle Seven and Eddie Chan, Bobby 2 Bad, Joice Heth, General Tom Thumb and Commodore Nutt, Tommy Blalock, Motion, Paul Kasmin, Donald Baechler, Lev Mikhailovich, J. J. Huneker and Sidney Falco, Cleveland Blakemore, Rashan Ray Perry, Benny and MoRitz, Dr. Davitt, Flo D'Arcy and Aug. Allaire, Calvin Palmer, Archie Smith and Satan, Sadie, Denise Denise, Stanford White and Evelyn Nesbit, Tracy Love, Bert Randolph Sugar, Fred Silver, Terry Malloy and Charlie DeVoe, Sister

Pearl, Lenny Schneider, Katy Freeway, Bob Anthony, Sarah and Serena, the Emerald Doyles, Emile Griffith, Jimmy Glenn, Texas Guinan, Tony Slydini, Mike Bornstein, Ray Crabtree and Richard Roffman, Dick Falk, the Great Herman." I gave it up. "Stuff like that," I said.

It was past five when I got back to the Hotel Moose. First light glimmered, but the windstorm kept up unabated. It did not seem that it would ever be done.

The corridors were deserted. Even Motion had ceased his gardening. Inside my room, Lush Life lay on her back with her legs stuck straight out and her hands folded in her lap. A single candle burned at the foot of the bed. It cast the shadows of her big feet, toes upturned, like upreared horses on the wall.

She did not move when I came in. My first thought was that it was true, she really was dead. But when I looked in her eyes, the pupils were dilated, compressed into tiny black holes.

An empty smack deck lay crumpled among the marigolds. On the wrapper, rubber-stamped, it said HARD CANDY. "Got any Heath Bars?" Lush Life asked. Her voice was as scratchy as an old 78. "Or a Butterfinger, maybe?"

"Out," I said.

"Milk and cookies would do."

"Out," I said. "Out."

"Ladybeard," she said. "What's the use?"

Her burn-scarred kimono lay plopped on the floor. I scooped it up blind, cast it at her nakedness. Its edge clung to her genitals like seaweed to a scallop shell; she started to scratch. "You wanna know something?" Lush Life said. "I'm glad."

She had met Tommy Blalock as appointed, at Tad's Steaks on Forty-second. It was their special place. For $4.39, you could get sirloin steak charbroiled, served with garlic bread and onions, a baked potato running with lard, and each table came with its own candle. Even the streetcombers who hung across your shoulder, ready to pounce on any scraps you failed to keep down, couldn't squelch the romance. But this day something did not smell right. "The grease wasn't rancid; there was no stink of lye," Lush Life said. And Tommy Blalock did not eat his baked potato. "I've been thinking," he said. It was the first time he'd ever referred to himself as anything but Tommy Blalock. "I just wondered," he said.

"Eat your bake," said Lush Life.

"I don't feel good." His tousled head was down, his nose stuck in his plate. "I got a sick headache," he said. "My blood's all backed up. Feels like it's flowing upstream."

"Kiss," said Lush Life. "Kiss my."

"I can't."

"Kiss my sweet lips."

"I just can't."

She put her hand out, her left hand, just touched him lightly on his wrist. Tommy Blalock threw it off him. But Lush Life refused to be shuffled. Again she touched him, this time his cheek. And now his head came up, he looked in her face, and his voice was so ugly, just mean. "Get your hand the fuck off me," he said.

Nobody living had to tell her that twice. Right then, she'd pushed her plate away, would not eat another bite. "No need to be nice," she said. "Just tell me."

So he told her. He had thought the whole thing over, looked at it all around, from his angle and hers, and the angle of his folks in New Iberia, his mom and all of her relations. And he'd decided it just wasn't right. "Why not?" Lush Life demanded.

"My mom," said Tommy Blalock. "She's kind of set in her ways. Old-fashioned, you might say. Prejudiced."

"So what?"

"She never met no Puerto Ricans."

It was the worst thing he could have told her. The worst thing you could say to any Dominican. Without a word or sign, Lush Life had stood up from the table. He tried to give her fifty dollars, but she threw it in his face. She didn't need his dirty money, she still had the two twenties she'd taken from his pants pocket in the night, and she walked them right over to Ninth Avenue. "Three dime bags. Three bags full," she said. "Plus ten for the powder room." Steadily, without impatience, she scratched her thighs, her arms, her groin. "A gay divorcee," she said. "If only I'd had my knife, I'd be a merry widow."

When I raised up my window and looked up, the small square patch of sky was a muddy brown, a paper towel soaked in spilled tea. The wind trapped in the airshaft swooshed and roared like shook foil.

"Take me," said Lush Life. Fumbling, she raised up off the bed. Her long nails scrabbled at the wallpaper, the nosegays of blue and pink roses. "Take me home," she said.

Her own room had not been disturbed. Though she'd left it, she had not checked out. "Saves time and trouble," she said, "And misunderstandings about the rent."

The cyclostyled note pinned inside her door, INTIMATE AC-COMMODATIONS FOR THE DISCERNING FEW, still overlooked a bunker. If anything, Lush Life's pallet on the floor, carved out of curtains, scarves, and wadded sacking, had grown more deeply entrenched with the months. Old Glory had been replaced by the Stars and Bars; and there was a Louisiana State Tourist Board poster of Bayou Lafourche at dusk tacked up where *Madame Butterfly* had been.

On the shellacked drop-curtain that masked the window, a blown-up photograph of a beaming Huey Long, captioned KINGFISH, hung askew. "Some old football player. Used to be Tommy's coach," Lush Life said. "Or his daddy, I forget." She tore it down without rancor, folded it into a paper dart, and launched it into the dawn. Instantly, the wind picked it up and swirled it off down the street, flailing into Times Square. "End around, flea flicker. Flushed out of the pocket," said Lush Life. "Sacked." She lost her balance, tumbled down on her Japanesque pillows. "Oh, those play-action fakes," she said.

A garbage truck came around. The exterminating thump of its compactors made Lush Life roll and twist, tuck her knees high and tight into her flat chest. "The other deck. It's in my shoe," she said, scratching, scratching. "We could share."

"I couldn't."

"Stiffs can't." She looked down her coiled body, wrapped tightly in walls of stuff. "Only embryos." But anger was too much like work. So was self-pity, grief, all things but smack. "Know something? I'm glad," she said again. Her Debbie Reynolds wig had slipped, and blonde flick-ups kept crawling inside her mouth. "I am just so thankful," she said.

For a minute or two, the drug enlivened her. She climbed back on her feet, came back towards the window, and she pulled aside the drop-curtain; she let the light touch her face. The air was grayish now, thick with grit, but she seemed not to feel its sting.

Her voice was a sandpaper rasp; then it was a dying motor. "Fresh air," she said. The skin across her cheekbones was drawn so tight, I could seem to read her ebb and flow, every flinch of her nerve ends. "Can you feel?" she asked. "Can you?" But she had started to scratch again; she was gone before I could speak.

A hundred yards along the street, Times Square was starting over. By leaning out and craning, I could just catch its throb, its gathering bloodbeat. "I'm falling," Lush Life said. The block was full of loose ends and flying dust. "I fell," she said.

Something blackish and acrid hurled into our faces. Lush Life squeaked and turned her head, buried herself in my neck. When I eased her back, away from the light, her eyes fogged over, drooped shut. The lids were a deep, bruised purple; a weak and ragged pulse twitched her throat. "Pity the poor sailors," said Lush Life, "out on a night like this."

Coda

THE MORNING I CHECKED OUT of the Hotel
Moose, it was warm and sticky and raining, a light drizzle like
Scotch mist. Crossing Times Square, I felt myself drifting in a
steam bath. It was noon; nobody was out but tourists and cops,
a few kids. At the foot of Father Duffy's statue, I sat down and
rested. One of the kids came up and asked me for the time,
while his partner tried to snatch my typewriter. "Early," I said.

"Seems late," said the kid.

In Jimmy's Corner, I sat waiting for Sasha. To pass the time,
I reread Irving Wallace's account of Chang and Eng, Barnum's
twins. To me, it was the tale of tales, the whole of Broadway.
"Chang and Eng were born in Meklong, Siam, a small village
near Bangkok. Their father was an impoverished Chinese fish-
erman. From birth, they were united by a thick, fleshy ligament
covered with skin, like a four-inch arm, connecting their lower
chests. At first, this band held them face to face, but as they
grew, it stretched to five and a half inches, allowing them to
stand and move sideways. The joint was sensitive but strong. If
it was touched at the middle, both boys felt the sensation. Yet
so sturdy was it that if one of the Twins happened to trip and
lose his balance, the ligament held him dangling but firm.

"With some difficulty, Chang and Eng learned to walk in
step and then to swim with considerable agility in the near-by

river. When they were nineteen years old, and a familiar sight to their neighbors, they were seen swimming one day by an American sailing-master, Captain Coffin, of the ship *Sachem*. Amazed at the sight, the Captain consulted Robert Hunter, a Scotch merchant, and together they determined to purchase the boys and exhibit them. They made inquiries. The father of the Twins had recently died, and their mother was prepared to bargain. In due time a contract was signed, money changed hands, and Coffin and Hunter took the Siamese Twins to England.

"After being shown on the Continent for many years, Chang and Eng were taken to Boston and then to New York. Advertised as 'The Siamese Double Boys,' they at once became a center of great interest and controversy. There was a rumor that they were not genuinely joined. The controversy attracted Barnum. He met them, was satisfied that they were true freaks, and bought up their contract. After that, they were shown at the American Museum regularly.

"The Siamese Twins were the most temperamental of Barnum's freak family. Nature had played more than one cruel joke on them. For though Chang and Eng were sentenced to each other, they were opposite in every way and disliked one another. Chang, the slightly shorter one on the Twins' own left, enjoyed wine and women; Eng, the more studious and intellectual, liked an evening of chess. Their differences were reported by the *Philadelphia Medical Times* in 1874: 'What Chang liked to eat, Eng detested. Eng was very good-natured, Chang cross and irritable. The sickness of one had no effect upon the other so that while one would be suffering from fever, the pulse of the other would beat at its natural rate. Chang drank pretty heavily—at times getting drunk; but Eng never felt any influence from the debauch of the brother. They often quarrelled; and, of course, under the circumstances their quarrels were bitter. They sometimes came to blows, and on one occasion came under the jurisdiction of the courts.'

"Left alone, they would brood in silence. Sometimes, they would agree to do first what one wanted, then what the other wanted. Their only interests in common were fishing, hunting, and wood-cutting. Although their abnormality had made them wealthy, they lived only to be free of one another. Countless doctors were visited, but not one promised them that they could live a single day cut apart.

"Once, after a particularily bitter quarrel, they decided to defy medical advice. According to the *Medical Times*: 'Chang and Eng applied to Dr. Hollingsworth to separate them; Eng affirmed that Chang was so bad that he could live no longer with him; and Chang stated that he was satisfied to be separated, only asking that he be given an equal chance with his brother, and that the band be cut exactly in the middle. Cooler counsels prevailed.'

"Enjoying American freedom and American dollars, the Twins agreed to apply for citizenship. At the naturalization office they learned that they must have a Christian or family name. They had no names other than Chang and Eng. An applicant standing in line behind them, overhearing the nature of the problem, offered his last name. It was Bunker. And so the Siamese Twins became Chang Bunker and Eng Bunker, American citizens.

"At last, wearying of the grueling Museum routine, they gave Barnum notice and retired to a plantation near Mount Airy, North Carolina. They relaxed and let their slaves do the work. Then, almost simultaneously, when they were forty-two, they fell in love with the young daughters of a poor Irish farmer in the neighborhood. It was a double wedding. Eng married Sally Yates, and Chang married Addie Yates. Now diplomacy and compromise were required. The Twins built a second mansion, a mile away from the first. Two separate households were established. Chang and Eng and Sally spent three days in Eng's house, and then, Chang and Eng and Addie spent three days

in Chang's house. Apparently the arrangement was not inhib-
iting. The Twins produced twenty-one children.

"The Civil War took their slaves and their wealth from them.
They were forced back into show business. They asked Barnum
to manage them, and he agreed. When their comeback proved
unsuccessful in New York, Barnum decided to send them
abroad. 'I sent them to Great Britain where, in all the principal
places, and for about a year, their levees were continually
crowded,' the showman wrote. 'In all probability the great success attending this enterprise was much enhanced, if not actually
caused, by extensive announcements in advance that the main
purpose of Chang-Eng's visit to Europe was to consult the most
eminent medical and surgical talent with regard to the safety of
separating the twins.'

"Again they were wealthy. And again they took leave of
Barnum and retired with their wives to the plantation near
Mount Airy. They were sixty-three years old, and though Chang
had been unwell, the future was bright. The end came suddenly,
and the *Annual Register* reported it in 1874 to the Twins' vast
English following:

" 'They were at Chang's residence, and the evening of that
day was the appointed time for a removal to Eng's dwelling.
The day was cold and Chang had been complaining for a couple
of months past of being very ill. On Friday evening they retired
to a small room by themselves and went to bed, but Chang was
very restless. Sometime between midnight and daybreak they
got up and sat by the fire. Again Eng protested and said he
wished to lie down, as he was sleepy. Chang stoutly refused and
replied that it hurt his breast to recline. After a while they retired
to their bed, and Eng fell into a deep sleep. After four o'clock
one of the sons came into the room, and going to the bedside,
discovered that his uncle was dead. Eng was awakened by the
noise and in the greatest alarm turned and looked upon the
lifeless form beside him, and was seized with violent nervous
paroxysms.

" 'No physicians were at hand, and it being three miles to the town of Mount Airy, some time elapsed before one could be summoned. A messenger was dispatched to the village for Dr. Hollingsworth, and he sent his brother, also a physician, at once to the plantation but before he arrived the vital spark had fled, and the Siamese twins were dead.' "

Done reading, I told the tale to the barmaid. She was busy washing glasses, she did not look up. "Don't talk to me about families," she said. "You never met my cousin Bruno." But before she could elaborate, Sasha came.

He walked in bleeding but happy. Hannah Sophia, his Hanoverian masseuse, had caught him with a right cross and dropped him for the count, then deposited him in sections on the sidewalk. It was the sign that he'd been awaiting. "My upwake call," he said. The O'Fays were leaving on a sixty-day tour of Texas and Oklahoma. Till this morning, he hadn't been sure if he should join them. Now he was, and the Greyhound was leaving at 4 p.m.

I would miss him. But he had already told me that he was done walking Broadway. North of Columbus Circle, it became a different game. Though there were ten miles left in Manhattan, four more in the Bronx, it was no longer a street of dreams. Citizens lived in those regions, civilians with jobs and families, responsibilities. Its history was not primarily of adventure but of consolidation; of neighborhoods and races, the Irish, the Jews, the African-Americans and Hispanics, and now the Koreans, the Cambodians, the Vietnamese; first and last, of survival: "Real people. Real life," Sasha said. "Was nice knowing you."

In warm, wet stickiness, we walked back together to Times Square. Sasha's drums were downtown, doing lunch with the other O'Fays; my suitcase was already on 125th Street. Through the haze we watched the ticker tape, one last time. THE REVEREND ORAL ROBERTS, it said, ANNOUNCES A RAIN OF TOADS.

I headed north.

Shelter Island, December 9, 1990
In memory of Geraldo Cruz

Acknowledgments

In addition to the persons in these pages, I met and was helped by many others. For their generosity, time, and patience, I would like to thank the following in particular: Neil Byrne, hansom-cab proprietor; Dee Dee Darnell, singer; Eddie Blunt, ex-boxer; Patrick Bedford, actor; Michael Amato, talent agent; Larry Brown, philosopher; Vicki La Motta, model; Jane Dentinger, writer; Charles Cook, dancer; Marina Voikhanskaya, trick cyclist; Seymour Foreman and Irving Edelman, lawyers; Jim Fleetwood, operatic bass; Jerry and Bea Gasman, Academy Clothing; Billy Gallagher, Broadway folklorist; Don George, songwriter; Leroy Goldfarb, Wall Street investor; Velma, mentalist; Rocky Graziano, middleweight champ; Steven Greenberg, investor; Eddie Jaffe, press agent; Jonah Jones, trumpeter; Frank Scully, saloonkeeper; Joe Kaliff, cartoonist; Jennifer Lewis, diva; Big Nick Nicholas, tenor saxman; Fred "Taxi" Mitchell, cab driver and musician; Earl McGrath, *boulevardier*; Eddie Murphy, gay activist; Madam Julia Drobner and Andy Anselmo, voice coaches; Maria Nelson, entrepreneur; Maurice Hines, dancer; Al Flosso, magic-shop owner; Milo O'Shea, actor; Joel Reed, film producer; Max Rosey, publicist; Marvin Safir, restaurateur; Peggy Doyle, restaurateuse; Whitney Reis, actress; Sandy Saddler, lightweight champ; Larry and Dorothy Speir, Memory Lane Music; Ken Smith, private detective; Seymour Stein, Sire Records; Bob Appel, the Knitting Factory; Bambi, pocket-sized Venus; Henny Youngman, comedian; Sister Rosa, spiritual healer; Sonny Sharrock, guitarist; Gustav Schoeffer, taxidermist; Gene Saks, theatrical director; Toma Holley, dress designer.

Robert Hughes, Michael Thomas, and Ken Auletta were invaluable in supplying background. Sean Doyle was my first guide and mentor. Geraldine Fitzgerald, a marvellous woman, gave me inspiration. Fred and Mary Parvin gave me shelter. Fred Flores gave me heart.

And my wife, Michaela? Don't ask.

Sources

My reading on Broadway was as haphazard as the journey itself. So I will make no attempt at a formal bibliography. There were certain books, however, that I borrowed from quite blatantly. Among them, in no particular order, I owe debts to *City for Sale*, by Jack Newfield and Wayne Barrett; *Plunkitt of Tammany Hall*, by William J. Riordon; *The Streets Were Paved with Gold* and *Greed and Glory on Wall Street*, by Ken Auletta; *Wall Street: Men and Money*, by Martin Mayer; *The Epic of New York City*, by Edward Robb Ellis; *The Night Club Era*, by Stanley Walker; *New York Nights*, by Stephen Graham; *The Empire City: A Treasury of New York*, ed. Alexander Klein; *The New Metropolis*, ed. E. Idell Zeisloft; *Lost New York*, by Nathan Silver; *Incredible New York*, by Lloyd Morris; *The Great Metropolis*, by Junius Henry Browne; *The Great White Way*, by Allen Churchill; *The Palace*, by Marian Spitzer; *Broadway*, by Justin Brooks Atkinson; *The Gangs of New York*, by Herbert Asbury; *Hell's Kitchen*, by Richard O'Connor; *Manhattan '45*, by Jan Morris; *Show Biz, from Vaude to Video*, by Abel Green and Joe

Laurie, Jr.; *Metropolis*, by Jerome Charyn; *Crossroads of the World: The Story of Times Square*, by William Laas; *Times Square: A Pictorial History*, by Jill Stone; *The Big Drag*, by Mel Heimer; *The Greatest Street in the World*, by Stephen Jenkins; *Broadway*, by J. B. Kerfoot; *Djuna Barnes's New York*; *Meyer Berger's New York*; *New York*, by Paul Morand; *Nothing If Not Critical*, by Robert Hughes; and *McSorley's Wonderful Saloon*, by Joseph Mitchell.

Of the volumes and stories that I have quoted directly, I would like to mention again *Evelyn Nesbit and Stanford White: Love and Death in the Gilded Age*, by Michael Macdonald Mooney; *The Fabulous Showman: The Life and Time of P. T. Barnum*, by Irving Wallace; and *View of Life and Things*, by Ray Crabtree. All three served me faithfully.

Richard Reeves's *New York* profile of Matty Troy was reprinted in his collection, *The Big Apple*. It was Reeves, not myself, who first saw the parallel with George Washington Plunkitt, and I trust he will forgive my thefts.

Tales of Times Square, by Josh Alan Friedman, is filled with lore on Hubert's Museum, the New Amsterdam, and other Forty-second Street splendors, and provides the fullest portrait extant of the Deuce in its death-throes. Specifically, it includes a chapter on Izzy Grove.

The Power Broker: Robert Moses and the Fall of New York, by Robert A. Caro, taught me more about the city and how it got that way than all other histories combined.

Lights and Shadows of New York Life, James D. McCabe's immortal survey, is available in reprint. As for the two great nineteenth-century New York diaries, those of Philip Hone and George Templeton Strong, some highlights are collected in *The Hone and Strong Diaries of Old Manhattan*, ed. Louis Auchincloss.

Two recent books deal specifically with walks up Broadway: *Broadway*, by Carin Dreschler-Marx and Richard Shepard, which served as Sasha Zim's Baedeker; and *On Broadway: A*

Journey Uptown over Time, by David W. Dunlap, encyclopedic and indispensable.

Finally, there is A. J. Liebling, and here my dues can never be paid. Many of his books— *The Telephone Booth Indian*, *The Honest Rainmaker*, and *Back Where I Came From*, in particular—helped me shape specific passages. But without *The Sweet Science*, which I first read when I was fifteen, it is likely that this book would not exist at all.

A Note on the Type

The text of this book was set in a digitized version of Simoncini Garamond, a modern version by Francesco Simoncini of the type attributed to the famous Parisian type cutter Claude Garamond (ca. 1490–1561). Garamond was a pupil of Geoffroy Tory and is believed to have based his letters on the Venetian models, although he introduced a number of important differences, and it is to him we owe the letter that we know as old-style. He gave to his letters a certain elegance and a feeling of movement that won for their creator an immediate reputation and the patronage of Francis I of France.

Composed by PennSet, Inc.
Bloomsburg, Pennsylvania
Printed and bound by
The Haddon Craftsmen, Inc.,
Scranton, Pennsylvania
Designed by Iris Weinstein